RAILWAYMEN OF THE WELSH VALLEYS
1914-1967

Volume 1

Pontypool Road loco shed basks in the autumn sunlight as viewed from Coedygric Road viaduct on 14 October 1962. In the foreground on the left are Coedygric Sidings, New Sidings on the right.
W. Potter, R. C. Riley collection

Cover illustrations

Front

Top left: The snowplough is seen in action at an unknown location in 1947 using No 7426, with a Pontypool Road footplate crew. Driver Harry Robins is seen second from the right, in the back row. *J. S. Williams collection*

Top right: Driver Tom Davis and fireman Terry Nicholls prepare 'Castle' Class 4-6-0 No 4098 *Kidwelly Castle* at the north end of the shed in 1959. *Ken Davis, Tom Davis, J. S. Williams collection*

Bottom: The Dowlais tanks cross Crumlin Viaduct, for Pontypool Road and beyond, on 9 August 1961. *Paul Chancellor collection (Colour-Rail)*

Back:

Left: Ex-GWR '46xx' Class 0-6-0PT No 4639 and '52xx' 2-8-0T No 5208 rest in the round shed on 30 December 1964. The Lift Road is in the foreground, followed by the Plough Road, Cabin Road, Through Road and Tap Road. The loco is on the road adjacent to the Tap Road in the north-west corner of the shed. *G. Vincent*

Right: Ex-GWR 2-8-0 No 3816, banked by '36xx' Class 0-6-0PT No 3663, approaches Pontypool Road South Junction in November 1963. The train is passing the Old Yard on the right, having entered the yard via Panteg Junction and the Up Low Level Goods line. *Photographer unknown*

Opposite: GWR '2021' Class 0-6-0PT No 2080 is seen in the south bay at Pontypool Road station circa 1934. *Phil Williams collection*

RAILWAYMEN OF THE WELSH VALLEYS 1914-1967

Memories of steam working from Pontypool Road shed (86G)

Volume 1

Philip W. L. Williams

SLP

A Silver Link Book

First published in 2020

British Library Cataloguing in Publication Data

A catalogue record for this book is available from the British Library.

ISBN 978 1 85794 488 4

Silver Link Books
Mortons Media Group Limited
Media Centre
Morton Way
Horncastle
LN9 6JR
Tel/Fax: 01507 529535

email: sohara@mortons.co.uk
Website: www.nostalgiacollection.com

Printed and bound in the Czech Republic

Bibliography

Copyright of photographs belongs to the photographers credited in the captions and acknowledged in the Introduction.
The following references have been used in the preparation of this book, as indicated by superscript numbers in the Introduction, in addition to recorded conversations with former railway employees and railway enthusiasts and written documentation supplied by them.

[1] Drayton, John *On the Footplate* (Bradford Barton Ltd), page 59

[2] Gittins, Sandra *The Great Western Railway in the First World War* (The History Press), page 62
[3] www.aslef.org.uk>information>history
[4] Drayton, John *Across the Footplate Years* (Ian Allan Publishing Ltd)
[5] Industrial Wales and Transport and Industry around the world – www.industrialgwent.co.uk
[6] The Steam Workshops of the Great Western Railway, by Ken Gibbs (The History Press)
[7] Pontypool Free Press (Vol 2)[5] Pontypool Free Press (Vol 2)

The Author

Local railway enthusiast Phil Williams was a contract structural engineer in the aerospace industry; a graduate of Cardiff University, and a Research Associate there in 1994-1996, undertaking research into carbon fibre wing panel design sponsored by Airbus and NASA. His father's uncle, Harry Miles, was a Swindon-trained locomotive fitter at Pontypool Road in the 1930s. His family also have interesting links to the mining industry. His great-grandfather was Thomas Williams, the Colliery Engineer at Tirpentwys Colliery from before 1902 up to 1912, then at Crumlin Valley Colliery, Hafodrynys (sunk in 1912), from 1915 when the first coal came up the pit, until he died in 1925 aged 76. The Glyn Pits were owned by Crumlin Valley Collieries Ltd, and were included as part of his daily duties. Phil's father's great-grandfather, Joseph Harper, was one of the 1890 Llanerch Colliery disaster rescue team; he worked at the British Top Pits. His father's uncle, William Harper, was the foreman of the wagon shop at the Big Arch, Talywain, when it was owned by Partridge Jones and John Paton Ltd. A lifelong friend was a former Pontypool Road locomotive driver Phil Williams (no relation), affectionately known as 'Full Load Phil', who inspired the author to have an interest in railways from a very early age. Sadly, the author died suddenly in 2017 before his book could be published.

Contents

Dedication

This book is dedicated to the memories of all those people who once worked for the Great Western Railway in South Wales, at Pontypool Road loco depot, in the Eastern Valley and on the Vale of Neath railway, as well as to those people who worked in the industries once served by the railway at those locations. Today the UK coal-mining industry is extinct, and the future of the steel industry is in doubt. This book serves to remind to future generations what a fantastic place the South Wales valleys once were for heavy industry and transport infrastructure; it is also a tribute to the pioneering 19th-century railway builders. It is now 50 years since the depot closed, in April 1967.

He joined the Great Western Society in the late 1960s and was asked to select engines from Barry scrapyard that were in the best condition for preservation at Didcot Steam Centre. Under his guidance No 5322 was transferred to the Caerphilly Railway Society in 1969 and later returned to steam; he also prepared 'Castle' Class No 5051 *Earl Bathurst* at Barry scrapyard prior to its removal by rail to Didcot in 1970, via Gloucester. At Caerphilly, the initial restoration of Ivatt 2MT 2-6-2T No 41312 was begun in 1974, after purchase from Barry scrapyard by the late John Mynors, who owned *Earl Bathurst* and No 7808 *Cookham Manor*, based at the Great Western Society at Didcot.

Peter Rich

I would also like to dedicate this book to my old friend Peter Rich, the well-known locomotive preservationist and renowned model engineer, who sadly passed away on 14 February 2014 from cancer aged 73. Peter Rich was born in Newport and one of his uncles had been a springsmith at Swindon Works. Peter joined the railway at Ebbw Junction, becoming a passed cleaner, but left to gain a trade as an apprentice at the Mount Stuart Engineering Company in Newport. He later left and joined Newport Police.

Ex-GWR '43xx' Class 2-6-0 No 5322 undergoes steam trials at the Caerphilly Branch of the Great Western Society on Tuesday 26 May 1970. It was returned to steam from Barry scrapyard condition under the guidance of the late Peter Rich. *J. S. Williams*

The new-build 'Saint' was Peter's idea way back in 1971, in a letter to the Great Western Society, and in more recent times he was responsible for preparing new drawings for new-build projects Nos 5391 (West Somerset Railway), 2999 *Lady of Legend*, No 1014 *County of Glamorgan* and 4-4-0 'County' tender engine *County of Somerset*, as well as the proposed GWR Dean Single Project. No 6880 *Betton Grange* and the LMS 'Patriot' locomotive *The Unknown Warrior* were his other new-build design projects.

In his hobby as a model engineer, Peter specialised in building super-detailed live steam models of the designs of William Dean. By 2007 he had been designing and building model locomotives for 45 years; in that year he had built 15 very finely scaled 5-inch-gauge locomotives, and had been twice awarded the Henry Greenly Award, twice the J. N. Maskelyne Trophy, and also the Crebbin Memorial Cup at the International Model Engineering Exhibition. Together with these awards he had achieved Highly Commended, Bronze Medal, three times Silver Medal and twice Gold Medal standard. In addition, one of his models, a coach, was chosen for display at the National Railway Museum at York. He exhibited many models, won Silver Medals for Nos 1118 *Prince Christian*, 3050 *Royal Sovereign* and 14 *Charles Saunders*, and a Gold Medal for No 3440 *City of Truro*.

Peter Rich was the most remarkably talented person I have ever met, being blessed with a genius to design and superb draughtsmanship, a brilliant model engineer and incredibly modest and generous to his many friends. His design skills were equally at home with full-size locomotives as with miniature live steam engines. My interest in Churchward engines is due to conversations with him. He was the best friend my father ever had, and we both miss him greatly. My friend David Lewis of Newport said recently that Peter should have worked in the Swindon Drawing Office – I agree with him!

Bob Gale

I must also mention the late Bob Gale of Newport Model Engineering Society, who worked at Newport Pill as a fireman in the 1930s, and at Ebbw Junction and latterly Severn Tunnel as a loco driver. He was another skilled model engineer, self-taught, and passed away aged 76 in October 1994. He was a Judge at the London Model Engineering Exhibition for many years, and won Silver Medals for his superb 3½-inch-gauge 9F 2-10-0 No 92000 (incorporating numerous railwayana artefacts), and his 5-inch-gauge GWR 2-4-0 'River' Class loco *Avon* (now owned by Pete Waterman); both of these models were based on general arrangements drawn by Peter Rich.

Bob's claim to fame in the late 1930s was to fire a 'King' Class engine up the Western Valley when the GWR used two of these engines on Newport (Park Junction) to Ebbw Vale Steelworks iron ore trains, to assess the possibility of constructing a 2-10-2T for this route; one 'King' was on the front, and one on the back as a banker. Bob fired the banking engine. Now, I never asked him in detail about that, but what a story that would make!

I am reminded that one Friday night in June 1980, looking from my parents' house in Griffithstown, I spotted 9F No 92220 *Evening Star* being diesel-hauled heading south past Pontypool Road Station South Signal Box; it was returning from the 1980 Rainhill Cavalcade Celebrations to Didcot Railway Centre. With my father and brother, we traced this engine to a loop west of Severn Tunnel diesel depot, where it was held for a path to Didcot Railway Centre. Travelling with it was the late John Bellwood, the Chief Engineer of the National Railway Museum, and the three of us were welcomed onto the footplate for a considerable time. By coincidence, Bob had arrived to book on, and joined us on the footplate. The diesel driver was Eric Price, and the diesel a Class 31. Bob related to John Bellwood about the use of railway materials in his model 9F No 92000, part of which was from Crumlin

Viaduct. Bob owned the smokebox number plate from No 92000, which now resides, I understand, with a friend of his in West Wales.

John Williams

After the initial submission of this book for publication, very sadly my father John Stanley Williams passed away very suddenly. A former Senior Lecturer in the Engineering Department at Pontypool College, he died aged 85 at 10.25am on Saturday 28 January 2017 in Nevill Hall Hospital, Abergavenny, after a short but brave battle against cancer; his cause of death was bronchial pneumonia.

He had been a railway enthusiast since childhood. Brought up in Abersychan in the 1930s, he provided numerous contacts, photos and information for Pontypool Road books and for my future publications *The Collieries and Railway Systems of the Blaendare Trading Company and John Vipond Ltd* and *The Collieries and Railway Systems of Partridge Jones and John Paton Ltd at Abersychan – Big Arch to Llanerch and Blaenserchan Collieries*. Without foresight in photographing the remains of the railways of the Eastern Valley from 1969 to 1982, many images in these books would have been lost forever, particularly his coverage of the Top Line Eastern Valley branch from Trevethin Junction to Blaenavon Furnace Sidings. Despite poor health in his last nine years, he remained enthusiastic and interested in railways and local history.

My father was born on 3 March 1931 at Melrose Cottage, Stoney Road, Abersychan, into a family with strong links to the mining industry. His father was Horace Williams, and his mother Caroline Harper. On his father's side, his grandfather was Thomas Williams, who was the Colliery Engineer at Tirpentwys Colliery and subsequently Hafodrynys Colliery and the Glyn Pits. Thomas's brother, Harry, was the engineer when the pit was sunk in 1878. On his mother's side of the family, his grandfather was Joseph Harper, who worked as a collier

at the British Top Pits, and was a member of the Llanerch Colliery Disaster Rescue Team on 6 February 1890. One of his mother's uncles was a railway inspector when the LNWR built its branch line from Blaenavon to Talywain in the late 1870s; he later worked in India, when railways were being built on that subcontinent – and sent postcards home from Poona, India. My father was named after his uncle, Armourer-Staff Sergeant Stanley Williams AOC, who was killed in action in the First World War in March 1918 and is remembered on a brass war memorial plaque opposite Pontypool Town Hall, which is adjacent to the Italian Gardens at Pontypool Park.

My father's interest in steam locomotives began in 1935, when he was taken to Talywain station by a family friend called Stan Porter. Vipond's engines would be seen in the sidings with trains of coal from Red Ash Slope and Lower Varteg Colliery. He gained a scholarship at Abersychan Grammar School and, intending to have a career in farming, went to Usk Agricultural College in 1947.

John began working for the NCB in November 1947, maintaining railway rolling stock at Big Arch wagon shop for 12 months. In January 1949 he became an Apprentice Fitter at Blaenserchan Colliery; this work included the installation and maintenance of all colliery machinery, above and below ground, and machine shop work. Further qualifications were obtained by attending Crumlin School of Mines. Promotion to Grade 2, 1 and Shift Fitter soon followed. He became a Mechanic of the Mine, which required the examination and testing of all colliery machinery, above and below ground. Finally, he became Mechanic of the Mine Class 1. This included examining and testing, together with carrying out duties of assistant and mechanical engineer in their absence. On the day shift, on summer mornings, he and John Waters would stand by the railings near the weighbridge at the screens to watch Big Arch loco driver Len Jones pull empty wagons for the screens towards Blaenserchan; Len Jones would give the engine full regulator if he had a day shift audience, and the loco would jolt sideways on the bad joints in the track!

Many jobs and memories were recalled: helping to fit the new fan shaft, changing both the pit wheels on No 2 Head Frame, descending the pit at Llanerch Colliery with the cage rubbing on the side of the shaft, and walking to Cook's Slope, the scene of the 1890 explosion. He looked after the Llanerch Pit Bottom Pumps, writing his name and date on the flywheel of the big steam-driven haulage engine at the bottom of the upcast pit. Lewis's Slope at Llanerch was situated under Llanilleth, and there was a fall in the roof so large that Talywain church could be fitted into it. Tom Hodge was the Foreman Blacksmith at Blaenserchan, and an uncle to Alan Hodge, a maths teacher at West Monmouth Grammar School. John became the spare hand pitman when the resident pitman was on holiday.

John met my mother Constance in 1953 and they married in 1960. His two sons, Nigel and Philip, were born in 1963 and 1966. In the late 1950s there was a series of local pit closures. Jim Harris, the colliery manager, said that John could have Will Howell's job (Assistant to Austin Jones, the Colliery Mechanical Engineer), and Austin's job when Austin finished. John decided to leave, and his departure allowed Len Giles to be promoted. John left the National Coal Board in September 1960, to begin a career in teaching, initially at Abertillery Technical College. He started at Pontypool College at the end of 1961, and worked there he retired aged 65 in 1996. He was the longest-serving member of staff at the college.

In 1964 he rode on the footplate of *Estevarney Grange* on the last day of the Vale of Neath line, at the invitation of Pontypool Road driver Bert Hale from outside Neath to Pontypool (Clarence Street); he recalled blowing the whistle while coming back over Crumlin Viaduct and through to Pontypool (Clarence Street). In 1965 he rescued railings from Crumlin Viaduct for Pontypool College car park. Gaining further qualifications, he was promoted to a senior lecturer in the early 1970s, and also acting Deputy Head of the Engineering Department until the early 1980s. He rescued the Tirpentwys Colliery spare pit wheel and reassembled it at Pontypool College in 1978, as well as the rev counter from the Tirpentwys Colliery steam fan engine.

He began taking photographs in the 1950s. Renewing this hobby in 1969 with 35mm film, he used his mornings off to record the railways and collieries of the Eastern Valley, with footplate rides on the NCB Big Arch engines at Abersychan, and on coal trains passing Panteg Junction or Talywain to Blaenavon. He machined boiler fittings free of charge for several well-known ex-Barry scrapyard engines – *Raveningham Hall* (for the Shildon Cavalcade of 1975), *Witherslack Hall*, *Hagley Hall* and ex-GWR Nos 2857, 4150 and 9681, as well as axle

My father, the late John Williams, is seen at Blaenavon Furnace Sidings awaiting a return footplate ride south on a Type 3 diesel-electric locomotive, with a loaded train of coal, circa April 1972. *J. S. Williams*

boxes for No 41312, and 56 firebox crown stays and nuts for *Nora*, the first steam loco to work at the Pontypool & Blaenavon Railway in the late 1980s.

Following retirement in 1996, he travelled on preserved steam railways as well as on main-line steam trips. In 2006 he renewed his friendship with opera singer Dame Margaret Price, the daughter of College Principal Glyn Price. He provided author Stephen Oakden with information about Blaenserchan Colliery and the Big Arch, Tirpentwys Colliery, and the name of an employee of the Blaendare Railway. Author Desmond Coakham was also provided with information about Blaenserchan Colliery for publication in the railway media.

Gordon Secker

I would also like to mention the late Gordon Secker, an Ebbw Junction Driver. My father first met him at Blaenavon Furnace Sidings in 1970 and until 1987 they shared a great friendship; Gordon would always offer my father and anyone with him a footplate ride whenever he saw him!

Without Gordon's help and enthusiasm, several unique photographs in this book would not have been taken, and these images would have been lost forever (among many others, the footplate views on the Blaenavon Top Line branch). My father used to see Gordon on the Blaenavon branch as well as the branch to Hafodrynys Washery. Gordon would work the same route all week, on a six-week roster. He proudly told the author in the late 1980s that the Blaenavon Top Line branch was his favourite route!

Terry MacTeer

Terry was a driver at Ebbw Junction when my father met him while taking photographs in the 1970s. He drove the last rail enthusiasts' passenger train to Blaenavon Furnace Sidings, on Sunday 13 April 1980. When the train returned from there to Newport station, my father and myself were on the footplate. Terry hadn't seen my father since the early 1970s, and said he would have given him a footplate ride if he had known he was on the train! Terry passed away in May 2017.

On Friday 27 August 1971 Type 3 diesel-electric locomotive No D6939, hauling the 08.10 train from Panteg and Coedygric Junction to Blaenavon Furnace Siding, has returned to Panteg at about 11.20. Driver Gordon Secker is standing in the doorway, while his secondman is at the controls. The guard was Bill Prowse. *J. S. Williams*

Introduction

This book has been written to record the memories of surviving former Pontypool Road loco depot staff, Aberdare loco staff and local railway enthusiasts. I have spent four years recording and writing the memoirs of 23 people spanning the years 1914-1967, researching photographs and writing up their memories.

My interest owes its origins to a former Pontypool Road locomotive driver called Phil Williams, affectionately known as 'Full Load Phil', who was a near neighbour when I was growing up in the early 1970s, and was then recently retired. My father, John Williams, got to know him around 1970 and Phil would tell me stories about the depot and locomotives. He started at Pontypool Road in 1923 and retired in 1968. My father often asked him to contact Bradford Barton Publishing, based in Truro, to record his memoirs, but alas he wouldn't.

My father has been a life-long railway enthusiast, and from 1965 to 1982 photographed the Eastern Valley railways in their decline. Since 1969 I have been visiting the remains of such places with him, and thus the seed of interest was sown. Footplate rides on empty coal trains to Blaenavon, heading north from Coedygric Junction to Blaenavon Furnace Sidings with Ebbw Junction driver Gordon Secker, a ride on a 'Hymek' loco from Talywain to Coedygric Junction with driver Mr Richins of Griffithstown, or a ride on a weedkilling train from Coedygric Junction to Hafodrynys New Mine are recalled. My own steam memories are limited to the NCB Talywain-Blaenserchan branch in 1969-70, Hafodrynys and Merthyr Vale Collieries in the 1970s, and Mountain Ash in 1978. For Christmas

1977, my father bought me a sound cine camera, which was used to record local railway scenes from 1978 to the early 1980s. The sight and sound of a braked coal train from Big Pit, Blaenavon, with wagons braked from Blaenavon Furnace Sidings heading south over the Big Arch at Abersychan in early 1978 in a fall of snow, and similarly the last train of blended coal from Hafodrynys New Mine on Sunday 1 April 1979, with brakes applied, passing the Mason's pub on Station Road in Griffithstown, are now lost forever.

Pontypool Road was a well-known depot in South Wales, and was located at the eastern end of the Vale of Neath Railway (VoN). The eastern end of the VoN from Pontypool to Quaker's Yard was constructed by the 19th century civil engineer and visionary Charles Liddell, for the Newport, Abergavenny & Hereford Railway, as its Taff Vale Extension, and was built to link with the Taff Vale Railway at Quaker's Yard, allowing South Wales coal to be transported to England and the Midlands. Crumlin Viaduct, designed by Tom Kennard, was the highest viaduct in the UK, the third highest in the world and, for its size, the cheapest ever built. During its construction Thomas Kennard lived in Crumlin Hall (later used as Crumlin Mining Technical School). On the Varteg hillside near Pontypool is a cast-iron memorial known as the Dog Stone, where Thomas Kennard accidentally shot his setter Carlo while out shooting on 12 August 1864. Crumlin Hall was in later years the name of GWR 'Hall' Class locomotive No 4916, and its namesake became the Crumlin School of Mines.

Pontypool Road shed was built as a

roundhouse in 1855, this fact being recorded on a roof supporting pillar located near the lathe in the north-west corner, cast by the City Basin Foundry[1]. The long shed was a later addition. The shed provided footplate staff for Pontrilas and Branches Fork engine sheds, the latter having branches with gradients of 1 in 22 and 1 in 19.

'Jellicoe Specials'

South Wales coal supplied the Royal Navy Grand Fleet at Scapa Flow throughout the First World War, and the trains carrying it were known as 'Jellicoe Specials', after Sir John Jellicoe, Admiral of the Fleet. Admiralty coal was one of the most important items of freight with which the GWR was involved. At the beginning of the First World War the Admiralty was dependent on colliers shipping steam coal from South Wales to fuel the fleet at Scapa Flow, and although arrangements had been made previously to send some of the coal by rail, it was not foreseen, at this point, the effect German submarines would have on the colliers while on their voyage from South Wales into the Irish Sea, then around Scotland. Many of the colliers were sunk, increasing the Admiralty's dependence on the railways to supply the fleet with coal.[2]

The coal wagons, most of which were supplied to the Admiralty by a hire company, were loaded with coal from the Aberdare and Rhondda districts and made up into the 'Jellicoe Specials' at Pontypool Road. Their destination was Grangemouth, a 375-mile journey that took around 48 hours. The trains were dealt with by the GWR as far as Warrington, and from there onwards the responsibility was shared by the railway companies en route.[2]

Pontypool Road thus became a location of strategic importance in the First World War. The first train ran on 27 August 1914.[2] Tom Davis, a Pontypool Road driver (see Chapter 5), recalled that 'at one period in the war, one train of coal left the Admiralty Sidings at Pontypool Road every hour around the clock for Chester and Liverpool, where the Royal Navy's ships were being bunkered, and similar trains of empties were being run in the opposite direction to South Wales. In addition to this traffic, all passenger and freight services were maintained. The backbone of this extra freight work was the "28xx" Class 2-8-0 engines, initially 24, but later increased to 32, which were stationed at Pontypool Road, for their power seemed unlimited and their free-steaming qualities enabled them to perform their jobs even when the clinker from dirty fires would be falling out of the firehole doors. These engines would haul trains of 45 10-ton coal wagons.'

Driver Phil Williams used to tell me that on a Sunday, a 'Jellicoe Special' coal train occupied every section of track between Pontypool Road and Shrewsbury.

'Castle' Class locomotives in the valleys

Driver Phil Williams also told me that 'Castle' Class locomotives have travelled across Crumlin Viaduct. 'Castle' Class locomotives on the Vale of Neath at Aberdare, Ystrad Mynach and Trelewis are well documented, and Phil recalled Winston Churchill travelling along the VoN from Pontypool Road to bypass bomb damage at Pengam in Cardiff in May 1941, being hauled by a pair of 'Castles', one of which was No 5038 *Morlais Castle*. Jack Everson, the son of Pontypool Road driver Dick Everson, recalled seeing No 4073 *Caerphilly Castle* taking water at Pontypool (Crane Street). The late Ken Harding, a railway enthusiast, worked as a fitter at Lower Varteg Slope, and in later years at Blaenserchan Colliery; he recalled seeing one of the class taking water at Talywain on the GWR Top Line branch from Trevethin Junction at Pontypool.

Notable Pontypool Road men

In 1865 North Eastern Railway footplatemen founded a union called the Engine Drivers & Firemen's Society. It unsuccessfully attempted strike action, as a result of which the NER was able to break up the Society. In 1872 an industrial union, the Amalgamated Society of Railway Servants, was founded with the support of the Liberal MP Michael Bass. In 1872 the ASRS reported having 17,247 members, but by 1882 this had declined to only 6,321.

By the end of the 1870s many UK railway companies had increased the working week from 60 to 66 hours, a 12-hour working day was common, and wages had been reduced. Of all the grades in the railway workforce, the engine driver enjoyed the highest pay and status of all but the Chief Engineer and a station master. The Great Western Railway had not increased wages since 1867, had increased the working day from 10 to 12 hours in 1878, and had then reduced wages for all but the most junior drivers and firemen in October 1879. In that year almost 2,000 GWR locomotive drivers and firemen signed an ASRS petition to the GWR Board of Directors requesting a restoration of the 1867 conditions of service and rates of pay. The GWR reacted by refusing to meet ASRS representatives and dismissing several of the petitioners from their jobs. As a result of this defeat, drivers and firemen from Griffithstown, Pontypool, South Wales, started to organise a craft union separate from the ASRS. At the time there were similar moves in other parts of England towards founding an enginemen's union, and ASLEF officially records Charles Perry[3], a Pontypool Road engine driver, as its founder. Other noteworthy Pontypool Road men included Arthur Hathaway, author of the GWR Rule Book, who was a Pontypool Road engine driver.

The most prolific example on record of any suggestion box scheme is that of John Drayton[4] (born 18 September 1907) of Newport, Gwent, who plied British Railways and the companies from which it was formed with a total of 31,028 suggestions between 1924 and 18 April 1984, of which one in seven was accepted.

Former Pontypool Road driver Jimmy

Watkins had the great foresight to take his cine camera to work in the early 1960s and recorded scenes that are now available on DVD from B & R Video, courtesy of his fireman Dennis Skinner. In the early 1980s he was kind enough to allow my father to borrow his films to show to students at Pontypool College. In the preservation era, in the early 1970s, Jimmy drove ex-GWR '96xx' Class 0-6-0PT No 9642 at NCB Maesteg, where it was restored and steamed occasionally.

Pontypool Road today

Pontypool Road loco depot closed to steam locomotive operation on 31 May 1965, but remained open until April 1967. Today it is the site of a bypass, and the station has a reduced island platform, with the remains of a spur to the down carriage sidings. The station's bays were removed at Easter 1978.

In 2016 Panteg & Griffithstown Station was removed for preservation by the Dean Forest Railway Society for future use on their railway. The alternative option for this building for the Canal Trust to use to re-line the canal bed as infill! Another local railway landmark now lost forever.

Panteg up and down loops exist below the old Panteg Junction, the Northern Sidings are overgrown and silent, and Little Mill Junction uses a single spur to store track machines. The only surviving example of Charles Liddell architecture is the old original station building at Pontypool Road. The Third Road partly survives between the canal bridge and the West Junction alongside the bypass through the yards; south of Coedygric Road viaduct remains a small area of land, formerly the New Sidings. At Pontypool, on the Pontypool to Hafodrynys bypass, the remains of Trosnant Sidings were removed to make way for a roundabout in 2016, and at Cwm Glyn the retaining wall at Cwm Glyn down loop remains in situ. The washery at Hafodrynys New Mine still exists; it was scheduled to become a restaurant but that scheme failed. The site of the dispatch sidings remains untouched. On the old Monmouthshire line at Llantarnam, at the bottom end of Cwmbran Drive, concrete sleepers survive beneath the Newport Road bridge and in the cutting. In the Eastern Valley, the only surviving part of GWR railway line remains buried, since December 1935, beneath the Llanerch Colliery tip on the Branches Fork to Blaenserchan Colliery branch. Crumlin Viaduct has survived, in part, thanks to a section of railings, complete with capping, being used as car park fencing at Pontypool College in 1965, when purchased by my father for the College; he also privately purchased from the scrapmen the signal box nameplate Crumlin High Level Station, but this was stolen from Pontypool College many years ago, and its current whereabouts are unknown. One piece of the railings now survives in my ownership, as do the signal box plates from Pontypool Road East Junction, Panteg and Coedygric Junction and a few Ponty cabside number plates!

Acknowledgements

In 2012 there was relatively little published information about this depot, apart from John Drayton's books and the odd magazine article. I must thank my father John Williams for his help in providing footplate staff contacts, and Harry Rawlins for shed fitting staff information and contacts. This book has been produced to record the surviving railwaymen's memories, primarily due to my lack of knowledge on this subject.

I would like to thank the following people for their assistance with providing information for this book, with great enthusiasm: my father John Williams, Harry Rawlins, Charlie Reynolds, Derek Saunders, Henry Williams, Gwyn Hewlett, Colin Polsom, Andy Atkins, Terry Target, David Williams, Robert Morgan, John Pring, the late Graham Merryfield, Arthur Edwards, Terry Warwood, the late Terry Jones, Terry Biggs, the late Bob Garrett, the late Ted Hounslow, Edward Freeman and Julian Brachii.

I would also like to thank railway enthusiast Keith Jones of Mountain Ash for his memoirs and for introducing me to ex-Aberdare firemen Terry Wilkins and Phil Marks, so that the western end of the Vale of Neath line and Aberdare loco shed can be remembered.

Finally, thanks to Ken Davies's widow Sheila Davies, for giving me Tom Davies's memoirs (he was Ken's father) so they can be recorded for posterity.

Special thanks are due to Harry Rawlins, Derek Saunders, Charlie Reynolds, J. S. Williams and Terry Target.

Harry Rawlins is a former locomotive fitter who worked at Pontypool Road from 18 August 1952 to November 1964. He undertook the majority of his apprenticeship at Pontypool Road, and spent one year at Swindon. He has since continued his interest in railways by joining the Dean Forest Steam Railway in 1995, undertaking some of the restoration of pannier tank No 9681 after 1995, when he was the loco's Chief Engineer for a few years. I first met him around 2001, and this friendship was renewed in 2012. He has collated a mass of information on Pontypool Road, and thus the idea for a book was suggested. Without Harry's friendship and enthusiasm this book would not exist and the information in it would not have been recorded.

Derek Saunders, a former Pontypool Road driver, began his railway career at Pontypool Road in 1944, and has recalled the war years up to closure; he has also provided footplate logs and pre-closure job roster information used by him in his efforts to prevent closure in April 1967. He undertook a personal attempt to save the depot when he was on the LDC, in his own time as homework, and his efforts in doing this must be recognised and applauded.

I met Charlie Reynolds in 2012. He fired the last tender engine to cross Crumlin

Viaduct, thus beginning a four-year period of research.

My father John Williams provided me with numerous footplate friend contacts and allowed me to use his extensive Eastern Valley archive of photographs taken between 1965 and 1982.

Finally, Terry Target first met my father in December 1982 while photographing a rail recovery train at Varteg station on the former GWR Top Line branch to Talywain, continuing as the ex-LNWR/LMS branch to Blaenavon. Having made a selection of Terry's photographs of the Blaenavon Top Line railway after closure, I am reminded of what a remarkable piece of civil engineering this branch was, from Trevethin Junction at Pontypool to Blaenavon Furnace Sidings. It is a tragedy that it was not preserved from at least Pontypool (Crane Street) to Blaenavon, as it would have made the finest preserved standard gauge line in the UK, with its fierce gradients, numerous curves, S-bends and incredible civil engineering, such as the 180-degree horseshoe curve, the Big Arch at Talywain, overlooking the site of the British Ironworks, and the outstanding Garndiffaith Viaduct.

The illustrations

I would like to thank the following for their help in writing the captions: the late Phil Williams (driver), Harry Rawlins, Derek Saunders, Gwyn Hewlett, Colin Polsom, Henry Williams, John Williams, Terry Target and D. K. Jones of Mountain Ash.

The Ordnance Survey maps are uncredited, but I would like to place on record the kindness of my old friend David Moores in making these available.

I would like to thank the following people for the use of photographs: Dick Whittington of Pro-Rail and Barry Hoper from the Transport Treasury; Harry Rawlins; Terry Target (Vol 2); my father John Williams, and other photos from the John Williams collection (Edgar Harvey, a latcher for PJ & JP Ltd at Blaenserchan Colliery in the 1920s and 1930s and the

late railway employees Dave Fry, Rollei Kinnersley (Vol 2), Dick Bassett (Vol 2) and Herbie Harrington (Vol 2); the late Desmond Coakham (Vol 2); David Postle from Kidderminster Railway Museum; Paul Chancellor from Colour-Rail; Mark Vrettos; Alastair Grieve; Lawrence Waters of the Great Western Trust for use of photographs from the Michael Hale collection; Tony from Rail-Online; and Rodney Lissenden for the R. C. Riley photographs in Christine Riley's ownership (I would like to thank Neil Parkhouse of Lightmoor Publications for kindly scanning this on my behalf).

A special thank you is given to Ken Gibb, who supplied a copy of the Pontypool Road Loco Depot Plan, and Bob Marrows for use of his photos at Pontypool Road and on the Vale of Neath. Keith Jones of Mountain Ash is thanked for extensive access to photographs from the Stan Brown and Sid Rickard collections and other photographers within his collection. John Bird of Southern Images, Colin Stacey of Initial Photographics, Graham Vincent, John Chalcraft (Railphotoprints) (Vol 2), Robert Hall of Griffithstown (Vols 1, 2) and Roger Phelps (Dean Forest Railway) for allowing use of photographs from their collections; R. M. Casserley (Vol 2), Joe Waterfield (www. britainfromabove.org.uk) (Vols 1, 2). To Chris Matthews for use of his photo of his father on his 100th birthday.

Finally, I would like to thank The Signalling Record Society, The Manchester Locomotive Society, R. K. Blencowe, R. S. Carpenter, Ralph Charles (Vol 2), Terry Walsh (Vol 2), Steve Davis (www. britishrailwayphotographs.com) (Vol 2), Barry Foster (Vol 2) and Terry Target (Vol 2) for making available photographs from their collections.

Mountain Ash 'Austerity' No 8 (LMR WD152 *Rennes*)

This engine is part of the history of the Vale of Neath Railway at NCB Mountain Ash, and is thankfully still with us and about to enjoy a new career as a preserved steam engine for future generations to enjoy. The restoration of the loco was approaching completion at the time of writing (December 2016), and was intended to spend the 2017 running season at the Dean Forest Railway. The owners would like to thank the following people who have helped with its restoration by providing legal assistance and loco parts: Hannah Davies of Newbold Solicitors, Steve Latham (LNWR Heritage Ltd) and Neil Booth of Stafford Railwayana Auctions for locating a nameplate from ex-LMR austerity loco *Caen*, allowing replica *Rennes* nameplates to be manufactured with accuracy by Newton Replicas. Finally to my brother Nigel, for

financing the final stages of its restoration using contract labour in 2016-17.

I would also like to place on record my sincere thanks to Silver Link Publishing for their support and enthusiasm in publishing this book, to be published in two volumes. Volume 1 recalls the shed, shed staff, shed yards and the Vale of Neath line.

Phil Williams
Torfaen
South Wales

'Saint' Class 4-6-0 No 2947 *Madresfield Court* is the backdrop for this Improvement Class photograph, taken in 1919 at the back of the coal stage. From left to right, the following staff have been identified with the assistance of Driver Phil Williams ('Full Load Phil'): Ernest Brakespeare is seen on the running plate, who in later years was to become the Shed Master at Barry loco depot. From left to right, on the first row beneath the running plate, are three unknown, Moses Austinfield, Albert Critchly, unknown, Albert Vinnicembe, Reg Baylis, unknown, and Russell Tucker (fourth, fifth, eighth, ninth and eleventh positions from the left). On the second row beneath the running plate are Bob Whatley, Bill Reed, unknown, Reg Irvings, Bert Oswald, three unknown, Bill Fry, Bill Jarrard (Shed Foreman), Fred Dicken, and two unknown. On the front row are Horace Howlett, Chris Chester, R. Martin, Fred Hayling, Geo Durrant, Harry Crabb, Len Hough, Bill Hough, Harold Hicks, Alf Lewis. *J. S. Williams collection, via the late Dave Fry*

Chapter 1: Overview - the shed and surrounding signal boxes

Notable dates for infrastructure modification

The following dates and titles are taken from official GWR or BR drawings, held at the National Archive, Wiltshire, and Swindon History Centre based in Chippenham. Drawing numbers are omitted.

Pontypool Road Engine Shed
1898 Pontypool Road: Coal Stage
1898 Pontypool Road, Neath, Gloucester: Coal Stage – Elevated Road
1898 Pontypool Road: Engine Shed – Arrangement of Smoke Troughs
1899 Pontypool Road: Locomotive Yard – Alterations
1914 Pontypool Road: Lifting Shop and Stores
1918 Pontypool Road: Water Supply
1920 Pontypool Road: Enginemen's Cabin
1928 Pontypool Road: Electric Lighting – (Plan of Locomotive Shed and Yard)
1936 Pontypool Road: Engine Shed – Electric Drive for Machinery
1936 Pontypool Road: Water Supply
1944 Pontypool Road: Alterations to Coal Stage – Installation of Coaling Lift
1945 Pontypool Road: Engine Shed – South End – Permanent Way Alteration
1957 Pontypool Road: Engine Shed etc, Water Supply Alteration

Pontypool Road Wagon Repair Shed
1930 Pontypool Road: Conversion – Wagon Repair Shed
1935 Pontypool Road: Alteration – Water Supply to Wagon Repairs Shop

Pontypool Road Yards
1908 Pontypool Road: Track Layout
1908 Pontypool Road (Payton's Yard): Water Supply
1913 Pontypool Road: Viaduct – Bridge over Panteg Goods Lines
1938 Pontypool Road: Track Layout
1946 Pontypool Road: Site of Proposed Locomotive Yard
1948 Pontypool Road: Land for Proposed Locomotive Yard
1948 Pontypool Road: Site of Proposed Locomotive Yard

Pontypool Road Station
Old Station
1899 Pontypool Road: Rearrangement of Station and Yard – Water Supply – including Drawing No 15435

1900 Pontypool Road: Station – Ticket Collector's Office
1907 Pontypool Road: Station Water Supply

New Station
1907 Pontypool Road: New Station – Plan, Elevations
1907 Pontypool Road: New Station – Track Layout
1910 Pontypool Road: Station Water Supply
1912 Pontypool, Tenby, Wrexham, Newton Abbot: Fixed Hand Crane – Arrangement
1922 Pontypool Road: Station – Proposed Extension of Refuge Sidings
1925 Pontypool Road: Station – High Pressure Oil Gas Main
1928 Pontypool Road: Electric Lighting – (Plan of Station)
1934 Pontypool Road: Water Tanks at Station
1964 Pontypool Road: Station – Water Supply

Crumlin (Vale of Neath Line)
1907 Crumlin Junction to Llanilleth Junction: Proposed Motor Service
1921 Crumlin (High Level): High Level – Water Supply Alterations
1923 Crumlin (High Level): High Level – Station – Track Layout and Lighting
1923 Crumlin (Junction): Junction Sidings – Electric Lighting – Track Layout
1929 Crumlin (Viaduct): Conversion – Double to single line
1933 Crumlin Junction: Water Supply

Train arrival and departure times

Within this book, reference is made to train times based on people's memories rather than accessing timetables of the period. Where there may appear to be a discrepancy in the text, relating to times referring to Pontypool Road station, it should be remembered that the time in question may be an arrival time or a departure time, which is sometimes not stated in the text. The following times are stated for selected train services at Pontypool Road station:

i) Manchester to Swansea – arrival at 1.25pm, depart 1.30pm (engine change for Cardiff; LMS engine turned and serviced).
ii) Liverpool to Plymouth – arrival at 1.38pm, depart at 1.42pm.
iii) Bristol to Shrewsbury – arrival at 3.15pm, depart at 3.20pm (Bristol engine removed, LMS engine attached to work train northwards).
iv) Bristol to Shrewsbury – arrival at 8.25pm, depart at 8.27pm (Ponty crew relieved by another set of Ponty crew. Return with the mail train from Crewe at Shrewsbury, arriving at Pontypool Road at 4.20am).

From left to right: John Pike (fireman), Terry Biggs (fitter), Harry Rawlins (fitter and turner), the late Malcolm Hewlett (fitter and turner), Derek Saunders (driver), the late John Williams (railway enthusiast), Gwyn Hewlett (fireman) and Peter Day (fireman). *Alastair Grieve*

Pontypool Road loco depot and yard, 1920. *Crown Copyright Reserved*

Note

O – Two lines at the east side of the triangle are the Up Main/Bi-directional Line and Down Main to Station South as recalled by Derek Saunders (the original main line)

Phœnix Galvanizing Works

3

L

K

M

E

D

O

2

No 1 Siding

C

G

East Junc

Middle Junction

B

F

Engine Shed

J

A

No 7 Siding

Allotment Garden

K

N (1920)

J

H I

Goods Shed

Viaduct

Tank

H I

1

Sidings Key

A - Loop Sidings

B - The Loop, Up/Down Goods

C - Loop Junction

D - Bi-directional Line to Station South

E - Hart's Yard

F - South Sidings

G - Birkenhead Sidings

H - Coedygric Sidings

I - New Sidings

J - Old Main Line, Up/Down Goods

K - New Main Line

L - Up/Down Goods

M - 'Third Road' to Loop Sidings

N - Up/Down Main

Signal Box Key

1 - South Sidings

2 - East Junction

3 - West Junction

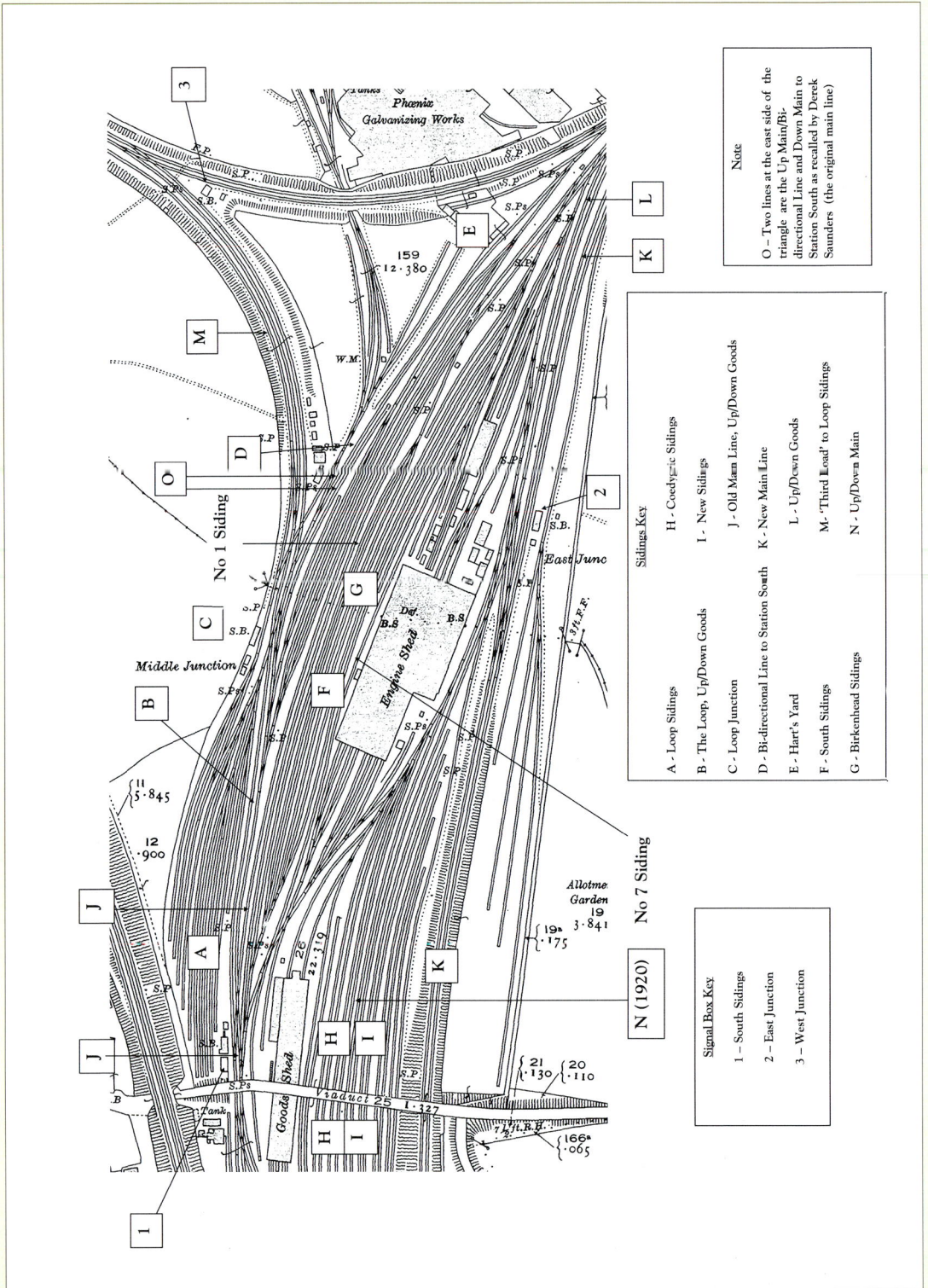

Pontypool Road loco yard and signal box locations, north of Coedygric Road Viaduct, 1920.
Crown Copyright Reserved

Sidings Key

A - Loop Sidings
B - The Loop, Up/Down Goods
C - Coedygric Sidings
D - New Sidings
E - Up/Down Main to East Junction
F - Up/Down Goods (South Sidings Junction to
Coedygric Sidings)
G - Up/Down Goods To Panteg Junction
H – Main line
I - Old Yard
J - Old Yard Weighing Machine
K – Eastern Valley Line
L – Down Loop

Signal Box Key

1 – South Sidings

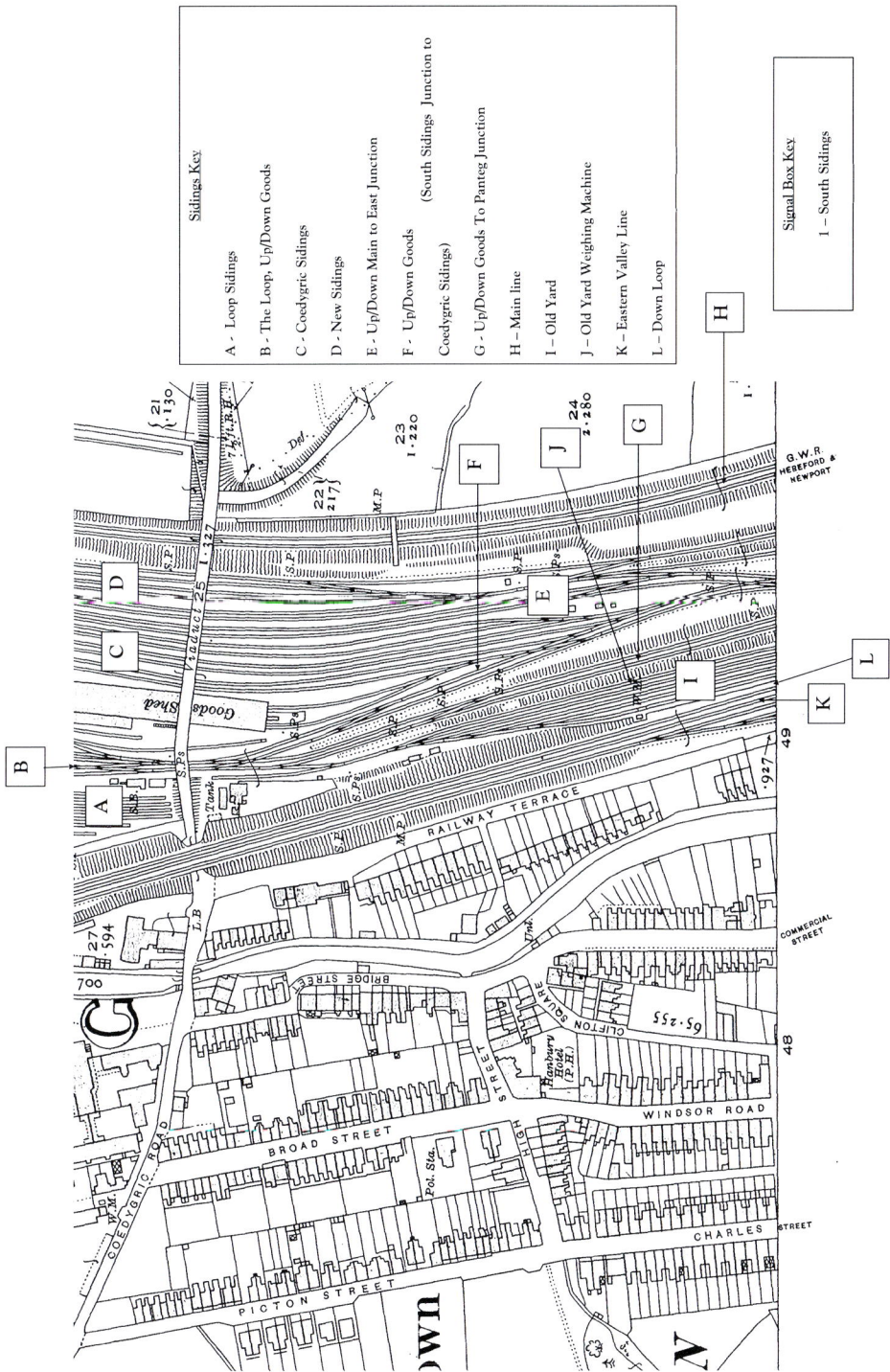

Pontypool Road loco yard locations, south of Coedygric Road Viaduct, 1920. *Crown Copyright Reserved*

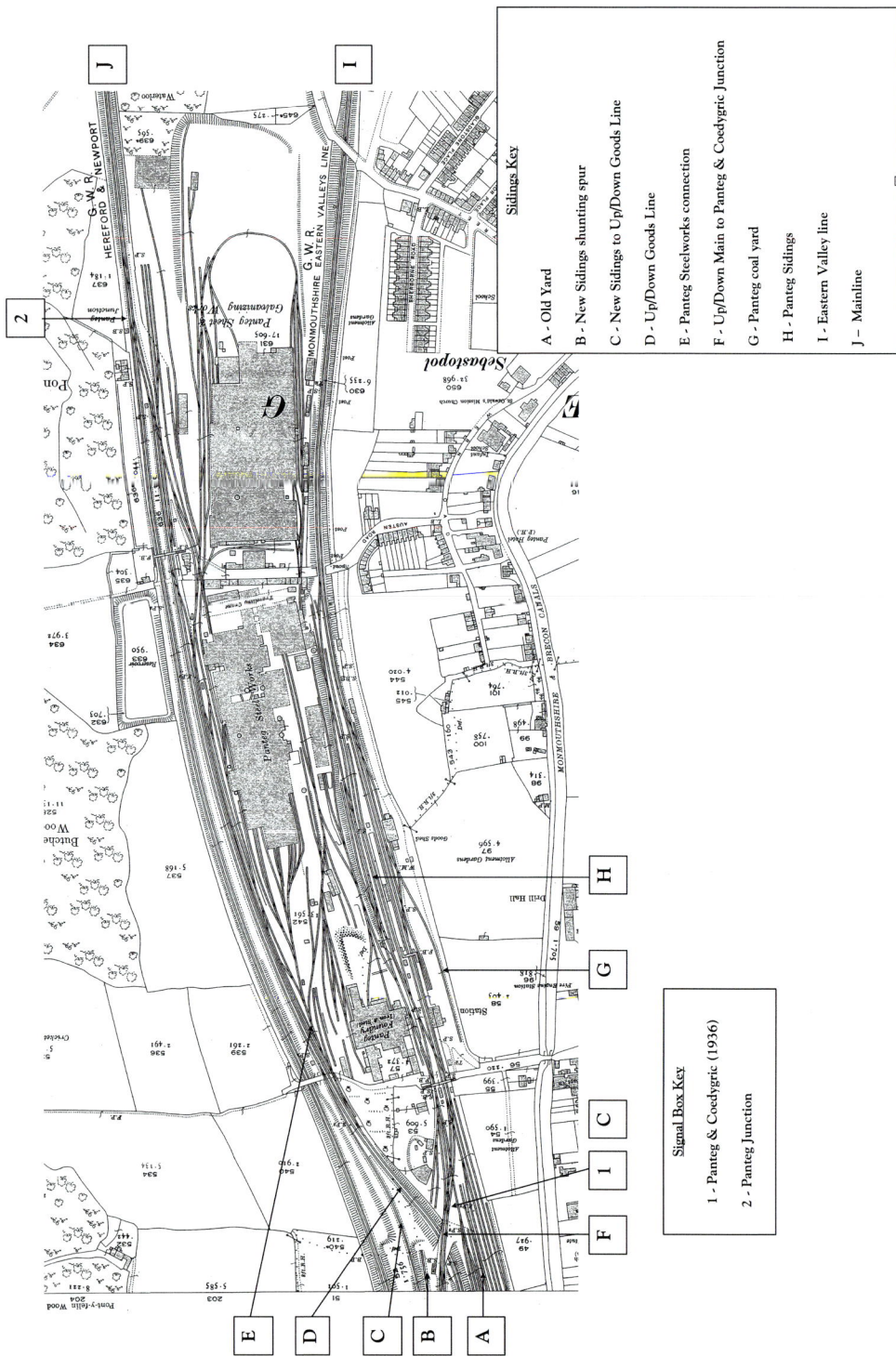

Sidings Key

A - Old Yard

B - New Sidings shunting spur

C - New Sidings to Up/Down Goods Line

D - Up/Down Goods Line

E - Panteg Steelworks connection

F - Up/Down Main to Panteg & Coedygric Junction

G - Panteg coal yard

H - Panteg Sidings

I - Eastern Valley line

J – Mainline

Signal Box Key

1 - Panteg & Coedygric (1936)

2 - Panteg Junction

Signal box locations and yards adjacent to Panteg Steelworks, 1920. *Crown Copyright Reserved*

An aerial view of Pontypool Road loco depot and yards, looking east to west, on 14 April 1959. *Terence Soames (Cardiff Ltd)*, *Phil Williams collection*

An aerial view of the gasworks, looking south on the same day; the Northern Sidings and New Sidings and their shunting spur are seen. *Terence Soames (Cardiff Ltd)*, *Phil Williams collection*

Panteg Steelworks, looking north on 14 April 1959, showing Panteg Junction and the Pontypool Road yards in the upper right background. *Terence Soames (Cardiff Ltd), Phil Williams collection*

The following signalling plans cover Pontypool Road station and the various yards surrounding Pontypool Road loco depot. Railway junctions at Little Mill, Llantarnam and selected locations from Pontypool (Clarence Street) to Penar Junction on the Vale of Neath line are also included.
The Signalling Record Society

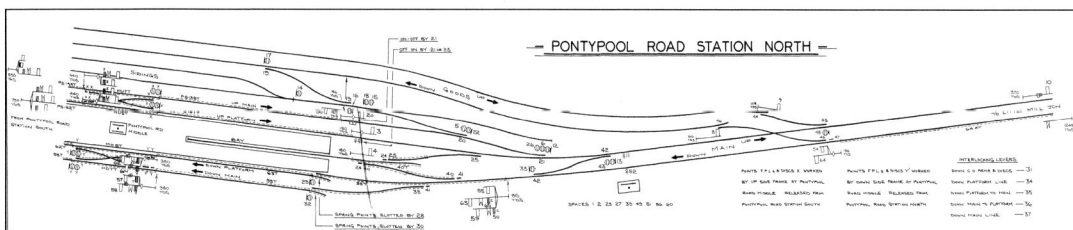

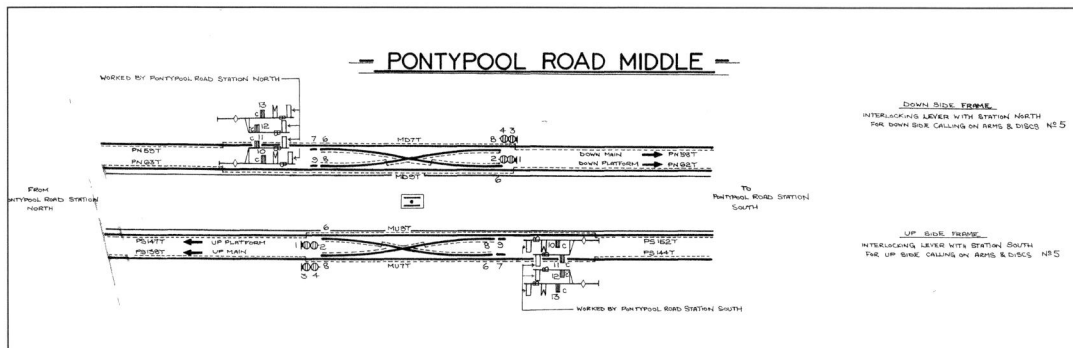

PONTYPOOL ROAD STATION SOUTH
1950

PONTYPOOL ROAD EAST JCN.

PONTYPOOL ROAD WEST JCN.
1955

PONTYPOOL ROAD SOUTH JCN.

Note that the Low Level Goods line proceeds to Panteg Junction, not Panteg and Coedygric Junction as stated on the Pontypool Road South Junction plan.

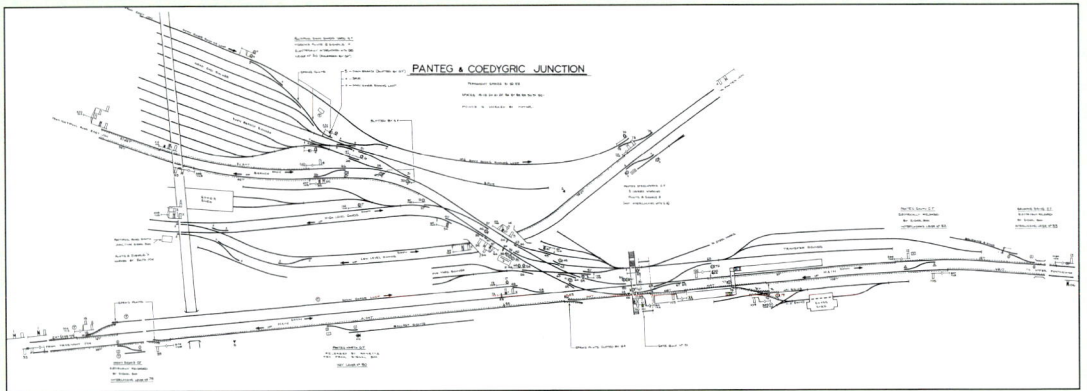
PANTEG & COEDYGRIC JUNCTION

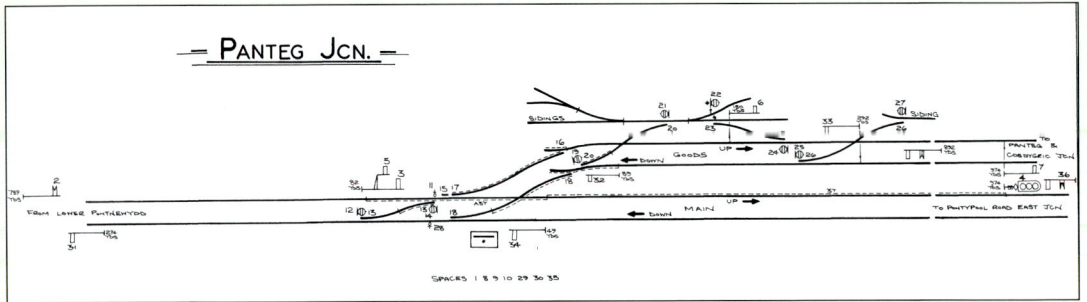
PANTEG JCN.

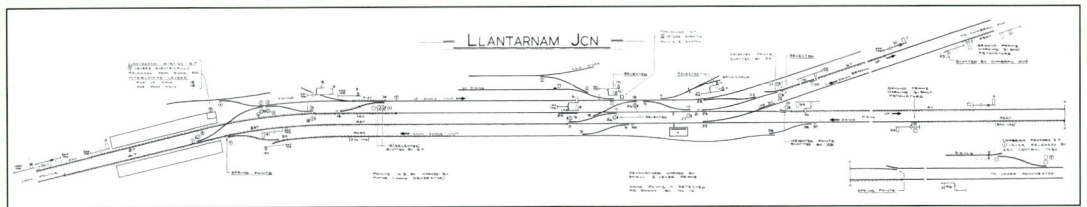
LLANTARNAM JCN.

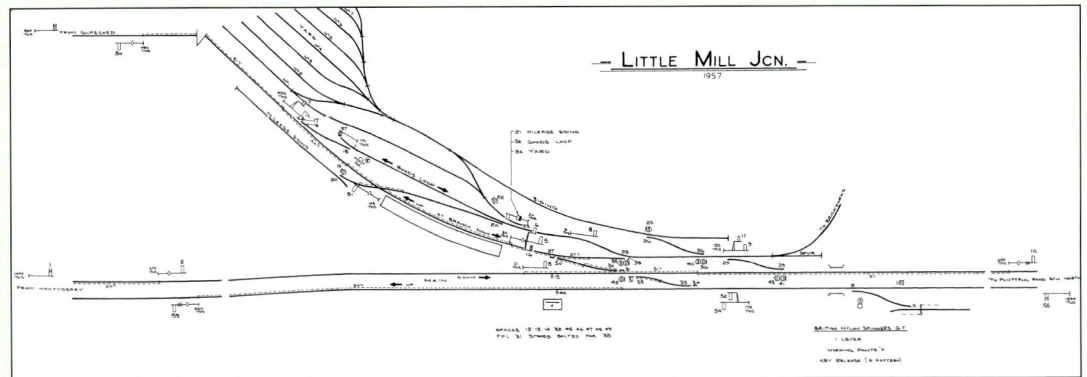
LITTLE MILL JCN.
1957

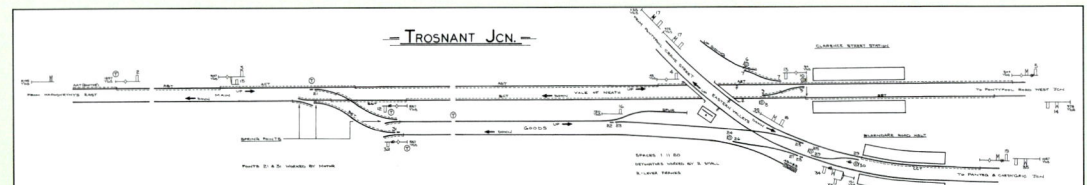
TROSNANT JCN.

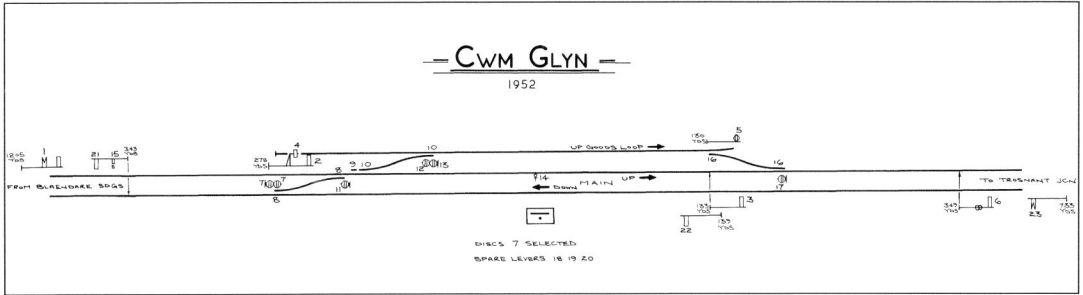

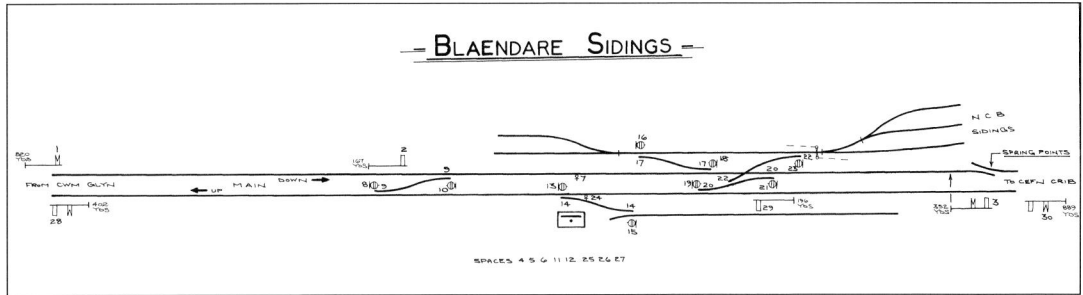

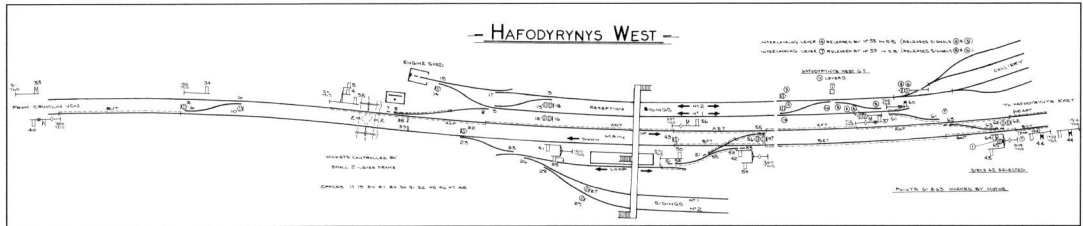

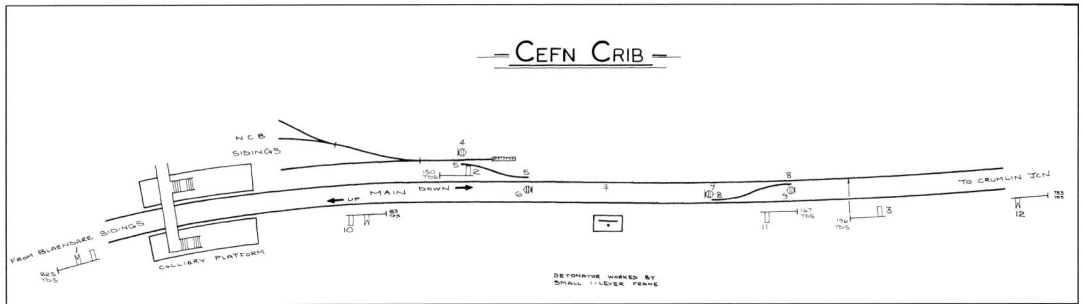

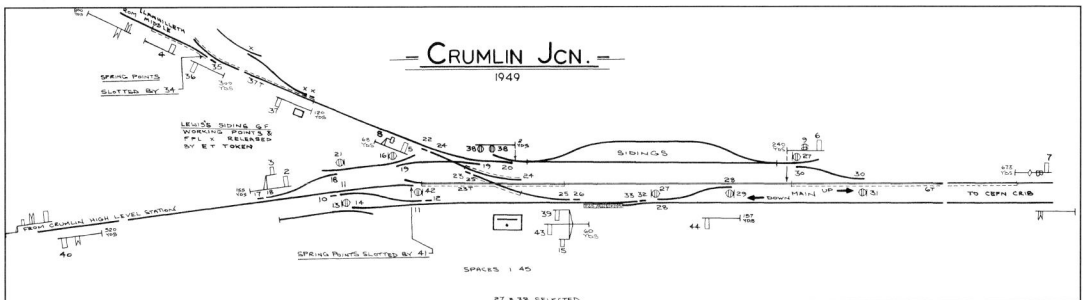

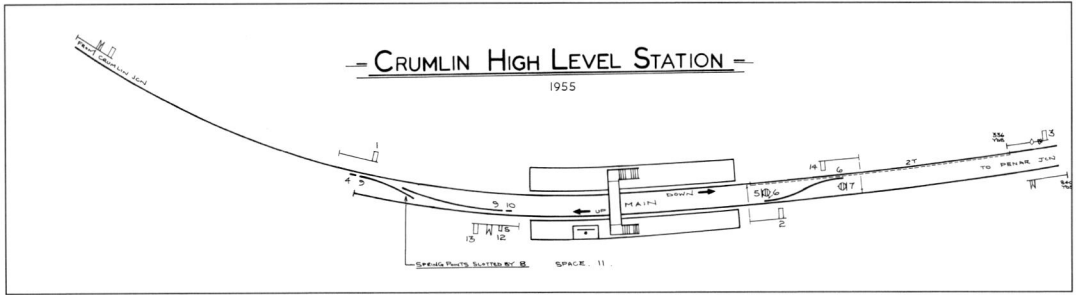

- CRUMLIN HIGH LEVEL STATION -
1955

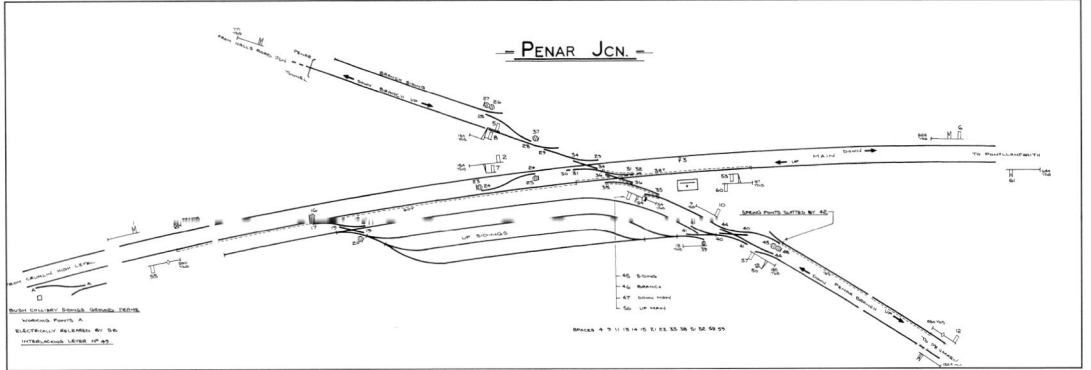

- PENAR JCN. -

Chapter 2: Pontypool Road shed

1. Driver Derek Saunders

My father Jim Saunders was a fireman (as a cleaner) on the Admiralty coal trains in the First World War. He came out of the line of promotion because at that time you only went to Swindon to pass out as a fireman when you had done 313 turns or your age came up. The shed master set the precedent as to when you could to go to Swindon to pass as a fireman, which required you to pass a medical. You were registered as a fireman as soon as you started to learn to fire, but the shed master could hold you back if he wanted to. As a result, when my father pushed to go to Swindon to pass, he was too old – when you turned 23 they wouldn't have you as a fireman. So he was a fireman on the shed, having done the 313 turns, but was too old. His job was moving engines on the shed and stabling them. You would normally be a fireman for 17 or 18 years before you became a driver.

Anyone could the join the railway to become a fireman. My father got me an interview, which I had in the shed master's office at Pontypool Road. If you were accepted by a shed for employment, you would receive notification from Swindon for a medical assessment, which included an eyesight test. This assessment lasted for two days.

I started on the GWR on 29 February 1944 at Pontypool Road shed, having been sent to Swindon on 21 February for a medical. I was sent back to Pontypool Road shed for 6 months to grow half an inch – I was 5 foot 2½ inches but you had to be 5

foot 3 inches. I went to Swindon the second time on 14 August 1944 for another medical. Pontypool Road shed had a fireman at that time who found difficulty in reaching the injectors as he was short in height.

Jim, my father, ran a sick club for employees at Pontypool Road. They would pay into this and claim sick pay if unwell. At Christmas time the fund would pay out a dividend to the members, and I would help my father pay out this money in brown envelopes, so I knew a lot of employees before I started to work at the shed.

When I started at Ponty, footplate men worked trains to Shrewsbury, Bristol, Neath and, towards the end of steam, to Swansea. Top link jobs from Pontypool Road were as follows: to Shrewsbury, such as the 8.27pm, the 1.25pm to Bristol (Liverpool to Plymouth), to Swansea from the 8:40am to Neath over the Vale (I can't remember what period), and to Cardiff, such as the 1.42pm (Manchester to Swansea).

I started as a fireman on 25 February 1946 at Hengoed. I would pushbike daily from Griffithstown, leave my bicycle underneath the signal box at Maesycwmmer, and relieve the 5.40am Rhymney from Ponty. I was moved back to Pontypool Road on 11 March 1946; I changed depots with a Merthyr fireman and got back earlier than expected – I had been away for only a fortnight.

I became spare leg on the coal stage on 25 March 1945, and joined the Pilot Link on 1 April 1946. I later joined the Banking Link, then did my National Service (Army) from 1947 to 1949. I did my practical driving exam on 18 April 1961, and passed for driving at Swindon on 17 May. I was made a driver at Cardiff on 20 July 1962, and moved there on 13 August 1962. I returned to Pontypool Road on 17 May 1965. When Pontypool Road closed I moved to Reading on 11 December 1967, as a put-back driver, classed as a fireman. I moved to Ebbw Junction as a second man on 15 January 1968, and was reinstated to driver at Severn Tunnel Junction on 11 August 1969. That closed on 10 October 1987, and I transferred to Newport High Street on Sunday 11th. I retired in March 1993.

Pontypool Road yard buildings

Timekeepers and guards occupied offices by the Coedygric Road viaduct. There were two timekeeper's offices, one by the viaduct for guards and shunters, and the other at the loco shed, for loco people. There was an Old Cottage by the viaduct where the Old Yard shunter lived, with pigeon cots in the garden. The cottage was split into two parts; the half near the viaduct was used as the Old Yard cabin, and the half near the pigeon cots was used as a house. A water tank by the Old Cottage supplied the water columns at the Old Yard. The Old Yard shunter would talk to the wagons!

Under the Old Yard water tank was the Ambulance Hall, a wooden building. Clem Ford, one of the storekeepers, was also the Ambulance man. His main job was taking ashes out of your eyes. He would turn your eyelid out and extract any ashes using a matchstick.

At the other side Coedygric Road Viaduct was the South Sidings signal box, but who worked there I cannot remember by name. Behind the box and adjacent to the canal was Coedygric Farm, which was kept by the Deakins family. They kept pigs at the bottom of the lane leading to the Skew Fields, at the back of the Loop Sidings. The Middle Junction signal box was located at the entrance to the Loop Sidings, and the brick wall behind the box acted as a boundary to the Skew Fields. Middle Junction signal box didn't exist when I started at Ponty in 1944; it was known as the Loop Junction when I worked there.

The Canteen started operating in the beginning of the 1939-45 war, and was also situated by the Coedygric Road viaduct. Also there was the wagon repair shed; in earlier times it had been a goods transfer shed, which closed in 1932. The lift by the wagon

Looking north, the last train of coal from Hafodrynys New Mine washery passes Coedygric Farm on Sunday 1 April 1979, hauled by Class 37 diesel-electric locomotive No 37230. *J. S. Williams*

repair shed was used for bringing machinery down into the yard; it was there from the 1950s.

There were six signal boxes controlling access to the yards: Station South, East, Panteg, West, South (known as the South Sidings), and Panteg & Coedygric. I recall the following staff at the Station South signal box: Jack Kitch, A. Driver and Arthur Wakeham from St Hilda's, Griffithstown. 'One at a time,' Archie Driver would say to me.

The tracks outside the East signal box on the main-line side were the Up and Down Main, and the Up and Down Relief. This box was opposite the east side of the loco shed. The gasworks located behind the East Box is seen in the photographs on page 23; it was built before the war when the site was just fields.

Panteg Junction was on the main line adjacent to Panteg Steelworks, and gave access to the yards via the South Sidings signal box at Coedygric Road Viaduct.

The West Box was situated at the western end of the triangle. The NUR Secretary, Bill Edwards, worked at the West box. Stan Filer worked as a relief signalman; he later went in the Goods Depot at Newport and came back to Ponty as a guard.

The Phoenix works was opposite the West box, although there were no buildings there in my time, as it had closed. Rail access was via a single-track underbridge in the triangle between the West Box and the Afon Lwyd, but there were no rails going through this bridge in my time when I started in 1944. The Phoenix works is now the site of the Tax Office. This line can be seen on the 1920 map on page 19.

Panteg & Coedygric Junction Box was situated at the southern end of the Old Yard, adjacent to, and giving access to, the Eastern Valley line.

The Monmouthshire Railway Company had a loco shed at Coedygric, and the buildings were still there in 1944, being used for wagon repairs, which continued for quite some time after I started at Ponty.

There were two air raid shelters, one between the bridge ('tunnels') by Coedygric

signal box and the south end of the New Sidings shunting spur, the other on the inside of the triangle, opposite the Skew Fields, south of the West signal box.

There was a sand drag at Pontypool Road between the West Junction and Station South Junction, alongside the Black Ash path. You entered it at the West Junction; it was full of gravel, and ended just before the main-line underpass for the Black Ash path. There was no buffer stop at the end, and no connection back on to the main line. If you landed up in this sand drag, an engine from the shed would pull you out. Another sand drag was located at Pontwalby on the Vale of Neath line.

Pontypool Road shed staff in 1944

These are some of the staff I recall:

Shed enginemen and firemen: Ted Heywood, J. H. Saunders, J. Smith, C. S. Davies, J. Meredith, A. Lovejoy (Foreman)
Shedmaster: Mr Rustell
Running Foremen: Joe Richards, Arthur Lewis, Bert Selwood
Locomotive Inspector: Jack Kersley
Shift foreman: W. S. Jones, A. E. Selwood, C. Hewlett
Office clerks: Reg Powell (Roster Clerk), F. P. Masey, Miss Stone, Mrs Milsom, Mr Daniels, H. Frances, C. Sumner (Stores Clerk), C. Ford
Lighters-up: H. Prosser, J. Howells, C. Davies
Mechanical Foreman: W. Wiltshire (his first name might have been Wilf)
Fitters: R. Jones, A. E. Morgan, W. Stafford, D. Powell
Shed man: W. Coggins, F. May
Fire-droppers: Bill Phillips, Bill Gittings, Bill Pugh, A. Williams
Boilersmiths: G. Samson, A. Stanley, G. Spencer
Tube runner (cleaner): B. Thomas, C. Churchouse.

Coalmen enginemen: J. Hewells, W.

Radnage, A. E. Aggett (who lived in Great Western Terrace)
Boiler washers: Ben Phillips, A. Giles
Ashpans and smokeboxes: Bill Sandell, Reg Middle
Coalmen: C. Mounty, A. Clapham

The shed master was Jack Rustell (known as Rusto), from Aberdare. He wore a bowler hat, and was strict, but didn't bother you if you were all right. He has his own office, and had a mania for the loco ashes from the ash pit. In the morning he would be seen watching the ashes – he would supervise the ash collection and have a bonus for this. A steam-driven crane was supplied for ash removal, but more often than not ashes were shovelled into a wagon by hand. He didn't like the clinker being mixed up with it.

Jack Kersley was a Locomotive Inspector and landed up as a shed master at Ponty. He later had an accident, being squeezed between two locomotives.

Engine numbers were allocated to rostered jobs by the shift foreman. An engine control did most of the work near the end of steam, while the shift foreman did the local jobs.

There were two chargeman for the cleaners, Ike Jones and Arthur Haymer, one for the day shift, one for afternoons. The men didn't do any cleaning at night.

The foreman fitter was Mr Wiltshire and he was a good chap. Les Norkett replaced him around 1949, after I come back from the army, but was not held in such regard. Dave Fry was a Swindon-trained fitter in 1944; he was later the foreman fitter and towards the end of steam got a supervisory job in the carriage & wagon shed. His office was in the shed that was used to store the diesel railcar.

The boiler washers were Ben Phillips from Abersychan, and Alf Giles. Cleaners would help out, and get extra pay as it was regarded as being shed duties. The tube runner was Bernard Thomas.

Mr Robinson was the foreman boilersmith. When I was a call boy I would go with some of the boilersmiths into the fireboxes of engines, to aid my knowledge. If the chief clerk wanted me for another task, he would wonder where I was.

There was one firelighter for each shift, and Harry Prosser, Cyril Davies and Jim Howells are recalled doing this job. When you booked on as a fireman, the engine had already been lit up by the firelighter. There was enough fire for a fireman to carry on raising steam, but sometimes you booked on to find a dead engine, with no steam at all.

Shed staff did the fire-dropping, and Bill Gittings and Bill Phillips are recalled. Fire-dropping would take place throughout all shifts. Engines would queue up on the fire pit waiting for their fires to be dropped. One person worked on smokeboxes and ash pans (Billy Sandell), the fire-droppers worked on fire-dropping, and the coal man loaded coal. Midland firemen would drop their own fires, but a Western man wouldn't. Crewe loco depot expected the fireman to drop the fire but Ponty men wouldn't do this.

Ex-GWR '7700' Class 0-6-0PT No 7740 is seen on the ash pit at Pontypool Road shed, date unknown. The coal stage building dominates the background.
Kidderminster Railway Museum

Ex-GWR 'ROD' 2-8-0 No 3042 is also seen on the ash pit road around 1952. In the background can be seen the ash pit shelter, built during the war. *Kidderminster Railway Museum*

Ex-GWR 0-6-2T No 6634 rests on the ash road, date unknown. A regular turn for this engine was the Crumlin Banker. *Southern-Images*

An ash pit shed was built during the war at the north end of the fire pit, opposite the coal stage. It was the length of a tender engine. The ash pit steam crane had its own driver. A water hydrant at the fire pit was used to cool the clinker from the ash pit, using cold water.

Frank May was the pit cleaner. He had a brush and shovel to load the wheelbarrow with the ash deposited on the ash road and load it into wagons. He could never keep a barrow, so he couldn't do the work – he would always put it in the way of an engine, which would smash it up. Mr Rustell thought he'd cure him by giving him an iron barrow – but he got rid of that as well.

Footplatemen frequently had nicknames, and these are a few that are recalled. 'The Moon Man' was Ernie Clee, 'The Hangman' George Norton, 'Ain't She Sweet' was Len Vickery, and 'Piccolo Pete' was Percy Bowen, who used to play the piccolo. 'Bubbles' would do his share of the firing, and was a good mate, 'Templegate' was Charlie Shirley, and Jimmy Watkins was 'The Panda'.

Around the shed

The shed was originally lit by gas lamps, but it was lit by electricity in my time – there were electric lights in the shed in 1944.

Originally the shed roof was wooden and had wooden chimney stacks, but the last one was replaced in 1945. There was glass in the north end for light, and the roof was raised by 18 inches in 1945 to get rid of the smoke – at the weekend, especially when lighting up on a Monday morning, the shed was full of smoke! The new shed roof was asbestos, but retained the original glass in the north end for light.

The shed had doors at each end, made of wood, but these were never closed. I can just about remember them. The south-end doors

The south end of Pontypool Road loco depot is seen here viewed from Coedygric Road viaduct. On the left are the South Sidings, with a row of wagons. There were eight roads at the south end of the shed, No 1 road on the left and No 8 road on the right. The line to the right of the wagons is No 7 siding, used to bypass the shed and for loco storage, while No 6 road was the through road to the round shed and coal stage. No 1 siding was adjacent to the old main line, the up and down line through the South and Birkenhead Sidings. Station South signal box can be seen in the top right-hand corner, and the East signal box on the right. *J. S. Williams collection*

The south end of the shed is seen again, looking north, in September 1936.
Kidderminster Railway Museum

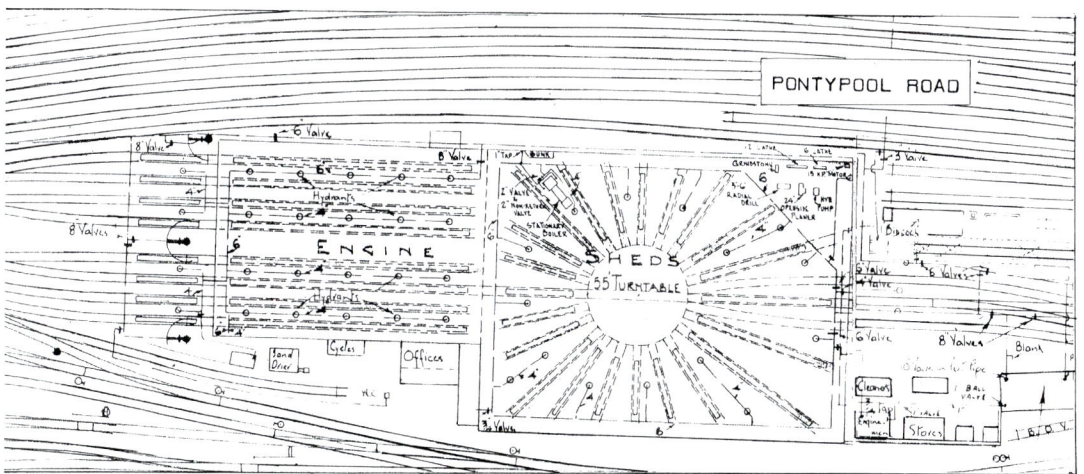

An official BR (Western Region) plan of Pontypool Road loco depot. The snowplough was kept on the shortest turntable road on the west side of the shed, adjacent to No 7 siding outside the west wall. When used with No 2385, it was stored on the plough road inside the shed. *Ken Gibbs collection*

On 15 May 1935 two 'Aberdare' Class 2-6-0s are seen on shed. On the left is No 2667 on No 2 road, and on the right No 2672 on No 5 road. *Kidderminster Railway Museum*

GWR 'Dean Goods' 0-6-0 No 2434 is at the south end of the shed on 15 May 1935. Coedygric Road viaduct is seen in the background, together with wagons in Coedygric or the New Sidings. One of these engines, No 2385, was used as the Crumlin Banker from Penar Junction to Cefn Crib, at Hafodrynys, and Llanilleth to Cefn Crib for many years. *Kidderminster Railway Museum*

Ex-GWR '5600' Class 0-6-2T No 5625 stands at the south end of the shed, circa 1960. *Kidderminster Railway Museum*

GWR 0-6-2T No 385 is also at the south end, on 24 April 1938. *Kidderminster Railway Museum*

In about 1960 ex-GWR '5600' Class 0-6-2T No 5659 moves off the south end of the shed, with the PR7 head code, and passes over a three-way point. Coedygric Sidings are on the left, with the wagon repair shed behind the engine. *Kidderminster Railway Museum*

were removed first, then the doors at the north end. At the south end of the shed, just inside between Nos 4 and 5 roads, was a urinal.

Clem Ford worked in the shed stores, as well as Clive Sumner, who was the stores clerk. The shed stores was located underneath the shed water tank (opposite the south end of the coal stage), with the office outside, on the north end of the base of the water tank.

The entrance to the shed store was at the south end, under

Cleaners and shed staff pose with GWR 2-6-0 No 6365 at the south end of the shed on No 7 road in 1944. Tom W. A. Bowstead, Arthur Edwards and Bill Morse stand alongside the engine. *J. S. Williams collection*

Above: Female cleaners are seen on the footplate of a GWR 'Hall' Class 4-6-0 at Pontypool Road station, with the former Civil Engineer's Office in the background, in 1942.

pints, 3 of general oil and 1 of thick oil. He'd ask for 3 and 1, or 3 and 2 of each type. All parts for engines and waste rags were stored on the ground floor; there were so many waste rags that some may have been stored upstairs.

The locomen's cabin was used for relief turns and spare men; it was for drivers and fireman only – cleaners were not allowed in. The cabin was situated outside the shed on the east side.

Situated in front of the drivers' cabin was the cleaners' cabin. This had no seats – you would use the boxes the piston valves came in. The fitters' cabin was alongside the cleaners' cabin and the stores.

Pranks were often undertaken; to initiate a cleaner a fellow cleaner would strip him down and plaster him with the jelly that was used to put on smokeboxes to make them shine black. If you saw a couple of cleaners scouting around the round shed you got out of the way. I was never caught out!

At the north end of the shed, looking north, were the Tap Road, the Straight Road and the Cabin Road, all connected to the north end of the turntable. At the south end of the shed were roads Nos 1 to 8. Outside, No 7 siding ran along the west side of the

the water tank. It had double doors, and as you went inside there were spiral stairs on the right. Drums of oil and paraffin were stored upstairs, pulled up using a hoist; the 40 gallon drums of oil and paraffin were poured through funnels in the floor and passed through pipes into three tanks on the ground floor, each with a tap from which to fill up bottles. There were two types of oil: thick oil for cylinders and general oil for lubrication. They didn't like giving the driver too much oil; the ration was up to 4

Below: Inside the south end of the long shed looking south, from left to right are roads Nos 8 to 5. The shed urinal is seen to the right of No 5 road. This end of the shed was rarely this empty, until after June 1964, which dates this photo to that period. *Arthur Tibbs, J. S. Williams collection*

shed and was used for storage at weekends when the place was full up with engines. Very rarely would an engine stored on the No 7 siding raise steam there as the lighters-up didn't like to work there. The fire-lighting men would get the shed turner to pick them up with another engine and move them into the shed for lighting-up.

The Tap Road ran in front of the coal stage; the water tap itself was behind the coal stage, in front of the sand house, and sometimes we'd wash there.

Most engines were turned at Ponty, and the turntable was operated manually (there was a vacuum-operated turntable at Shrewsbury). '29xxs' were turned on the turntable, and also '26xxs', known as the 'Aberdares'. A '38xx' could only be turned

At the south end of No 7 siding on an unknown date are ex-GWR 0-6-0PT No 9797, '6600' Class 0-6-2T No 6675 and 2-8-0 No 3854; on the right is ex-GWR '5600' Class 0-6-2T No 5645. *Kidderminster Railway Museum*

GWR 0-6-2T No 6666 resides on No 7 road on 15 May 1935.

GWR '1854' Class 0-6-0PT No 1705 and GWR '2021' Class 0-6-0ST No 2021 stand on No 7 road at the back of the shed in September 1936. Behind No 1705 is the round shed, and behind No 2021 the straight shed. The cabin for lighters-up, boiler-washers and the shed turner are behind these engines; Derek Saunders's father had a locker there. *Kidderminster Railway Museum*

Ex-GWR 'Hall' Class 4-6-0 No 6946 *Heatherden Hall* is seen at the north end of the shed, on the Tap Road, date unknown. Wagons for the coal stage are seen on the ramp behind the locomotive. No 6946 is waiting to be prepared, and has been stabled (it carries no lamps). Once prepped it will work a train northwards. *Kidderminster Railway Museum*

BR 'Britannia' Class 4-6-2 No 70051 rests on the Tap Road on 29 March 1964. *R. K. Blencowe collection*

Ex-GWR 0-6-2T No 6677 stands at the north end of the shed on the Cabin Road on 22 July 1962. *Rail-On Line*

if the tender was three-quarters full of water, to balance the turntable. I can recall hearing that an engine once fell into the turntable pit, but I never saw it. I recall maintenance to the turntable – it was lifted two or three times between 1944 and 1962. In the centre was half a ball bearing, which used to wear.

The shed master told the Superintendent that he couldn't deal with 'Castles' at Ponty – they were too long for the turntable and had to be turned on the triangle. 'Saint' Class '29xxs' had most of the passenger work, but 'Castles' were replacing them. A lot of the passenger work was therefore lost, and there were a lot of '29xxs' at Ponty before the war.

The Paint Road was situated between the ramp for the coal stage and the fire pit, and was rarely used. There was no buffer stop at the end of this siding, only turned-up rail ends; if you went through the end of the siding, you would land up in the fire-droppers' cabin underneath the north end of the coal stage! If an engine came on shed full of fire, it was stabled on this road.

Pits were unlit and not very deep, and it was difficult to oil the motion of the engines.

You would use a flare lamp at night when in the pit. Oil was taken from the shed stores. The driver would draw about 3 pints of engine oil, and 1 pint of thick oil for the lubricator, of which you would maybe use 3-3½ pints. A few 'Castles' occasionally came on shed, and you didn't take a feeder under there, you took a whole bottle, as a 'Castle' would use more oil.

The Stores Road was used for stabling engines at the north end of the shed, in particular one that was prepped for a duty later in the day and awaiting its crew to book on duty. I can remember seeing No 4264 on this road in early 1944 after it had run away from Blaenavon High Level and was diverted to the Gwenallt Loop at Cwmffrwdoer. No 4233 had been the first to do this, the previous year. It was a Pill engine, driven by Bill Dauncy and fired by Jack Lawrence, and had run away from just above Talywain to the Gwenallt Loop. I didn't see that on Ponty shed. [Author's note: information given to me by my father John Williams, who spoke to the fireman on the phone a number of years ago, and was given the driver's and fireman's names and the engine

Ex-GWR 'Grange' Class 4-6-0 No 6803 *Bucklebury Grange* is seen on the Stores Road at Pontypool Road shed, circa 1960. The shed water tank is seen on the left, with the stores office underneath. The coal stage dominates the background. The 'Grange' may be waiting to work a train north to Shrewsbury. Usually the Bristol engine was on this road all day long. *Kidderminster Railway Museum*

number. Details of both these accidents are recalled in Volume 2.]

No 4264 was a Pontypool Road loco, with driver Edgar Charles and fireman Ted Ashman. After the runaway incident it was taken onto the shed where it was on the Stores Road for two or three weeks. The brake blocks were worn away, there was damage to the brake gear and the boiler might have moved in the frames. The whole bunker was lifted up and had broken all the rivets. It was sent to Swindon for repairs. Edgar Charles worked on the Pilot engines at Ponty following this incident.

The Ash Hole Road, at south end of shed, extended along the east side of the shed, adjacent to the sand house. A wagon of sand for the sand house, and an empty wagon for ashes, would be stored here; it was also used for stabling engines.

There were two sand houses, the one at the back of the coal stage and another by the big office, at the south end of the shed.

At the south end of the sand house was a platform. An empty wagon would be shunted into the ash road and positioned next to this platform, then the shed man would wheel ashes in a wheelbarrow onto the platform and fill the wagon. There was no signal to this road – although a photo exists of No 9607 on this road, showing the 'dummy', I cannot recall it. We'd ask the signalman for permission to use the ash road and collect the wagon; the signalman would set the

Ex-GWR 0-6-0PT No 7724 is seen on the sand house road at the south end of the shed. On the right, the Up and Down Goods line from Coedygric Junction is seen, continuing towards East Junction. A train is seen climbing through the cutting on the main line on the right. *D. K. Jones collection*

Ex-GWR 0-6-0PT No 5756 is also seen on the sand house road, date unknown. *R. K. Blencowe collection*

GWR Dean '2021' Class 0-6-0PT No 2077 stands on the sand house road, with No 2160 in the background, on 24 April 1938. Due to a locomotive shortage at Vipond's Lower Varteg Colliery at Talywain, these two engines would later be hired to the railway system from Lower Varteg Colliery to Red Ash Slope, at Varteg Hill, Pontypool. *Kidderminster Railway Museum*

GWR 0-6-0PT No 743 is seen at the south end of the shed, with the sand house visible behind the wagon of sand. *R. K. Blencowe collection*

points and we'd go in and pull the ash wagon out.

The shed's stationary boiler was fired with small coal. The Webb 'Coal Tank' No 1054 is recalled as being used as a stationary boiler in the late 1950s, at the bottom end of No 1 road, where the old stationary boiler had once been.

The shed water tank fed all the water columns, using water from the canal.

The coal stage

No 7 siding ran at the back of the coal stage, extending the length of the shed. Next to this were two dead-end sidings that were used for anything; a loco would stable loaded wagons of coal before pushing them up the coal stage. Immediately behind the coal stage was a sand house, with its own siding.

Tommy Howells was a regular on the coal stage, together with Harold Powell and Bill Radnage. If he didn't have regular mates, the fireman would coal up. There were three chutes; the south chute was used before 1946, when an electric hoist was installed for the middle chute, which was then used all the time. The south and middle chutes were used. The north chute was never used in my time.

The coal stage coal shunt was done on the morning shift. A few runaways from the coal stage are recalled. Wagons would run out of the catch point at the bottom end of the coal stage ramp; the ramp incline was continuous, with a small slope through the coal stage building. Shunting was done by

Looking north, the coal stage is seen in September 1936, with GWR '7400' Class 0-6-0PT No 7402 being coaled. Note the 20-ton wagons of loco coal at the top of the stage. There were four rooms underneath the building. The first, nearest the shed, was a cabin for the driver and fireman who worked on the coal stage. The next room was the long lamp room, near the coal tipper on the second floor. The third was where the ATC batteries were kept, and the fourth, at the station end of the building, contained lockers for the coal man, fire droppers and the ash pan man. The upper floor was the coal stage. The toilet block is seen south of the stage on the left. There were two doors at the south end – that on the left was for the shed master, shown here with the wooden surround (so he couldn't be seen entering or leaving); the doorway on the right was for office staff. Everyone else used the side door. The louvres were for ventilation! *Kidderminster Railway Museum*

Ex-GWR 'County' Class 4-6-0 No 1013 *County of Dorset* passes the coal stage on the Up Goods Relief line, via the Eastern Valley at Panteg and Coedygric Junction. It will have entered the Eastern Valley line via Llantarnam Junction. *Kidderminster Railway Museum*

Awaiting their turn at the coaling stage are Nos 5092 *Tresco Abbey*, 3864, 7722 and 3851 on 3 June 1963. M. *Hale, Great Western Trust*

GWR 0-6-0PT No 6400 is seen at the coal stage on 10 May 1936. *Kidderminster Railway Museum*

the crew of the 6.42am Nelson turn, after a '48xx' or a pannier on the auto-train returned to Pontypool Road shed and came off the pit.

The coal stage used coal from any of the pits – what they could get. There was a shortage of steam coal and this was kept for certain jobs. Coal 'ovoids' are recalled; these were obtained from Abercwmboi and consisted of small coal and building cement mixed together. Coal was also available as brickettes, which were obtained from Cardiff; they had the word 'Cardiff' stamped on them.

Coal was also used from stock, in Hart's Yard (two or three roads at the back of the shed), but it was not as good as fresh coal. During the war coal was also stored in the Northern Sidings, and later on the ground at the Northern Sidings near the Black Ash path, at the bottom end, by Coedygric Road viaduct.

The coal was often terrible. It was very rare that you had good coal. You had all sorts of coal. Phurnacite was the worst – the 'oval eggs' would burn your eyes.

The coal was shovelled from a wagon into tubs. The tubs were then emptied into the bunker of a tank engine or the tender of a tender engine. The tubs held half a ton, and five or six tubs were loaded on a tender. Engines never came back on shed without any coal, so only a few tubs were needed to top up what remained in the tender or bunker. The coal man would lift the tub on his own; one tub at a time was tipped. The tubs were all the same type.

A loco would push half a dozen wagons up, and the coal stage men would drop them down on to the coal stage as required. Bunkers would be trimmed before going off the shed. Fireman Henry Williams once fell off the cab of a loco after stepping on a coal ovoid and fell into the pit – he could have been killed. Wagons of coal for the coal stage were used straight away as the wagons would be required for use elsewhere.

As a young fireman, I had a turn on the coal stage. Our proper job was to trim coal in the bunker and brush off any coal that had fallen onto the cab roof of the engine. I'd help coalmen to fill the tubs from the wagon in the coal stage, and lift the tub to drop coal into a tender or bunker.

There was a roller shutter at the shed end of the coal stage ramp, which would be lowered in bad weather. Arches under the coal stage at the north end were used to store smoke plates (which should have been in the stores.)

South of the coal stage was the shed toilet block. An early photograph of the coal stage shows a wooden surround at the south end of the toilet block, but I cannot remember this. There were two doors on the south end of the toilet block. The left door was used by office staff, the right door by the shed master. The door on the side was used by everyone else.

Coal field storage in the yards

Coal was also used from stock, from coal stockpiled on the ground, during the war, and coal was still on the floor when I started in 1944. Coal was stockpiled on the floor at two locations.

i. Hart's Yard
This was a yard having five sidings, inside the east side of the triangle, just below Station South Junction. It was accessed from the Up Main/bi-directional running line. The Up Main/bi-directional running line started at the South Junction, through the Loop Junction, to Station South Junction. There were two sidings for coal storage, adjacent to the embankment to the West Junction, and three for the engineers, which extended south, towards the Loop Junction; these three sidings held engineer's wagons of

sleepers, bogie bolsters with track parts and a brake van or two. At the bottom apex of the triangle at this location were the Wagon Examiner's and Wagon Greaser's cabins. During the war Henry Williams (who joined the railway in 1949) recalls seeing colliers emptying these wagons of coal, onto the floor, on a Saturday and a Sunday.

ii. Northern Sidings
Coal was also stored on the floor of the Northern Sidings near the Black Ash path, at the bottom end, by Coedygric Road viaduct.

Shed offices

The main office was in the bottom right-hand corner of the round shed, when looking north from the straight shed towards the station at Pontypool Road. The engine notice board was through a doorway on the left, in the round shed. Engine numbers were chalked up on the board.

You never clocked on. You would go to the window of the office and tell the boy your number, and he would record it in a book. This applied to all footplatemen. Clocking-on checks were used only for shed staff. You took a check out at the start of the shift, and handed it back at the end.

In 1944 the shed staff wages were put on the 12.02pm auto-train to Crane Street

Exiting the round shed, looking north across the turntable, are from left to right the Tap Road, No 6 Through Road and the Cabin Road. A 'WD' 2-8-0 loco stands on the Plough Road (also used for storing the snowplough), and an ex-GWR 'Hall' is seen on the adjacent Lift Road. The gentleman with the hose is undertaking boiler-washing duties.
Arthur Tibbs, J. S. Williams collection

GWR 'Buffalo' Class 0-6-0PT No 1600 resides in the round shed in September 1936. A water hydrant for boiler washing is seen on the left. *Kidderminster Railway Museum*

from Pontypool Road station, and the train would be stopped outside the East signal box to unload it. Money was put into round tin boxes. In BR days wages were brought from the station in a wheelbarrow.

In the shed office were W. S. Jones, Bert Selwood, Joe Richards and C. Hewlett. I had two 'reports' from Joe Richards, one of the Running Foremen when I was a fireman, one for being late off the shed, and one for waiting for tools, but on that shift was the tool man from Abergavenny, who was nicknamed 'The Snake'! I had been accused of hitting the tool man and this had been reported. I got a representative, Driver Tom Davis, who was my mate at the time and on the LDC (Local Departmental Committee). I was never aggressive, and went to see Joe Richards. The tool man accused me of striking him, but when I came out of the office I said to Tom, 'This is either a put-up job or mistaken identity – I haven't touched him.'

Tom said, 'Hang on a minute, there was a driver witness,' and went back in to see Joe – but wouldn't tell him who the witness was. Joe said, 'He'll have to be produced at the inquiry at Newport.' The witness was Harry Robins.

In the meantime I went to see 'The Snake'. I said, 'I've been accused of hitting you.'

'It wasn't you,' replied the tool man.

I wanted a written statement to take to the Newport Enquiry to confirm that I hadn't hit him. At Newport I met with my representative, the Sectional Council man from Cardiff (he was a bit raw – illiterate in writing). I said to the Super, 'We've proved to you this is a load of rubbish – the best thing you can do is withdraw it.' The Superintendent ignored the Sectional Council man, and turned to speak to me, saying, 'Something wrong here, fireman – I'll come to Pontypool Road on Monday and sort it out.'

I said, 'Thank you very much,' and away he went.

On the Monday there was a hell of a row in the traffic office, where clerks and the shift foreman were working. The Superintendent said it was the worst thing he had ever done, giving Joe Richards that job! The Superintendent was appointed by Swindon. Harry Robins, the driver, was standing by Jack Ford, his fireman, and it was Jack Ford who had hit the tool man.

Preparing engines

When getting an engine ready you would check if the loco had tools on the footplate. Tools were normally taken off the loco when the fire was being dropped, and were rarely left on the engine for its next turn of duty. As a young fireman you would take tools off an engine coming on shed; this was also the tool man's job.

The tool man would go to the lamp room to get any tools that were there – if they were missing, he would find them and bring them to you. Reginald Bolt was a former fireman, but was incapacitated. The footplate staff would help him, and he would also trim the loco lamps.

There was a shortage of tools on engines in the war, and the tool man would take them off the engine. In the 1940s and into the '50s tool boxes were sometimes locked, which was a great help; the tools could then be left on the engine and the tool box key returned to the lamp room.

Sometimes there was a queue of engines waiting to have their fires dropped when going on shed. I would put the tools in the tool box and my driver and I would leave the engine to await its turn on the fire pit and would book off duty.

During the war blast pipe jumper rings would seize up, and wouldn't work. To release it I would lift it up and twist it around to make sure it was working. I would then pour paraffin around it and set it on fire. I would do that quite often.

Steam was raised on locomotives at any time. An engine would be stone cold after a washout. Sometimes you booked on for a job and did not have much fire in the engine, while at other times there would be plenty of fire.

Leaving the shed

From the north end of the shed, to the station, the Northern sidings or the Birkenhead and Loop Sidings, you would use the Up or Down Relief, controlled from the Station South signal box. You could also leave the shed from the south end, a movement controlled by the South Sidings signal box; this exit was used for pilots – the Panteg Pilot, the PR2, and engines for Coedygric and the New Sidings.

If the north end was blocked at the fire pit, you would leave via the East signal box. The whistle code was blow three and one to leave, and blow one and three for the disc for the signalman in the East box. When leaving the shed to go outside the station on the Relief line (if the pit was blocked and you couldn't get off that end) it was blow one, then three. More often than not the signalman wouldn't take much notice, then you would have to walk back to the phone and tell the signalman. Sometimes they would pull the 'dummy' signal off to come back, and you would stop outside the East box and shout and tell him where you were for, the Northern Sidings or the station.

For the Loop Sidings, you could leave the shed using three of the shed exits: north, east or south ends.

Mr Buckingham and Mr Waldren worked in the East box. The latter had suffered an injury and had been put on light duties. One day, after working a train from Hereford and taking the engine back to the shed with Driver Sid Webber, I recall the signal coming off sharply, and realised what was wrong; I knew that Mr Waldren was in the box, and that he had fallen over.

The phone for going off shed was on the lamp post at the north end of the shed, but wasn't used very often as a whistle code was used instead.

There were two phones at the north end of the shed; one allowed you to leave via the East Junction, while the second was on the signal for leaving the fire pit and allowed you to leave the shed by ringing the Station South signal box, to leave via Station South Junction.

Three ATC ramps were located off the shed at the signals – one at the station south end, one at the east, and one at the south sidings. There were two ramps at each of these locations; the first ramp was dead, and the second ramp was live. When passing

The fireman of GWR 'Buffalo' Class 0-6-0PT No 1600 rings the East Junction signal box for permission to leave shed via East Junction on 15 May 1935. Telephones were seldom used – the whistle code of 3-1 was used instead. *Kidderminster Railway Museum*

On 15 August 1962 ex-GWR 0-6-0PT No 4668 has reversed from the Cabin Road to leave the shed while its fireman rings the East box for permission to leave. Wagons of ash are to the left, and ex-GWR Nos 6335, 9611, 3682 and 3815 are seen in the background, awaiting fire-dropping on the ash pit. *Phil Williams collection*

over these, the buzzer would sound first, then the bell. Ramps were situated beyond the signals at the three shed exits – at the north and south ends of No 7 siding, and at the east side of the shed.

An engine could be failed before going off shed. I do not recall many engines coming off the main line as failures.

Wartime recollections

Ambulance trains from Southampton are recalled, going north. These trains would be double-headed, with a Southern engine attached at the front, and fitted with a Westinghouse brake. These trains ran with 'H' codes, and 'H36' is recalled. The engines were rough – trains would often struggle with dirty fires and a lack of steam. I was in the office as a call boy, and remember a train requiring a banker as the train engine was doing rough. I can recall that the foreman decided to change the engine. That was just as bad – the train was then stuck at Nantyderry, of all places!

There were also Government Stores Trains, and near D-Day trains of tanks were seen, as well as tanks going by road down through New Inn.

When I started my career at Pontypool Road, women cleaners and Italians were present. The latter, being prisoners of war, weren't allowed to go underneath locomotives as management was afraid of sabotage. There were six to ten women cleaners at Ponty during the war. They had a mess room up the wooden steps to the room above the Carriage & Wagon Supervisor's office and change their clothes there.

American soldiers, black and white, lived in the Polo Grounds, while Indian troops would take mules out for exercising.

I remember the 'Lend-Lease' 'USA' locos when I was a cleaner. The whistle valve would stick open when the engine was cold; when you were cleaning them the whistle would begin to blow, giving an indication that the engine was making steam; I would climb onto the footplate to shut the whistle off.

These locos had a lot of trouble when running tender-first; they would come off the road, with their four-wheel tender bogies, even on the straight goods line (opposite the Old Yard) between the South Junction box (South Sidings) and the 'tunnels' at Coedygric (refer to the lower picture on the back cover, and the straight double track behind the cab roof of the '38xx'; the goods line is between the wagon repair shed and cutting to just before the 'tunnels', where it joined the Up and Down Main (Goods Relief line)). They were seldom cleaned, as they were new engines. They would be used on '28xx' turns; they were not run over the VoN, just on the main line, up to Shrewsbury and the Midlands. When towing them around the shed, the couplings were that stiff that they would rise up out of the hook and become uncoupled. The shed turners would then have to run as the engine would run down the slope on its own. 'Austerity' locos were the same.

The best thing about these engines was the American whistle; it wasn't a 'chime' one. For New Year's Eve celebrations I would hang a shovel on an engine's whistle chain, and the engines would sound their whistles and run over detonators. The 'USA' engines had a unique-sounding whistle and were ideal for these celebrations!

Arthur Edwards was a fireman on a 2-8-0 'Austerity' engine in the war. It was being got ready in the round shed. Arthur couldn't see the water in the gauge glass, nor could his driver, so he called the foreman, then the fitter to have a look. They couldn't tell where the water level was, but concluded it must be full. The engine was taken off the shed in the belief that the boiler was full, and driven to the Loop Sidings, where it took a train for Hereford. Arthur was putting the injector on occasionally to top up the water.

As they were climbing Nantyderry they heard a bang, and the fusible plug was dropped. The engine was brought to a stand by Nantyderry signal box. The station master at Nantyderry had a bit of a garden in front of the signal box, and Arthur dug it up to throw in the fire to damp the fire down.

Night work was no good in the war due to the blackout. There were lights – shaded lights – but the round part of the bulb was painted black.

During the war I had a close shave in the dark. The Ebbw Vale train came off the West Junction, to Ponty station, and was propelling back into the Northern Sidings; opposite the South box trains would be propelled by the train engine across the main line and reverse into the Northern Sidings behind the East box. I was walking from the station to the shed, with my back to this train. There were two lamp posts between the Down Relief and Up Main, and the connection to the Northern Sidings crossed the main line between them. The guard spotted me and shouted – a close shave!

I also once accidentally walked into a pit at the engine shed in the dark, there being no lights. You only did that once!

Aberbeeg men worked double-headers on the 'Dump' trains. There were about six trains to the 'Dump' (ROF Glascoed) each shift in the war; if the first train was delayed, being rough for steam, it would delay all the rest of them.

Rhymney and Merthyr men would work double-headers and struggle for steam. I once worked to Hereford on the inside engine as a fireman, but not as a driver. It was very rare in steam days to have a double-header.

During the 1940s a new steam shed was planned for the Skew Fields, but this proposal never came about.

Pontypool Road yard sidings and freight lines to Panteg

The roads between North Junction and Pontypool Road Yard were as follows; the terms Up and Down Goods lines are used to describe the goods routes between the station, various yards, Coedygric Junction and Panteg Junction for freight:

i. Main line and Up and Down Relief lines: these served or bypassed the platforms. Scissors crossovers were provided halfway down each platform face.

ii. Up and Down Goods lines: these were to the west of the station, and could send you to the Vale of Neath line; on to the shed; to the Birkenhead Siding (to arrive at the bottom end of the South Sidings); and around to the East Junction. At the South Junction, Up and Down Goods lines would take you to Panteg Junction, via the cutting; or to the bottom end of the New Sidings. The latter route was used by the Coedygric Pilot to service the south end of the wagon repair shed.

From East Junction you could proceed as follows:

i. Cross over to the Down Main line to Newport
ii. To the New Sidings via a reception line parallel to the main line. You could join the main line at Panteg Junction by using the New Sidings connection to the Down Goods Line from South Sidings to Panteg Junction, adjacent to the New Sidings shunting spur.
iii. To Coedygric Sidings
iv. To Coedygric Junction

A train would enter the yard using one of four reception roads west of the shed – Up and Down Loop, and Up and Down Goods Line – before being marshalled by the South Pilot or Loop Pilot (at the other end) to the South or Loop Sidings respectively. These four lines were kept clear by the two pilots so that arriving trains could be split and marshalled. Typically trains from the Vale of Neath via the West Junction to South Sidings signal box, trains via Panteg Junction, or freight traffic from north of Pontypool Road would use these four roads for marshalling into the South or Loop Sidings.

The Up Loop and Down Loop lines were two running lines extending from the South Sidings signal box to Hart's Yard. They were adjacent to the South Sidings signal box, and used to be part of a loop extending round to the West Junction, hence their name.

Looking north towards the station the

This view from across the tracks shows Pontypool East Junction signal box. Note the two fire buckets hooked onto the bottom of the steps, and the gasometer beyond. The signal box opened in October 1900, and closed on 9 February 1969. On 19 April 1936 it was recorded as having 70 levers in four frames. *Kidderminster Railway Museum*

Up and Down lines were to the right of the Up and Down Loop lines. These two lines were the original main line down to Newport via the old Monmouthshire line, before the main line to Caerleon and Newport was built.

The Loop line ran between the Loop Sidings to the Up and Down Goods Line (at the South Junction). It became the Up and Down Goods line to the West Junction.

Stop boards were located at the reception sidings, and there was also one at the New Sidings, one in Coedygric Siding, and one protecting the Loop from Station South.

There were catch points everywhere, for example opposite the Station Road refuge sidings (Ballast Siding on the up line), and one at the south end of Pontymoile Viaduct, on the up line.

Northern Sidings

These sidings were situated behind the East Junction signal box, and were accessed via the Up Relief line at the Station South

Junction. When using the Northern Sidings, the train engine would propel its train back into them. The Ebbw Vale train would propel back in using this method of working. No 1 Siding was next to the main line.

South Sidings

These sidings started at the South Sidings signal box, opposite the timekeeper's office, and continued until you arrived at the chimney of the furnace for the lighters-up at the long shed. The South Sidings shunters' cabin was next to the South Sidings signal box. The sidings lay between the bi-directional line between the Loop Junction and Hart's Yard, and No 7 siding, adjacent to the loco shed, and they fed the Birkenhead with wagons.

If a train arrived in the Loop from the West Junction, the engine would stand by the South signal box. The wagons would be uncoupled and propelled into the Loop Siding by the Loop Pilot, or the South Pilot would push them into the Birkenhead

Siding. Alternatively the Northern Pilot would pick them up and put them in the Northern Sidings for the glassworks.

The Panteg Pilot used these sidings for goods for Panteg station, Weston's Biscuits in Cwmbran and Girlings. No 1 siding was next to the old main line (the Up and Down line).

The Up and Down Goods lines between the South Junction and Coedygric Junction were kept clear. There were two or three sidings south of the wagon repair shed, and wagons were shunted in via the Up and Down Goods.

During the night shift the Coedygric Pilot would have an engine exchange, when a fresh engine would come off the south end of the shed, couple onto the South Pilot, and double-head a train destined for the West of England out to Coedygric signal box (using the Up and Down Goods alongside the repair shed and cutting to Panteg Junction), then propel it back into Coedygric Sidings or the New Sidings. That was the first job on the night shift; it was the 11.45pm, and we'd clock on at 9.45pm for the 10 o'clock shift.

Birkenhead Sidings

These sidings were named because the trains using them used to go to Birkenhead. They were installed before the Northern Sidings were built and were at the top end of the South Sidings, nearer to Hereford. They held northern traffic, while excess traffic from them was shunted by the Northern Pilot into the Northern Sidings. Birkenhead and Chester trains started here until they moved over to the Northern Sidings, which were a later addition, before my time, to make more room at the Birkenhead Sidings. No 1 Siding was next to the old main line (Up and Down Goods line).

Loop Sidings

These were situated between the South Sidings signal box and the Skew Fields. They started by Coedygric Road viaduct, and ended before the triangle of lines, opposite the demarcation of where the South Sidings finished and the Birkenhead Sidings started. The Loop Siding was at the end of the 'Third road'. The Loop cabin was on the border of the Skew Fields, opposite the wagon examiner's cabin, but nearer to the South Sidings signal box. Trains for the Vale of Neath started at the Loop Sidings, as well as some northern trains. Coal trains for the Midlands also started here. The 11.40am Bordesley (Birmingham) started here, and we worked it as far as Hereford, being relieved there. Before the war, Ponty men had worked this train right through to Bordesley. No 1 siding was behind the South Junction signal box.

Freight would enter the yard from the

In September 1936 GWR 'Aberdare' Class 2-6-0 No 2667 is seen on the uni-directional line between Loop Sidings and Station South Junction, in the process of being turned on the triangle. *Photomatic Ltd*

Vale of Neath line at the West Box. Wagon brakes would be adjusted twice after leaving Cwm Glyn, and the brakes would still be applied from the West Box to the South Sidings box. The train would stop at a stop board protecting the line going across the Loop, where the brakes would be 'picked up'. Sometimes you were called on, and you would go as far as you could before the brakes stopped you.

In the other direction trains were banked from the Loop Sidings around the curve to Skew Fields by the Loop Pilot.

Loop Junction to Hart's Yard and Station South

Derek Saunders recalls the Up and Down Loop and Up and Down Main (the original main line before the main line to Newport was built) as starting together, north of the South Sidings signal box, running parallel to each other through to the Loop (Middle) Junction. The Up and Down Loop continued to the West Junction, whilst the Up and Down Main continued as two parallel roads through to Station South

Junction. The Up Main was also the bi-directional line to the Loop Siding, and also used for turning engines on the triangle. To the right of the down Main, when looking north, were the yards at the back of the shed, i.e. the South Sidings and the Birkenhead Sidings. This layout is not what is shown in the 1920 map in Chapter 1, or the aerial photographs, as they reflect a different period in time

When we were cleaning, we had a shed turn (a labourer's turn), and earned extra money, shovelling coal off the floor into wagons at the coal field in Hart's Yard.

The Control banker was kept at Hart's Yard (where the roundabout is now).

Engine turning on the triangle

To turn an engine using the triangle of lines south-west of the station, you came from Ponty station, through Station South Junction and up to the West Junction. You reversed there, and proceeded along the Down Goods line to the Loop Junction. You then went forwards, along the single-line bi-directional Up Loop, past Hart's Yard,

Ex-GWR '29xx' Class 4-6-0 No 2937 pilots a southbound passenger train. In the background the Control banker, an ex-GWR '72xx' Class 2-8-2T, rests in Hart's Yard awaiting its next turn of duty. *Rail-On Line*

through Station South Junction and back to the station. The 11.40am Bordesley used this line from the Loop Siding.

Wilson's Leg and Dead End Siding

This was a siding outside the main office by Coedygric Road viaduct, and extended beyond the viaduct and alongside the wagon repair shed. It stored wagons for the repair shed, and could be accessed from both sides of the viaduct, although the north end was not used very often as the track was overgrown; I only recall wagons entering from the south end.

The Dead End Siding was west of Wilson's Leg and terminated in a stop block immediately south of the Coedygric Road viaduct. It was used to stable engines from the shed.

Old Yard

This was double ended, and could be accessed from both the north and south. No trains ran direct from the Old Yard. The Old Yard Pilot would take trains from here to Pilkington's, the Loop Sidings, or Panteg Works.

To work a train from the Old Yard to Pilkington's glassworks, you would leave the Old Yard, go up the Loop (alongside the Loop Sidings) to Station South, onto the Up Goods, then push back into Pilkington's.

There was one road connecting the Old Yard with the South Sidings box.

New Sidings and Panteg Junction

These were next to the cutting for the main line and would receive trains from Hereford (which might also go to Coedygric Sidings). No 1 siding was next to the main line, and there was a dead-end spur to give the pilot engine room to shunt 40 or 50 wagons in the New Sidings.

From Panteg Junction, the Up and Down Goods line, taking you to the South Sidings junction, was between the main line

and the back end of Panteg Steelworks, to which there was a connection. It then passed through an underbridge (which looked like a pair of 'tunnels') and through a cutting to reach the South Sidings signal box. These 'tunnels' were used by a train at night from East Usk, as well as one from Severn Tunnel and Cardiff. The Old Yard or South Pilot would bank trains from Panteg Junction through these tunnels into the Old Yard, the Loop or the South Sidings. The Panteg Pilot from the South Sidings would go down the cutting, via Panteg Junction, to Llantarnam biscuit factory and Girlings, as well as to Panteg Steelworks. A sloping spur, which had a set of catch points on it, connected the New Sidings to the Up and Down Goods line south of the 'tunnels', by running adjacent to the New Sidings shunting spur. The 6.15am Exeter train, later classified as the Severn Tunnel train, used this route from the New Sidings, as well as the afternoon tunnel train.

Panteg Steelworks had a connection on the Up Low Level Goods Line, between the 'tunnels' and the New Sidings sloping spur.

One day, working as a young fireman with Harry Watts on the Panteg Pilot, the steam pressure wasn't rising as expected, which concerned me. We just made the Old Yard from Panteg Junction to take water, and I discovered the damper had shut! Some dampers needed to be propped open with a spanner, as they dropped down without you noticing.

Coedygric Sidings and the East banker

The East banker worked the bottom end of Coedygric Yard. It used to do a bit of shunting and banked from there. It did one shift only, in the morning, pulling the 4.35am Merthyr train from Coedygric Sidings to Station South Junction and banking it from there to the West Junction and Cwm Glyn. The 6.10am Abertillery started from the Loop Sidings, and was banked from the Loop, up around the West

Junction to Cwm Glyn. A pannier would do this.

Panteg & Coedygric Junction to Station South Junction

A freight train coming up the Eastern Valley for Pontypool Road Yard would come off the Eastern Valley line at Panteg & Coedygric Junction. It would pass Coedygric signal box, go over the bridge (the 'tunnels'). It would then divert left onto the High Level Goods Line (which Fireman Henry Williams calls the 'South Road'); it would proceed past the western side of Coedygric Sidings, past the wagon repair shed on the right, under Coedygric Road viaduct to the South Junction, and up to the Loop Junction for one of the pilot engines to shunt off the train.

Freight trains from the north for Pontypool Road Yard would enter the Down Relief Line at the North Junction, pass through Station South Junction and the East Junction and continue south and divert off the main line. The train would enter the New Sidings Reception Road, adjacent to the main line, or would continue on the Down Relief and divert onto the Coedygric Reception Road.

No freight trains used the relief lines from Coedygric through to the East Junction, which passed the canteen, alongside the wagon repair shed, or in the opposite direction – East Junction through to Coedygric.

Passenger trains that joined the Eastern Valley line at Llantarnam Junction, or the ROF Glascoed train from Blaenavon,

would come off the Eastern Valley line at Panteg and Coedygric Junction. They would pass Coedygric signal box and go over the bridge (the 'tunnels'). They would proceed past the connection for the High Level Goods Line to and from South Sidings, then divert along 'the branch', a pair of up and down lines to the west of Coedygric Sidings, going alongside the east side of the wagon repair shed and under Coedygric Road viaduct. They would proceed to the east side of the loco shed, and go through to the East Junction, joining the Up Relief and connecting back onto the main line alongside the signal box at Station South Junction.

Two passenger trains are recalled working in the opposite direction. The engine rostered to work the auto-train for Blaenavon would leave shed and proceed to the south or north bay to pick up the auto-coaches. It would be better if the auto-train was stored in the north bay, as the engine would be on the correct end for working up the Eastern Valley. If picking up the auto-train at the north bay, it would proceed to the North Junction, and propel its train through Station South and the East Junctions onto 'the branch', past the canteen by the viaduct (alongside the wagon repair shed), under the viaduct and onto the running line to Panteg and Coedygric Junction, over 'the tunnels', past Panteg & Coedygric box and out to Panteg & Coedygric station. It would pick up passengers as per the timetable. On a Monday morning a '41xx' would leave shed, go to the station to pick up coaches for Blaenavon; the station pilot would pull these out of the siding, the '41xx' would back on and propel them to Panteg & Coedygric

On 15 May 1935 GWR '4200' Class 2-8-0T No 4274 hauls a train of sand for Pilkington's glassworks; it will be propelled into the Northern Sidings at the back of East Junction signal box. *Kidderminster Railway Museum*

GWR 'Bulldog' Class 4-4-0 No 3382 *Maristow* is seen at the old Pontypool Road station, before the new one was built in 1909. Under the 1912 renumbering, the loco became No 3309. *J. S. Williams collection*

Junction and take them to Blaenavon. This was undertaken as no coaches were left in the sidings at Blaenavon Low Level after a Saturday night, for fear of vandalism. After working the train to Cwmbran for Girlings, the '41xx' would take the carriages back to the sidings at Ponty station for cleaning.

Other sidings in the Pontypool Road area

Pilkington's glassworks was built before the war on the site of the Admiralty Sidings; it was always there in my lifetime, even when I was a small boy. Trains would be propelled into the sidings, with the engine coming to a stand at the back of the Station South signal box. Pilkington's had its own engine to take the train into the glassworks.

Panteg Sidings, opposite Panteg & Griffithstown station, were used to store empty wagons for Waenavon. These were known as the 'transfer sidings'.

Panteg Steelworks had a siding that was accessed on the up low level goods line, from Panteg Junction, between the New Sidings slope to the low level goods line, and 'the tunnels'.

Griffithstown Station Road refuge siding (Ballast Siding) was located on the left side of the running lines north of the footbridge at Panteg & Coedygric Junction. Although used very rarely, empty wagons were stored there as an overflow for Panteg Sidings.

ICI had a siding at Mamhilad, and the Little Mill Pilot would place coal wagons in it.

There was a siding at Little Mill

Brickworks, but it was not used.

The Cold Storage in Llantarnam was built for the war, for cold meat storage, and was located by the footbridge at Llantarnam.

I also remember Pontnewydd tinplate works and Chapel Lane pipe works, but never did any shunting there.

Pontypool Road station

The red-brick building on the station approach had been the District Superintendant's Office in Driver Phil Williams's day. The office later moved to Newport, and the upstairs part of the office was rented out as flats.

At the top of the steps to the platform in front of you was a ticket collector's office opposite the step gates. Behind that was the Lost Property Office, the shunters' cabin, the guards' room, the Station signal box, the Refreshment Room, Waiting Room, and toilets at the far end. The Station Master was Mr Clements.

There was a lift to carry heavy items for the Refreshment Room. It had a steel rod to lift it up or down.

The carriage sidings stored coaches for the Eastern Valley passenger trains, and for 'strengthening' passenger trains when required. No coaches were ever slipped there.

The North Bay was never used after the line to Monmouth closed.

There were four water columns at Pontypool Road station, one at each platform end; they were fed from the canal. At one time there were pits at the ends of

Passengers wait on the old Pontypool Road station, date unknown. *Phil Williams collection*

the up and down main platforms, as well as in the bays. They were all removed in the early 1950s. The pit in the Down Main at the platform was for going under the engine to clean the fire, but was later filled in – I can't remember anyone using it.

There were Up and Down Goods lines to the north-west of the station, and trains coming down (south) would be routed to Ponty yard or the West Junction. Trains going north would be for Little Mill, Chester, Shrewsbury, Crewe or Worcester depending on the time of day. The Up and Down Main lines bypassed the island platform, and the roads serving the platforms were known as the Up and Down Platform lines.

On the Up Goods line trains would stack up behind each other until the 1950s, as traffic was so busy. They would be looped at Abergavenny, Pandy and Pontrilas on the way to Hereford. Tram Inn only had a down loop.

On the Up Goods line, later called the Up Relief, there was a conical water tower opposite the North signal box where Oliver Payne got wet, possibly with a '68xx' 'Grange' locomotive.

The main station building was a two-storey red-brick building, at the bottom of the approach road from the Highway Road, in New Inn. You purchased a ticket from the ground-floor booking office, and walked through the subway and up steps to the platform.

A siding immediately south of the main station building on the down side and adjacent to the station approach road was known as Butt's Siding. It was accessed from the carriage siding that ran alongside the main station building and was used for carriage storage before the war. Butt's Siding was installed around 1946, and was adjacent to the main station building, where Driver Arthur Butt lived in one of the flats, giving his name to the siding. South of the main station building was a cabin that looked like a small signal box. On the door was a plate that read 'Signal and Telegraph Linesmen'. North of the main station building there were three sidings, with several gas tank wagons placed at the end of one of them, the one nearest to the Down Main. These wagons were there when I started in 1944, and were redundant wagons used to supply gas to coaches that had gas lamps. The down carriage siding still remains, in truncated form, and is the only remaining siding from Pontypool Road Yard and station.

At the end of the South Bay, between the bay road and the Down Platform line, was an engine spur, which wasn't used very often. If a train was to split at Ponty, the train engine would proceed with the front half of the train, then the engine in the spur would back on and take the remainder of the train to its destination.

A single siding for storing passenger trains was present on the west side of the platform, between the Up and Down Relief, and Up Main and Up Platform roads.

The Station Pilot would shunt the station and assist any trains to Hereford. A '41xx' tank loco was used on this job.

Opposite Station South signal box were the Station South Cattle Pens. Traffic did not go in there very often. There was also a

North of the Highway Road bridge, the new Pontypool Road station is seen after construction in 1909. The Up and Down Goods Relief lines are on the left, in the process of being laid. *Phil Williams collection*

line to a scrapyard, which was disused but still laid down. Driver Ernie Melverton used to live in a cottage opposite the signal box.

Fatalities and incidents

Sydney Walker, a locomotive cleaner, drowned at Symonds Yat in the Wye Valley in 1944.

Driver George Grey was killed at Clarence Street station, Pontypool, cause unknown.

Hubert Jones, another driver, was killed in the late 1950s by No 6818. His engine was coming off Neath shed to work back home on the 5.59pm service from Neath. His fireman, George Holloway, was driving the engine, and Hubert was squashed between the cylinder and the side of the shed.

Alf Morgan was a driver who lived in Florence Place or Gove Place, one of the streets off Kemys Street in Griffithstown. One day he came out of the Open Hearth pub by the canal, intoxicated, fell in and was drowned.

A platelayer was killed in the New Sidings, his head being squashed between a wagon and a stop block.

Bryan Wilkins, a relation of Henry Williams, was caught between the buffers of two engines on No 7 road in the shed. When

they were parted he fell down, but wasn't hurt. Tommy Smith was crushed between two engines at the water column at the south end of the loco shed.

Ray Callow, a driver at Ponty who lived in the old Panteg station building at Panteg Junction, was knocked down early one morning by a tank engine working the Abergavenny mail train near the Station South signal box; he was thrown against the ladder of a signal and severely injured. He spent a long time in hospital, eventually returning to work, but didn't last long before passing away.

Charlie Chivers was killed at Pontypool Road station. A train was split on the main line next to the platform, and an engine was going to go on the back end, and ran over him.

Tommy Vennard lived in the station flats and was killed under the road bridge by the station. A driver was killed under the same bridge on the Relief line.

Calling and cleaning

I wasn't yet 16 and could only work days and afternoons, from 7.00am till 3.00pm, or 3.00pm till 11.00pm. I did two years as a cleaner, and the first engine I cleaned was No 4932 *Hatherton Hall*. After two or three weeks cleaning I was sent out calling.

I covered the calling area of New Inn, Pontymoile, Griffithstown and Sebastopol. The D-Day landings happened at this time and there were a lot of troop trains running around. So I was going out taking notes telling drivers and firemen what time to come to work and what job. Once you had worked 12 hours you had to have 12 hours rest before booking on again. A lot of rosters were disrupted, and men were being called out for hospital trains and Government Stores trains – described on the advice notes as 'GS'.

When calling I remember Driver Bill Cole, who was a fussy old devil. He was always up when you called, but you still had to call him. You would open the letter box and say 'Bill,' and he'd reply, 'Right-o boy.'

Identification badges were issued during the war as the Army were patrolling different places; at Severn Tunnel, for example, both ends were covered. My father's identification number was 102434, and I would polish this up at one time.

There were many 'Saint' Class '29xx' 4-6-0s at Ponty when the shed had a lot of passenger work. I remember two in 1944, *Saint David* and *Lady of Lynn*. 'Saint' turns to Blaenavon Low Level had finished by this time.

I recall that one day in 1945 or 1946, before I was made a fireman, a 'Saint' working the 9.06am Birmingham service was passing Llantarnam, travelling towards Pontypool Road, when the connecting rod little end broke. It knocked the cylinder end out, but the connecting rod stayed in the slide bars. I only worked these engines to Hereford about six times.

The '26xx' 2-6-0s were known as 'Aberdare Castles' and were used on coal trains. They would hold a barrow full of sand in the sandbox, and the steam reversers had to be kept adjusted as they would work themselves into full gear. No 2667 is remembered. I worked on them as a cleaner but they had gone by the time I was made a fireman in 1946. [Author's note: No 2667 was still at Ponty in 1949 and was the last

'26xx' in service; it was withdrawn on Thursday 27 October 1949.]

When calling I would go to the station with letters, riding down on an engine from the loco shed to the South Bay. My first footplate ride was on No 6309 used for the 7.45am Aberdare train; the driver was Mark Cray. Nos 5322 and 4303 are also recalled; they were used on freight work.

Hubert Jones worked the 2.25pm stopping passenger to Hereford. At 7.00am one Friday morning I managed to finish early when calling, and rode with Hubert and No 6818, the best engine at Ponty, to Hereford, stopping at every station. At Hereford the crew turned the engine and worked the 6.30pm express to Cardiff. I stopped with him all day. At Cardiff we returned light engine. This particular day, they asked Hubert if he knew the Monmouthshire line via Dock Street. He said he did, but he was a passenger man and did not work this route often.

I was dropped off at the steel works at Panteg and went to bed that Friday night. I overslept till Sunday dinnertime. My father had come home from work and gone back to work while I was still in bed. I didn't know it was Sunday, but the Sunday papers were through the door. I was calling that afternoon, but managed to get there in time. My bosses weren't surprised as another call boy had slept a weekend.

I was a cleaner for two years. Only the passenger engines were cleaned – the others were in a bit of a state. In my last year of cleaning I worked with Bob Crump; we cleaned the diesel railcar before breakfast, and No 6818 *Hardwick Grange* after breakfast. The cleaners would sit on the wall by the stores, and watch this engine go down at 6.30pm on the express – it would work the 2.25pm stopper to Hereford, and the 6.30pm express to Cardiff. It was gleaming! One driver came up and put his hand behind the side rods, and others would check behind the connecting rods to check that I had cleaned the back of them!

The diesel railcar, No D30, was housed in the wagon repair shed by the viaduct;

the diesel tank was outside, and kept away from the steam engines (the tank later went to Severn Tunnel). The railcar worked to Monmouth. You only cleaned the bottom half – the carriage & wagon cleaner cleaned the top half. The railcar had been used to the Blaenavon bottom line, but was too light for the Vale of Neath line. I used it from Sebastopol station to go to Newport before the war, before I worked on the railway. It was used as an economy measure for a while.

I recall one incident involving it. There was a loco on No 8 road on the shed and the fireman hadn't turned up. I got on the engine and had hardly taken off my jacket when the engine started to move up to the signal. At the same time the diesel railcar was coming on to the shed on the wrong road – this was very rare. The two locos touched one another, and there was a bit of damage to the diesel.

When my uncle, Ivor Williams, was booked to work on the afternoon Monmouth goods, he would have to prepare No 6818 for the 2.25pm Hereford train, before travelling to Monmouth to work the return goods train to Pontypool Road. I was able to tell him that there was no need to go underneath as I had already done its oiling, thus avoiding oil spillage.

Brick dust was used to clean the safety valve cover and the copper rim around the chimney, name plates, number plates and whistles. Cleaning materials were unlimited, and engines would be cleaned anywhere, inside the shed if it was raining. There were a dozen cleaners on the shift, and a seniority list to become a senior cleaner. Recruitment for cleaning was still being undertaken in December 1964, near the end of steam, when engines were still being cleaned.

The foreman cleaner had a big oil can for the cleaners – he would pour some in a bucket, and you would soak waste material in it. You would clean everything, with dry waste in one hand and oily waste in the other.

After you had done sufficient cleaning turns you became a senior cleaner, and you had the opportunity to get a shed turn. Some cleaners worked as boiler washers, or on ash pans and smokeboxes. I did fire-carrying, and this was before we had 'faggots'. This involved fire-carrying for the lighters-up. There was a little furnace by the stationary boiler, that had to be kept going, together with some scoops. You pushed the scoop in, got a scoop of fire, then put it over your shoulder and carried it to the engine. The fire-carriers would fire the furnace, and it remained in use until the shed closed.

The lighters-up would put a bed of coal in the firebox, and I would get fire to them to light up. Bundles of wooden kindling, known as 'faggots', came later after the war. They were made from redundant sleepers. There was limited relaying of sleepers during the war as there was insufficient wood about; only essential relaying was undertaken. Later, just wooden sticks were used to start the fire, without the use of hot coals.

A little tank engine was kept on the top end of No 1 road as the stationary boiler, and was possibly in use when the roof was being lifted. The cleaners and sometimes firemen would fire the stationary boiler, and it would blow off very occasionally. A wagon of coal was shunted next to it inside the shed when the coal stocks ran low, and was unloaded by hand, between the stationary boiler and the furnace. The coal was kept in a bunker inside the shed – it was a screened-off area, and held about a wagon load of coal. You tried to throw the coal off the wagon straight into this bunker, but you'd miss, as you couldn't quite reach it. Then it would have to thrown on the floor, then thrown into the bunker. The bunker would be refilled about once a fortnight.

Management used to put some cleaners with the boiler washers – it was a dirty old job, and I avoided it.

The shed was cold in winter, and in frosty weather two or three bonfires were lit inside the north end and the heat would travel down to the south end. Looking after the frost fires in winter in the 'fire devils' under the water columns was another shed turn as a cleaner. We did all the water columns, even those at the station. We lit them up with coal or coke, and every 4 or 5 hours topped them up.

I remember Arthur Edwards started cleaning, and was made up to a fireman in no time at all. However, he didn't know how to put the injector on when he started. Some firemen couldn't reach the injector on a '49xx' or a '68xx'.

As part of the learning process I would go around with the fitters and boilermakers in the shed and go around with them when they were expanding tubes. The boss, the Chief Clerk Mr Belson, was looking for me one day in the office. They played hell – I shouldn't be in a firebox! But I liked to know about other jobs and was eager to learn.

When I started at Ponty, Ted Kilby, Ted Broard and Reg Dimry ran Mutual Improvement Classes, which were held in the 'Oily Rag' in Griffithstown.

Everyone belonged to the union, which was mainly ASLEF, although we had about half a dozen men who were members of the NUR. ASLEF was started by Mr Perry, a Pontypool Road engine driver who lived in York Place, Griffithstown (now called Park

Street). Derby was the first place to register, but it was formed at Ponty. When Ponty closed, all the correspondence and books had to go to Head Office at Arkwright Road; the Union collected them.

Firing from 1946

I finished cleaning and started firing turns in 1946. You were sent to Swindon to pass for firing and in Great Western days you were given a registration number – mine was 32307. You would then pay half a crown to join the pension scheme, which was provided by Provident Mutual. You paid in weekly and the earliest you could retire was 60 years of age.

My first firing turn was on the New Sidings Pilot with Driver Harry Watts. He was fussy but likeable. I told him it was my first time out.

'Get hold of that hand brush and give it a bloody good sweep up,' he said.

Harry had a stomach complaint and was always taking Dewitt's Powder.

In those days you had to go where

YOUR REF.		BRITISH TRANSPORT COMMISSION BRITISH RAILWAYS WESTERN REGION	OUR REF. **94**	B.R. 3/5
DATED			DATE **SW.2/133**	

TO Fireman D.H.Saunders.
Pontypool Road.

FROM C.J.Hewlett.
Shedmaster,
Pontypool Road.
Extn.

Compensatory Rate Clause 5 (iv) of Manning Agreement in relation to assumed date of appointment to Fireman as a result of S.C.
Mon. 2S/2447.

Referring to your application in connection with the above, I am pleased to inform you that your assumed date of appointment to Fireman has been decided as 12.2.45 and I will advise you when retrospective payment will be made.

Shedmaster.

Derek Saunders's promotion to fireman at Pontypool Road loco depot, as signed by shed master Charlie Hewlett, on 2 February 1945. *Derek Saunders* they sent you, on promotion. I was sent to Hengoed, an outstation of Pontypool Road, for a fortnight. I worked to Elliot's Colliery in New Tredegar, from Maesycwmmer Junction. I relieved a turn from Pontypool Road, the 5.40pm Rhymney, which was a middle turn. They then relieved you in the evening to work back home to Pontypool Road. A '46xx' or '37xx' pannier tank would be on the job. In the afternoon I cleaned the fire on the dinner hour, and worked the 2.05pm colliers' train to New Tredegar and return to Elliot's Colliery, then worked the coal down to Maesycwmmer Junction for the Ponty men to take back to Pontypool Road. This was a shift's work. I did that for two weeks. I then went back to Pontypool Road.

I was in the Army in February 1947, and returned in 1949 to work in the Branch link. While in the Army I missed the Abergavenny Banking Link altogether, as well as a little bit of working to Monmouth. There was a change of staff at Ponty to get out of the war – the essential works order was on. I was one of the first to go eventually, but the exemption paper I was sent I put in the firebox. Chaps older than me didn't go. I was fed up with firing, but after the Army I never thought of packing up the railway job. There were two things I missed – mountains and the smell of steam and oil! When I was home on leave, the first thing I did was go down to the shed! I was a keen cyclist before I went in the Army.

While in Dusseldorf I recall seeing stations with no roofs on, and engines on their side. There were rows and rows of debris. Occasionally you'd see a pipe coming out of this debris with smoke coming out of it – people were living in cellars underneath it all. The place was stinking.

On my return I did 74 turns spare firing. Spare firemen would pack the valve spindle glands on tank locos if they were spare. In Great Western days the driver would write down loco repairs in a book outside Mr Wiltshire's office. In BR days repairs were written by the driver on a repair card, and deposited in a box by the office. I was given three cards instructing me to pack the valve spindle glands on one shift. I did one and returned the other two cards to the foreman. It was a horrible job. I would take 2½ hours to clean around the valve spindle before changing the packing.

There were three Branch Links, and I worked in the Top Branch link, to Porth, Stormstown and Pontypridd, and Ebbw Vale, Abertillery, Penar and Oakdale Colliery. Oakdale coal was used on the railway at Wolverhampton and Shrewsbury loco sheds, and also on the coal stage at Pontypool Road. The best coal was from Lady Windsor Colliery. Coal was also sent to Tyseley, but this train was only worked to Hereford. I had good mates to work with. George Turley was the driver in this link – he was really good.

I then went into the Relief Link in 1945-46, firing on Pilot turns. With the Pilots you could tell who was on them by the head and tail lights. Bob Crump worked on the Pilots at the same time as me. I did it by the Rule Book – a lamp at the bottom of the chimney, and a lamp on top of the bunker in the middle. If the lamps were in this position they knew who it was.

I fired on Pilot duties as follows:

New Sidings Pilot: Driver Harry Watts, engine Nos 2728, 3717, 8755, 1847, Monday 13 to Friday 17 February 1945. Shift was 1.13pm-10:00pm.
Birkenhead Pilot (Northern): The Birkenhead used to shunt on the west side of the coal stage. Driver Mark Cray, engine No 4639, 3 March 1945. Shift was 1.13pm-10.00pm.
South Pilot: Driver George Richards, engine No 8776, 24 March 1945.
Driver Teddy Barcus (who had thick eyebrows, like a hand brush!), engine No 2728, Monday 7 to Friday 12 April 1945. Shift was 1.45pm.
Driver Bill Cole, engine No 2739, 5 May 1945. Shift was 1.45pm.
Driver Mark Cray (the 'Scrap Man' – he had bits of scrap on the engine), engine No 2728, 23 June 1945. Shift was 5.45am.
Driver Dicky Loveless (his father worked at Branches Fork), engine No 2035, 4

September 1945. Shift was 1.45pm.
Driver Bill Jones, engine No 7426, 24 to 29
September 1945. Shift was 1.45pm.
Driver Jim Smith, engine No 2728, 27
October 1945. Shift was 1.45pm.
Driver Teddy Barcus, engine No 2041, 10
November 1945.

Little Mill Pilot: Driver Bill Southcot
(Pontypridd), engine No 5768, 13-14 April
1945. Shift was 1.05pm on midday.

Coedygric Pilot: Driver Jim Smith, engine
Nos 7426 (16-17 April 1945), 1730, 4611,
8755 and 1730 (18-21 April 1945). Shifts
were 5.12am on 17 April, the remainder
being 5.45am.
Driver Dicky Loveless, engine No 7721
(LTS – Llantrisant), 4 August 1945. Shift
was 5.45am. This engine would work traffic
alongside the New Sidings; it would go over
to the South Sidings and bring over a raft of
wagons on the night shift.

Loop Pilot: Driver Tommy Loudon, engine
No 7720, 5 September 1945. Shift was
1.45pm.
Driver Bill Jones, engine No 7724, 8
September 1945. Shift was 1.45pm.
Driver Sid Jones, engine No 2739, 19
September 1945. Shift was 9.45pm.
Driver Ted Macey (Cardiff driver), engine
No 3674, 12 October 1945. Shift was
9.45pm.

Old Yard Pilot: Driver Ron Day (passed
fireman), engine No 1847, 11-12 July 1945.
Shift was 5.45am.
Driver Jack East (passed fireman, who later
went to Banbury), engine No 1847, no date
recorded. Shift was 9.45pm.

Pilot workings away from Pontypool Road
yard, at Little Mill and Usk, are recalled. No
385 was a regular engine on the Little Mill
Pilot; it would work Little Mill only, and was
OK. Little Mill Sidings were used to store
trains for Cardiff and the Vale of Neath. A
lot of trains would terminate at Little Mill,
coming down from Hereford. Little Mill
Brickworks is not recalled as being shunted
in my time on the engines.

There was a train to Usk at 7.10am. The
Usk Pilot would go to Usk, then to ROF

Glascoed. Usk goods yard was where Jack
Drayton ran away down the slope and hit
the buffer stop, and nearly landed up in the
allotments; that was in 1947. When I was
courting, my girlfriend would arrive at Usk
station and have a ride on the pilot engine
from the station into the goods yard. Driver
Jack Drayton would ask the footplate men
at Ponty, 'How long is the turntable?' A lot
of them didn't know, but they would reply,
'About the same length as it is from the top
of the bank to the stop block in Usk Yard'!
Jack had been in every catch point and sand
drag that was about. The engine would be a
'46xx' pannier on the Usk Pilot. Perishable
traffic went into Usk goods yard, as well as
wood from there.

A '45xx' 'Prairie' would be used to work
empties into ROF Glascoed, and pull an
ammunition train out. The train would
initially proceed to Pontypool Road Yard, but
was destined for Newtown, near Chester.

There were two goods trains to
Monmouth, one in the morning and one in
the afternoon. The morning goods was the
7.50 working, while the afternoon goods
would require the footplate crew to travel to
Monmouth to work back.

I have worked to Monmouth, Ross and
Mitcheldean on the way to Gloucester. You
would then run around the train at Ross, to
go to Mitcheldean. This was a train of coal
and the loco would be a '45xx' tank engine.
You would use a bunker of coal and come
back via Ross. I never worked Monmouth
Troy to Symonds Yat with steam, but have
worked the Class 37 diesels to Tintern
Quarry when based at Severn Tunnel
Junction diesel depot.

The Abergavenny banker was one of the
turns in the banking link. No 349 was the
bad one, and was put on the Abergavenny
banker. It was a bugbear and wouldn't steam
very well. I had it on the Abergavenny
banker, with driver Les Mathews. At
Abergavenny Junction, when banking a
train, it started to blow off. 'I take my hat
off to you,' said Les. I said, 'Wait till I put
the feed on – it will be good night!' It was a
hopeless engine. Les was the only driver to

take his hat off to me!

In the snow of 1947 No 7426 was used as the snowplough engine with another engine behind it. The 6.30am passenger stopper from Hereford worked tender-first with a '29xx', and got as far as Panteg, after passing through the yard.

I recall working to Brynmawr in the snow that year. From Brynmawr the snow was up above the cab. Driver Charlie Shirley (known as 'Templegate', who looked for horses in the *Daily Herald*) worked to Brynmawr in the same winter. He was lost in the snow for three days and left his engine up there, walking home. Mixed traffic was worked from Brynmawr with a '72xx'; no '42xxs' worked to Brynmawr, only to Hafodrynys Deep Mine.

Engines with water leaks – which would use too much water – were known as 'Water Carts'. Drivers would complain about wasting water.

When firing you had to regulate the fire so that the safety valve on the boiler didn't lift. One of the GWR Directors lived opposite the station in Hereford and was a railway enthusiast; he would take photos of engines in the station. You were warned by your driver not to let the engine blow off in the station. By Ayleston Hill signal box there was a notice asking firemen not to let the engine blow off. The Director was subsequently sacked for publishing a photo of an engine on a train at Hereford that had been 'scrapped' months before!

In 1955 there was a railway strike; they were mainly NUR men, striking over differentials. Pill men kept the Eastern Valley open. I stayed on strike for three weeks; drivers got an extra shilling but firemen got no pay increase. I was annoyed – if they'd given the driver 10d and the fireman 2d, and that would have satisfied the firemen. The view was that the firemen would eventually become drivers and would then have the shilling.

Trains in trouble on the main line would have a pilot attached at Ponty station, or the train engine maybe replaced by a fresh engine If a train we were working was in

trouble coming up from Newport, and if they were in a rush on shed, they'd throw fresh coal on an engine that hadn't yet had the fire cleaned, and just throw new coal on the tender. The fire wouldn't be touched. We'd change engines at Ponty and the fresh engine would be worse than the one we'd just had! They'd do all sorts of tricks.

Drivers

There was no practical exam for driving on the Great Western, but one was introduced on BR. Dai James said they had a few dressmakers as drivers! A lot of drivers relied on the fireman.

I worked with many drivers when I was a fireman and in the spare turn. In a link you had a regular driver. On the whole they were good men – the worst were Oliver Payne and Bill Luxton.

I worked with Oliver Payne in the Relief Link. He had no idea about working an engine, but the driver was the boss – he had the power to say you were no good and you could be sacked. One day I wanted a cup of tea from the canteen – I had been on 4 or 5 hours. I had just bought a cup of tea when in walked Harry Robins: 'Your mate's got a job.'

I said, 'Where's he going?' but Harry didn't know.

I charged down to the drivers' cabin by the shed stores to ask the same question – nobody knew. I took a chance and went down to the station. Nothing was coming into the yard but I noticed a train at the north end, and there was nothing to Hereford at that time of day.

Oliver was just relieving the crew of a train in the Up Goods line, and said to me, 'I thought you weren't coming.' I laughed it off, and Oliver could see I had been rushing. He then said something I couldn't understand: 'I don't reckon to look after the fireman.'

I said, 'You're joking – it won't take me long to show you that this is a two-man job.'

We were taking water to go to Hereford from the conical water column opposite the North box. I was filling the tender and Oliver was on the ground. Oliver said, 'I'm getting wet down here.'

'Well, book it,' I said.

That's how the job started in the Relief Link. The loco may have been a '68xx'.

I recall going to Cardiff via the old Dock Street with Oliver on another job (Dock Street was accessed via Courtybella to Cashmore's scrapyard). The train was being worked down the old Monmouthshire Railway to Newport. The line passed under the main line at Newport, by the castle. At this location you went down a steep slope under the main line and back up the other side. Oliver would let the train run through, as the man he learned the road from had done it. When passing Newport Castle (now underneath the road by the green crossing) there was a hell of a tug at the train. Oliver was concerned and I said, 'The best bloke I worked with under here was driver Monty Harris.' (Monty Harris and Tom Davis were regarded as real good men.) I said that Monty would pull the train out from under the main line.

'The man I learned the road with done it this way,' said Oliver.

I said, 'You picked the best bloke to learn the road with, did you?'

I pointed out that I worked with many drivers and there were other ways of doing the job.

I was at St Philip's Marsh at Bristol on another occasion with Oliver. I said, 'Shall we go back for coal?'

'Got enough there,' said Oliver.

I then shovelled it forward and Oliver got the wind up, and went back for more.

We were working from St Philip's Marsh at night. At Pilning we were put in the loop. There was a white light in front. Oliver got down to have a look – it was a stop block! I said, 'It was a good job I was looking out.'

We had such a long train that we had to pull towards the dead end to get the back end in, then push back inside the signal – we could see the guard calling us back. That showed you how much Oliver knew about the road.

Oliver often tried to come from Llanvihangel to Pontypool Road in less than 15 minutes – but he never did it. With a '63xx' loco on the job he came round Penpergwym curve so hard that the loco lurched to the left down on to the axle boxes – if we had had a full boiler it might have overturned. It put the wind up Oliver and he put the brake on.

I said, 'You daft devil – by the time that takes effect we'll be halfway up the bank and be struggling.'

By the time the brake did take effect we had gone around the bend. It frightened Oliver – he didn't like that, did he?

One day when working a train from Hereford I recall cleaning the fire at Pontrilas. I was throwing clinker out and the guard came down to ask what I was doing. I told him I was earning my differentials!

On another occasion, after putting a train in the sidings, I was returning from Little Mill to the shed light engine with Oliver. A guard, Dewi Fry, caught hold of the regulator at the invitation of Oliver, and I dropped off the engine, saying, 'You don't want me, then.' Oliver had to stop the engine and wait for me to walk back to it. I said, 'I've been doing this job for 10 years and will probably do it for another 10 before I'm allowed to do that.' Oliver looked daggers at me.

While working from Stretton to Leebotwood and Dorrington to Shrewsbury with a 'Castle' driven by Oliver, he showed the speedo reading to me – 100mph. Trains would come down from Craven Arms at a fair lick too. The Locomotive Inspector asked Oliver what the speed was outside the shed when the diesels were brought out – he didn't know.

Tommy Lovejoy was another mate, known as 'Tommy Needle' as he was so thin. He would let the shunter drive on the South Pilot, in front of the offices. I said, 'I don't like the idea of you letting the shunter drive.'

'Mind your own bloody business,' said Tom.

I said, 'I asked you not to do it – now I'm *telling* you, or I'll do something about it.'

When I was working with him regularly Tom would say, 'When I'm gone, you'll be one of my bearers, taking me to Panteg.'

I said, 'I won't! If I'm up there, I'll take you to Pontypridd!'

When Tom passed away, all his previous mates were bearers, and so was I.

When there were speed restrictions signalmen kept the Distant signal on, to make sure the driver reduced his speed. The rule was later changed so that all the Distant signals came off if you had got the road. The drivers played hell. I said, 'This is extra responsibility – extra money for it!'

On one occasion, from Shrewsbury heading towards Leominster, the station was shut and unmanned, and the Distant signal was left on. You were not going to stop at the signal, but you were afraid of losing time. St Devereux was always shut at night. One driver, George Norton ('The Hangman') was working a seasons train in the morning, and went through the section without stopping.

The Liverpool to Plymouth train was worked by a Shrewsbury engine, and would be relieved by Ponty men, who took it to Bristol, leaving Ponty at 1.25pm. It would normally be a 'Castle' or a 'County'. This engine would return with the 7.15pm from Bristol Temple Meads. From Bristol Stapleton Road you were allowed 59 minutes and drivers would be worried about losing time coming back, as train timings were tight. It would arrive at Ponty at 8.25pm.

You would work the 8.27pm from Ponty to Shrewsbury (the 7.15pm from Bristol, which arrived at Ponty at 8.25pm), and would return with the 1.25am from Crewe. Ponty men would take the train from Shrewsbury with a 'Castle' or a 'Britannia'. The last day a man was hanged at Shrewsbury I was working with 'Tommy Needle'. I was pulling coal down on the tender and Tommy said, 'He won't have long now,' referring to the man being hanged. The train arrived in Ponty at 4.20am, where you were relieved. The 1.25am Crewe passenger would be met at Ponty by the postman to pick up mail.

You always had enough coal to get to Shrewsbury and back, so would not very often go to the shed to top up during a shift – maybe only once or twice during your career

with steam. When working to Shrewsbury you turned the loco at Abbey Foregate and put it in the bay to wait for the 1.25am from Crewe to come in. While waiting you did a bit to the fire, and pulled some coal down to bring you home. The Crewe engine uncoupled, and we backed on and took the train to Ponty, where we had relief.

I recall having hard coal on one occasion and there was not enough to come back with, so we had to go to Shrewsbury shed for coal. It was like burning paper! Coal was the bugbear of firing. The best coal at Shrewsbury was kept for the Newton Abbot turn, which was a 'double home' job.

Driver Ted Loveridge once went onto Shrewsbury shed for coal and said, 'I want that coal.'

'You can't have that – it's for the Newton,' was the shed staff's reply.

'I'll have that or none at all,' said Ted, so we had a few of the boxes they were keeping for the Newton men.

The Manchester to Swansea was a through train that left Ponty at 1.38pm; it would arrive with an LMS 'Royal Scot' or 'Jubilee', which would be taken off the train. The LMS engine was turned and coaled, then worked the 3.15pm Penzance to Manchester Piccadilly train. A Western engine would take over, to take the train onwards to Cardiff. The Ponty engine for Cardiff would wait on the Down Main at Pontypool Road station to changes engines (I have only ever once seen an engine waiting in the siding at the end of the south bay to change engines to go south). You would have a '68xx' or a '49xx' on this job, but sometimes a tank engine was rostered. I was with driver Bill Luxton one day, and he was an expert on vacuum brakes. We had an ex-works '68xx', which we had taken from the shed to Ponty station, awaiting the arrival of the Manchester to Swansea train. The ex-LMS engine uncoupled and went to shed for servicing and we backed onto the train. Bill could get no more than 16 inches of vacuum. The pipe between the engine and tender was twisted, and it was declared a failure. This fault had not been picked up on shed by the driver, and it should have been. We had another engine to replace the '68xx'.

Jack East fired to Driver Tom Brown for four weeks but they didn't get on. Jack would arrive at work, see he was booked to work with Tom Brown and go back home again. Later, he went driving at Banbury, and ended up a foreman there.

Jack Davis is another driver I remember. He had been a driver on the Romney, Hythe & Dymchurch railway during the war, and had worked the armoured train there in connection with the undersea pipeline 'Pluto' project.

Bill Oakley was a good chap to work with, and was ex-Branches Fork.

I used to fire '29xx' 'Saint' Class engines to Hereford. They were good engines as far as steam goes and the harder you hit them the better they liked it. I recall working with Jack Drayton. I said, 'You carry on from Pontrilas like you did from Ponty and you won't see Hereford today.' I was sitting on the seat, and wouldn't get off it. Passing through St Devereux there was plenty of steam, and I was still sitting on the seat. I tapped Jack on the shoulder and said, 'Much better way of working, isn't it, Jack?'

I remember a trip with Jack Drayton on a '28xx' tender loco with hard Staffordshire coal, which would burn quickly. I had filled the firebox three-quarters full, to prevent the engine from blowing off; there was no fire at the front of the firebox. Jack had pulled a train out of the Loop Siding to go to Hereford and as we went past the Station South box I looked back to receive the signal from the guard that he was in his van after leaving the Loop, and give that instruction (the 'tip') to the driver. On this occasion the guard was a long time giving the signal to say he was in his van after we pulled out of the Loop, so I hadn't given that instruction to Jack. Jack would talk in riddles and not use the correct words. In America the fireman is called a stoker. Jack said to me, 'Stoker tip.' I said, 'If you want the tip, get it yourself.' The front of the fire had gone out, under the brick arch. I said to Jack, 'I haven't any fire under the brick arch – it is only half way over the

box.'

One day when coming towards Llanvihangel with a '63xx' or '68xx' on a train from Hereford, the 6 o'clock from Chester, I was doing some firing and realised I was on the footplate on my own. I thought Jack had fallen off so I looked down his side of the engine and there was no sign of him – but a train was coming towards us going to Hereford. I thought Jack had fallen off in the 'four foot' and that he would be run over. Just as I was going to make up my mind to get the gauge lamp off the water gauge, Jack appeared from in front of the smokebox – he had been having a walk round. He didn't say a word to me. I was quite abrupt to Jack about this.

Jack used to get firemen to put glass bottles in the firebox. He gave me a bottle one day and asked me to throw it in. I wouldn't do it as it would block up the firebars. He had some funny ideas and I couldn't get on with him.

Driver Alf Batley came from Banbury, and lived in a caravan. He was nicknamed 'the Gypsy'.

When I fired regularly with Driver Fred Stanley, a Newport man who fought in the war, I wasn't good at getting up in the morning and would often sleep late. Fred would be 'off the road' regularly on the Coedygric Pilot – he would pass the signal for the road, and run into the catch point. Of the drivers at Ponty, some were from Newport and Cardiff. In the war, drivers were pushed through for promotion, and Fred was one of them. He said to me, 'I don't know much about this job, but I've got the garden under hand.' When not on afternoons, Fred would catch the 8.30am train to Newport and go home, but didn't book off till 10.05 or 10.10am. I have worked the Llantarnam banker on my own as a cleaner. I went to Llantarnam to bank the 261 up – the Bristol to Manchester freight – from the Llantarnam loop. The only train banked from Llantarnam was the 261, which would go into the Northern Sidings, and the Northern Pilot was used as the banker. The Northern Pilot would wait in the up loop at

Llantarnam for the 261 to pass on the main line, and stop beyond the north end of the loop. The Northern Pilot went up behind the train, *but we was not* coupled to the 261. The Northern Pilot banked the train over the brow at the East Junction, and returned light engine to the Northern Sidings. The train would then be propelled into the Northern Sidings using the train engine.

Driver Harold Pearce was firing a '68xx' at Penpergwym bridge once and missed the firehole – half a shovel full of coal went on to the footplate instead of into the box. He shouldn't have been firing there.

Driver Ted Kilby was coming up from Neath towards Resolven on a '63xx' and the firebox caved in as there was no water in the boiler – apparently the fusible plug had already gone before he left Neath.

I worked with an Abergavenny driver Dai James, another good driver. When I was a passed fireman we would swop over. On the night Shrewsbury I backed on and Dai coupled up the coaches. Running towards Condover, the Distant was on. Dai said, 'I know what's the matter – I didn't take the tail light off the tender – keep going!' Dai walked along the tender and took the tail light off before we got to the box. He was taking a chance doing that.

Another time Dai was working a train of vans back from Swansea on the Vale of Neath. At Crumlin High Level he said, 'I'll get the staff,' but he missed it. He said, 'Go on, keep going, I'll get on the van.' Dai got the staff and rode in the van over the viaduct, while I remained on the engine.

I once fired a '63xx' to Hereford with Driver Sid Webber and never got off the seat; I was just flicking the shovel. Sid was a fusspot. 'I wonder what was coming off there,' he said.

Driver Bert Hale was a 'money bags'. I was the fireman with him on a train to

In March 1961 a freight train is being banked from Llantarnam Junction by ex-GWR '5600' Class No 6690. The Northern Sidings are in the background. *D. K. Jones collection*

Gloucester on a Saturday night – the 7.30pm Oxford. We pulled into Bullo Pill, as there was a loop there. The first thing Bert thought of was to put the bag in the tank. I had hardly put it in when the board came off. Bert said, 'Don't take any notice of that,' so we had our water. This was a Saturday night to Sunday morning job, at time-and-three-quarters.

We left the loop and the signalman said, 'Get a move on – the parcels is behind.'

Bert said, 'Can't help that – we are leaving here at so and so.'

I said, 'No need to worry Bert – we won't catch that passenger.'

We made 12 hours that night. Bert got off at Panteg, as he lived near the station, and gave me the ticket to put in. Horace Francis was in the office, and saw me clock Bert in. Bert was docked 16 minutes walking time from the station to the shed, which he complained about.

This train to Oxford ran all week, via Worcester, but on a Saturday it would sometimes be diverted. There was a morning and night train to Oxford. The loco would be a '28xx', a '63xx' or perhaps a '49xx'.

Len Hough was another money man, but he was all right, but. He had a brother Harold, a shift foreman in the shed.

Steam locos had three different types of smoke plate – 1, 2 and 3 – which fitted in the top of the firehole ring. Most tender engines had a No 3, which was oval by the firehole and tapered out flat. Sometimes a No 1 smoke plate was fitted on a tender loco, but was the wrong one and you couldn't get in the corners of the firebox to fire the engine.

I was with Driver Bill Luxton and the engine wasn't steaming well. I threw the smoke plate into the tender. Bill didn't know the difference between a No 1 and a No 3.

When Port Talbot station was being altered, Driver Bill Jancey and I were waiting for a passenger and went into the shunters' cabin on the platform to have our food. The shunter complained and Bill went outside to eat his food on the platform, in the rain. He didn't want any animosity, but I stood my ground. I said, 'Here's my particulars if

you want to complain,' and stayed put in the cabin. Bill was Henry Williams's father-in-law, and was a special constable in his spare time.

Bill would always ask you the time. He once asked a guard what the time was as they stood under the station clock – the guard put his bag down and got his watch out.

Curly Franklyn was a driver at Ponty; he'd gone to Old Oak as a fireman and came back with a London accent. When leaving Newport on a passenger I would knock the clock back to 160psi and would then have a decent trip. If you kept it on the mark, he'd hammer you.

Other drivers I remember were Dicky Loveless, who worked at Branches Fork, and W. S. Jones, a Newport driver. Ernie Brakespeare was a Ponty driver before being transferred to become the shed master at Barry loco depot. Driver Charlie Hewlett later became the shed master, and his son Gwyn was a fireman at Ponty. Arthur Edwards started his railway career at Neath and arrived at Ponty in 1941. Driver Harry Crabb lived at 77 Stafford Road, and Edgar Charles worked on pilot engines after the Blaenavon High Level runaway.

Driver Jack Page came from the South West of England and ran the fish and chip shop at Sebastopol in his spare time. A photograph of Jack Page and Jim Saunders on a 'Star' Class loco, taken at Pontypool Road station, is on the wall of the present-day Page's fish bar in Sebastopol.

I never worked with Phil Williams ('Full Load Phil'), who was a driver before I started in 1944 and ran the Locomotive Improvement Classes. He lived in 95 Stafford Road. He is remembered for throwing a feeder can in the south-west corner of the shed – maybe a cork had been rammed down in the little end of the connecting rod of his engine.

Ron Voyle was a Newport man, but worked at Ponty as a driver in 1945/46, when in his early 30s or 40s before returning to Newport Ebbw Junction. Men were there from all over the place. He had come to Ponty as there were vacancies there as an intermediate step towards his own depot. When he was at Newport, he became a locomotive inspector.

Arthur Hathaway was the Royal Train driver, and worked one to Monmouth in 1937.

Ponty men would work the 8.27pm from Ponty to Shrewsbury. This train was formed of two trains assembled at Ponty station in the evening. Earlier in the day, Ponty men worked a train to Bristol, then in the evening they brought an engine off Bath Road shed to Platform 3 at Bristol Temple Meads and backed it onto the at 7.18pm train for Ponty; sometimes it would be a 'Castle', or maybe a '49xx'. When I was a fireman on this train we stopped at Stapleton Road station in Bristol. You were allowed 59 minutes to get to Pontypool Road and drivers would be anxious about keeping to this scheduled time. In the meantime, another train would come up from Cardiff. The Bristol train had a Post Office van next to the engine, which had come up from Plymouth.

We would be relieved at Ponty and fresh Ponty crew would take over the Bristol train, and back onto the Cardiff train in the station to form one train, with the Bristol portion, and thus the Post Office van, next to the engine. The train would then be worked to Shrewsbury and back by the fresh Ponty crew.

Pontypool railway enthusiast David Williams recalls this train being assembled at Pontypool Road when he was a trainspotter in the 1960s. The Cardiff train would arrive first and stop at the Newport end of the station; the engine would uncouple and come off the train. The Bristol train would arrive on the Up Main, alongside the Cardiff train, and cross over in front of it at the north end of the station. The station pilot would then propel the Cardiff portion forward against the Bristol portion, the two halves were coupled up and the Bristol engine took the train to Shrewsbury. In the meantime, the Cardiff engine would be turned on the triangle by the West signal box, and arrive back at the station to await

a train from the north, which was split into two parts – one for Cardiff and one for Bristol. The Cardiff engine worked the Cardiff portion back to Cardiff from Ponty.

The 8.27pm train arrived at Shrewsbury around 10.30pm, and the engine worked the 2.25am back to Ponty; this was the 1.25am passenger from Crewe. The morning Post Office van would still be behind the engine. We worked this train using a Cardiff engine, maybe a 'Castle', a 'King' or a 'Britannia'.

One night Arthur Hathaway was shunting the Post Office van onto the train in the up platform at Ponty station when he reversed a bit hard and damaged it; his fireman was Allan Foster.

Learning to drive

I learned to drive when I was firing, and I used to drive the 'Swansea Vans'. I would start with oiling round, then take the loco to Neath. It might be a '28xx', '68xx', '63xx' – anything. I remember 'Halls' going over the viaduct at Crumlin.

Drivers would say to the fireman, 'You don't value the last 10 pounds on the clock.' When I was passed as a driver, I would tell other drivers that they didn't know how to use the steam when they got it!

Joe Field was the Inspector at Swindon who passed you as a driver. If you passed you were given a piece of paper for the doctor; it had your name on it and the word 'passed'.

Driver Tom Davis was a regular mate, and I said to him, regarding driving methods, 'Well, Tom, I see how this job is done, but tell me how it should be done!' He put me in good stead for how it should be done. He later retired to live in St Blazey in Cornwall, and married the sister of guard Dick Kendall.

I remember working with Driver Tom Davies on the PR2 with Pontypool Road '72xx' tank loco No 7206. After leaving Blaenavon High Level station with wagon hand brakes pinned down, I put 5 inches of vacuum in the brake. When travelling through Varteg Tom blew the brake off and reapplied it when the gradient demanded it. I learned a lot from Tom, which put me in good stead for my future.

When I was a fireman some drivers wanted you on the hand brake to buffer up, but I would use the engine brake when I was driving. A lot of skill was needed on the steam locomotive. The retaining valve was used in the brake system, to maintain pressure.

My last Ponty firing turn was with Bill Luxton. I was firing an express, the 2.25am from Shrewsbury, and at about 4.10am at Penpergwym I said, 'I don't know how you are going to manage at Cardiff.' We hadn't been speaking. I had been relaying the signals to him, but wouldn't give him any tea or anything. He had to make his own. I said, 'I can see the bump [redundancies] coming at Pontypool Road, and I'd rather go away as a driver than as a fireman.' And that is what happened. I wasn't at Pontypool Road when they had the first 'bump' in 1963, but came back in 1965 as a driver, and was there until it finished in 1967. I got driving and was equal to any of them.

I started driving at Pontypool Road and the first engine I drove was one of the pilots, No 8493, when I was a fireman, but 'spare driving'. My fourth spare driving turn, with engine No 6872, was with a fireman from Aberbeeg, who had never been out of the yard. I drove No 4639 when the track was being removed at Ebbw Vale North, and

the railway was accessed from Abergavenny Junction. I worked No 6926 to Cardiff from Ponty in July 1965.

Charlie Reynolds was my fireman sometimes when picking up track on the line from Abergavenny Junction to Brynmawr. The ganger would ask for coal to go in the cabin as it was wintertime, but somebody told me he was taking the coal home instead. So Charlie filled a sack with ballast, put some lumps of coal on top and gave it to the ganger!

Charlie once opened the drain cocks on Ponty shed and let waste oil drain into the pit. This was dangerous if anyone went into the pit and slipped on it. I made him clean it up before we went off shed.

Fly shunting was used to speed up shunting operations, when working in the yards. When I was driving and working to rule, I pushed every wagon to where it was wanted – and drove the shunters wild!

After promotion to driver, I transferred to Cardiff. My job on the pilot at Cardiff Canton in 1962 involved piloting engines off the main line to go into Cardiff East Dock loco shed, as Canton was being closed for steam. I was the pilot for Driver Bill Luxton once, and had half-a-dozen 4-foot rockets on the engine for Guy Fawkes Night. Bill saw red as he thought he was earning good money! He asked his fireman, Bill Boon, to

The acknowledgement of a driver vacancy application made by Derek Saunders, as received from the Newport Divisional Superintendant's Office. *Derek Saunders* break the sticks of the rockets with his feet!

Mr Wagstaff was the shed master at Canton at the time steam finished, and his duties covered Cardiff East Dock. I signed on at Windsor Road, by Newtown goods shed in Cardiff, when I was working at East Dock and the diesels came in.

An incident is recalled regarding prepping a 'Castle'. We had an agreement the union that getting two 'Castles' ready warranted a prep jacket. I was set up on this particular day. I always wanted a prep jacket when I went to East Dock. I was asked to prep a 'Castle' in a filthy condition, but I said, 'I'm not prepping no engine – I've got no prep jacket.' I was sent back to Windsor Road and told to go home.

I said, 'Thank you very much. I'll get my

Derek Saunders's driver's report log for his first driving turn on 19 June 1961, on engine No 8493 as the Crumlin Banker. *Derek Saunders*

BRITISH RAILWAYS   B.R. 87219

Mon 16 October 1961   0.6.30. Train from MJH

Engine No. 4639   Fireman's Name K. Hicks 351

STATIONS	Actual Time		Shunting Time						Loco. Duties away from H'me Shed	Time Lost by Loco.	Load		Delays	
			Coaching		Freight		Departmental				Vehicles	Tons or Equiv. No. of Wagons		Cause
	arr.	dep.	H.	M.	H.	M.	H.	M.	Mins.	Mins.			Minutes	
Shed.	0615	0650												
West Yd	0655	0705												
Abergavenny Jct	0730	0820												
Brecon Road	0825	0830										3	3		Class 3
Brynmawr	0910													
			Relief 1210											

REMARKS

The log for Derek's driving turn on 23 June 1961, on engine No 6872 on a trip from Pontypool Road to Shrewsbury. *Derek Saunders*

money – I know what I'm doing.' I was back home just after six.

The following Thursday, pay day, I went to see Mr Wagstaff and said, 'I don't mind ferrying, but I was down East Dock and they asked me to get a "Castle" ready. I said, "I expect to have a prep jacket – would you like to go underneath a "Castle", then travel as a passenger next to your wife in filthy overalls?'

He could see what I was getting at. I said, 'You know the state of those engines, and you know I am travelling to get to work. I could do it another way. I could

clean my way in, but it would take me over 8 hours to do it.' Mr Wagstaff put out an instruction for prep jackets to be issued.

Much later, in December 1982, I drove the last train from Cwmffrwdoer with Class 37 No 37098 onto the Blaenavon branch at Llantarnam to collect and haul a train of recovered all-welded rail from the Horse Shoe curve at Cwmffrwdoer. This was the tail engine of a train with locos at both ends, and the last train off the Eastern Valley.

My second man was Brian Mathew, while the driver of the lead engine, No 37214, was

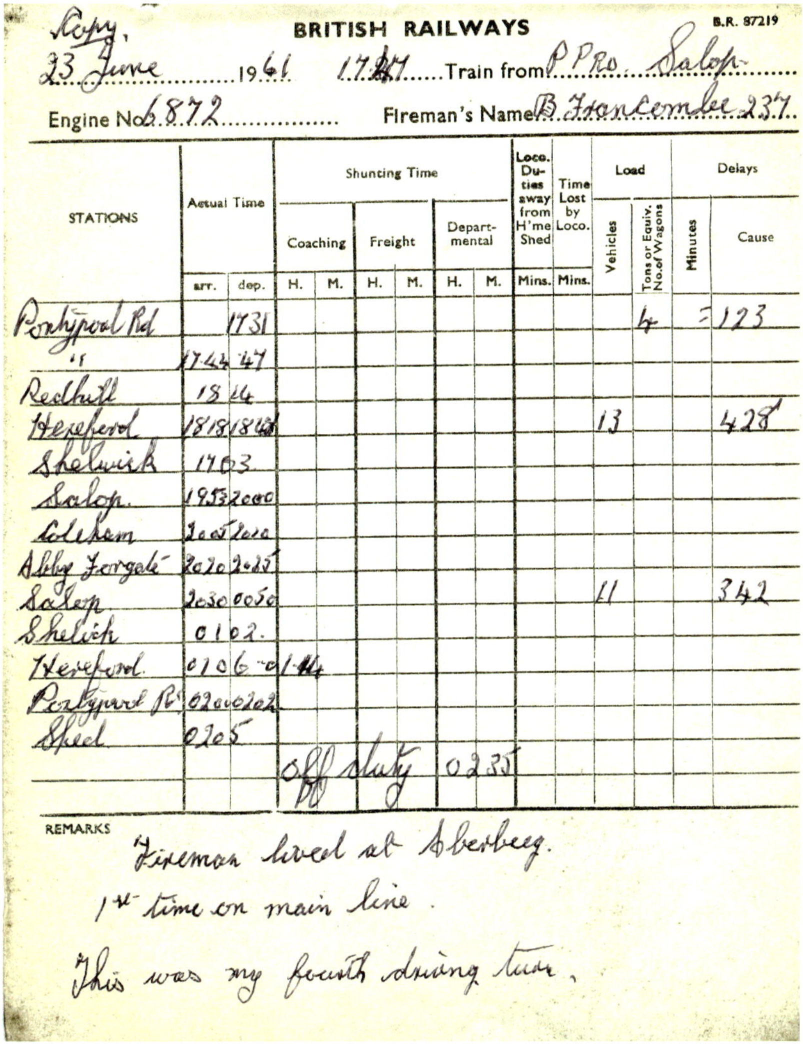

STATIONS	Actual Time arr.	Actual Time dep.	Coaching H.	Coaching M.	Freight H.	Freight M.	Departmental H.	Departmental M.	Loco. Duties away from H'me Shed Mins.	Time Lost by Loco. Mins.	Load Vehicles	Load Tons or Equiv. No. of Wagons	Delays Minutes	Delays Cause
Pontypool Rd		1731									4			=123
"		1744 47												
Redhill	1814													
Hereford	1818	1843									13			428
Shelwick	1753													
Salop	1953	2000												
Coleham	2005	2010												
Abbey Forgate	2020	2025												
Salop	2030	0050									11			342
Shelwick	0102													
Hereford	0106	0144												
Pontypool Rd	0200	0202												
Shed	0205													
	Off duty 0235													

BRITISH RAILWAYS — B.R. 87219

Copy, 23 June 1961 1.7.27 Train from P PRO Salop

Engine No. 6872   Fireman's Name B. Francombe 237

REMARKS

"Fireman lived at Aberbeeg.

1st time on main line.

This was my fourth driving turn."

The log for a turn on 16 October 1961, on engine No 4639, while undertaking track removal between Brynmawr and Abergavenny on the ex-LNWR line from Abergavenny Junction to Merthyr. *Derek Saunders*

Len Salter, a Severn Tunnel man. During the war he had been a fireman, and while carrying out 'Rule 55' at Gloucester station in the dark he had stepped off the footplate and fallen 30 feet over the parapet of a railway bridge. He survived but his health was affected.

On the way back I rode in the back cab of No 37214 and took some cine film, while Len drove No 37098.

1. Loco Fitter Harry Rawlins

From 18 August 1952 to 9 May 1957 I served my apprenticeship as a fitter and turner, and between June 1959 and November 1964 was a fitter at Pontypool Road MPD, 86G. Between 29 May 1957 and 1959 I served my National Service in the RAF (Cardington in the first week, West Kirby for 8 weeks, Weeton outside Blackpool for 4 months, then to Malaya for 15 months). I left the RAF on 14 May 1959, 14 days early.

The following recollections are from the period August 1952 to November 1964.

Trainspotting memories

I was an enthusiastic locospotter in my early teens and would collect engine numbers at Abergavenny Monmouth Road. I befriended signalmen in local Abergavenny signal boxes, and spent many hours in Abergavenny Brecon Road loco sheds, Abergavenny Mon Road and Abergavenny Junction. My time at Brecon Road was

Surviving members of the Pontypool Road fitting staff reunite in 2004. From left to right, they are Brian Ford, Harry Loveridge, Bobby Garrett, Brian Farr, David Hall, Harry Rawlins, Terry Biggs, John Garrett, Gwyn Lewis, Clive Morgan, the late Malcolm Hewlett, Averyn Walbank and Alec Davis. *Harry Rawlins*

spent with a man called Harry Rice (who instigated my railway career), while at Abergavenny Mon Road and Abergavenny Junction was Harry Jones, a relief signalman, who also worked Pontypool Road Middle (in the station), which you couldn't visit, as well as at Llanvihangel signal box (which I visited once).

A 'Star' Class engine worked an evening train from Abergavenny to Ponty, then return to Shrewsbury on a return working. The mail train going light back to Shrewsbury often had two engines on it, as well as the Travelling Post Office; a 'Castle' would be the train engine and a 'Star' as the pilot, the latter being a Shrewsbury engine. This train would pass Abergavenny at around 9.00pm in the dark. In later years, after dieselisation, this train would stop at Abergavenny Mon Road.

Llanvihangel Summit is recalled, where there was a refuge siding and a little goods yard. The refuge was used for parking trains, if Pandy loop was full and an express was coming; the train would be pushed back into it.

For the 1.42pm train to Swansea, Monday to Saturday, the LMS engine would be changed at Ponty, then the train would continue to Cardiff, usually with a Ponty '68xx' 'Grange' loco, returning to Ponty at approximately 5.30pm.

Four coaches would go on at Ponty, and four would be held back to join onto the back of a train that left Bristol at 4.09pm, having originated at Penzance. The 6.00pm at Abergavenny was the combined 4:09pm from Bristol and the returning train from Cardiff; it then went on to Crewe, with a coach for Glasgow. For a long time it was headed by *King George V* (which worked from Bristol Bath Road to Shrewsbury, returning with a night mail train; it rarely failed on this turn. By 1950 it was painted blue, and was still on this turn when I started at Ponty in 1952). Before then it used to be a Bristol 'Castle' and a Pontypool 'Bulldog' as far as Pontypool. (I can recall 'Bulldogs' *Calcutta*, *Skylark* and *Seagull* at Ponty. *Calcutta* was withdrawn first, and *Seagull* and

Skylark were the last there. *Seagull* alternated between Hereford and Ponty. *Skylark* and *Seagull* were later transferred to Reading, to work a few specials, and were then withdrawn and scrapped.)

The LMS engine was turned and coaled, then worked the 3.15pm Penzance to Manchester Piccadilly train, passing through Abergavenny around 3.30 to 3.45pm. A 'Castle' brought the Penzance train into Ponty, where it came off, working back to Bristol on another job.

There was a 50mph restriction over Penpergwym river bridge; engines would kick like mad going over it. An LMS man brought a train back early in the morning, and they went over it at about 70mph. Driver Jack Drayton recalls a '45xx' tank loco coming off the track on the bridge, and jamming in the platform at Penpergwym; the driver was Harry Oswald (who was known as 'horses head').

A 'double home' arrangement was worked by Abergavenny Brecon Road men on freight train workings. The job was from Abergavenny to Crewe, or Abergavenny to Harlescott, north of Shrewsbury. After Abergavenny shed closed all the fitters from there came to Pontypool Road, and the footplate crews booked on in a little room at Abergavenny Mon Road station, at the end of the down waiting room. This was a sub-shed of Ponty, used for booking on after reading the notices. 'Super Ds' were used on this working, and in later years Ponty '28xxs'. Booking on at Abergavenny Mon Road continued to the end of steam.

Before Abergavenny Brecon Road shed closed, a train was worked from Abergavenny at 9.10pm to Crewe, the engine returning with another train the following day. This working was originally the Dowlais Top ammonia train, worked from Merthyr to Abergavenny Junction in the evening, then sent from Abergavenny Junction to Crewe, for Billingham-on-Tees, where ammonia was used to make explosives and fertiliser. The plant at Merthyr had been built just before the war as two separate factories to manufacture ammonia for explosives.

Two trains came down in the evening to Abergavenny from Merthyr – one with general freight and the other with ammonia tanks. Sometimes they both comprised ammonia tanks, and would be joined at Merthyr, with two brake vans on the back and maybe 20 tank wagons (there were two brake vans as there were two trains coupled together). Two 'Super Ds' would work this train to Abergavenny Brecon Road. The weight of one full ammonia tank wagon was equal to two tank wagons. The two brake vans were removed, and the two Merthyr engines would then return to Abergavenny Brecon Road shed. A fresh 'Super D' from Brecon Road worked the train on to Crewe. The train would be formed of a fresh train engine, usually a 'Super D', ammonia tanks, other odd wagons and a fresh brake van. A loco from Brecon Road shed would bank the train to Abergavenny Junction, and would continue to bank to Llanvihangel, then begin its night work as the 9.00pm Abergavenny banker, banking trains from Abergavenny Mon Road to Llanvihangel as required. I saw this in the early 1950s.

On a Wednesday night a vacuum-fitted van was used to bring stores to Abergavenny Brecon Road shed on a weekly basis from Crewe; it returned on the 9.10pm train to Crewe. It was propelled from the shed to Abergavenny Junction with the banker, and there was put on the front of the 9.10pm. This train was mostly ammonia tanks and ordinary freight.

When the Heads of the Valley line closed, the train went from Merthyr to Hay with two panniers, until that route was also closed. A train of empty tanks from the north was worked to Ponty during the day, and was left behind the loco shed. A Ponty '56xx' tank went off shed at midday, taking empties up to Merthyr and returning with a train of ammonia, which it worked through to Hereford, returning light engine to Ponty. [Author's note: These trains were routed over the Vale of Neath after 5 December 1960 for about a period of two years, and to Merthyr via reversals at Bargoed and Pant.]

LMS 8Fs went to Brynmawr, but it was usually 'Super Ds' on freight trains, although occasionally a 'Black Five' would go as far as Brynmawr. This would be a Crewe engine working a 'double home' job, or if a 'Super D' had failed on the way south.

Before the war, Abergavenny shed had worked through to Birkenhead.

An ROD tender with four wheels was stored in an excursion siding at Abergavenny Brecon Road as a water carrier when the railway to Brynmawr was being lifted (the middle pair of wheels had been removed). It was stored where the hairdresser is now situated by the roundabout. Water was taken up the line, the tender propelled by a little steam engine.

A train of coal from Ponty was worked through to Harlescott, a yard north of Shrewsbury, on the line to Crewe. Ponty men would work it to Harlescott, take the engine to shed, stay overnight, and come back with the same engine working a different train the next day.

There were three trains to Ebbw Vale from Ponty. The 1.30am had a '56xx', and the 12.30pm had a '72xx'. (Aberbeeg parts were sent on the front of the engine before it left the shed, smokebox first, down the Llanilleth line, known as the 'muck hole'). There was also one in the evening.

The Abergavenny banker

The Great Western had a locomotive shed at Abergavenny until 1932, when it closed; during the war it was an outstation of Reading Signal & Telegraph Works. Until then the GWR engines undertook banking duties at Llanvihangel. Three old GWR tank engines were kept there, undertaking banking and also a couple of odd passenger trains. Upon closure of the shed, the banking duties were subcontracted to the LMS, using engines from Abergavenny Brecon Road shed. In the early 1950s about 90% of banking was undertaken by the LMS, with the Great Western using the engine from the 1.00am mail train, originating at Newport with a Ponty engine. At that time the Abergavenny mail train was hauled by a '55xx'. The engine ran light engine to Newport, with one coach to Abergavenny, then it would stop at Abergavenny and start banking duties throughout the night for the remainder of its shift. When Abergavenny shed closed, Abergavenny men continued to work this job using Ponty engines, which would stop out for 26 hours, using two sets of crew. A third crew would take the engine back to Ponty, and return to Abergavenny 'on the cushions' (as passengers on the train).

The banking engine for this turn at Ponty was always a '72xx' 2-8-2T, due to the amount of coal required to stay out for 26 hours; the fire would be in a state when it returned to the shed. When the LMS was doing the job, it would be 'Super Ds', a Webb 'Coal Tank', or sometimes a Class 3 Stanier. When he was a loco inspector, Jack Kersley of Pontypool Road got the Webb 'Coal Tank' removed from this duty. He travelled up on the train engine, hidden under a coat in the corner of the cab, then when they got to

Abergavenny he dropped off the loco as they were going past Triley bridge and counted how many wagons the 'Coal Tank' banking engine was actually pushing as it went past – it was just the brake van! I can recall being in Abergavenny Junction box and seeing the Webb 'Coal Tank' lose the train – it was a couple of yards behind it. The signalman shouted to the driver to stop at the signal box rather than try and chase the train up the bank.

Triley bridge was the source of water for Abergavenny Brecon Road engine shed, in pre-British Railways days. Water tanks were also located Abergavenny Mon Road, fed from Triley until BR come on the scene, when they were fed from Abergavenny Junction. Water was pumped up from the river to Brecon Road shed, and from the shed to Brecon Road station, and possibly from there to Abergavenny Junction. Then they tapped into the line coming from Triley, and ran it down to Mon Road.

Before I started at Pontypool Road engine No 385 was used on the banking work. One

Ex-GWR 2-8-2T No 7227 is seen at Pontypool Road Station South Junction on 15 August 1962, acting as the Abergavenny banker, and freshly coaled up. *Southern-Images*

Friday night the driver wanted to get home quick, and ran the engine really fast from Llanvihangel summit back to Pontypool Road. However it ran the metal out of the big ends by the Horse & Jockey Pub at Abergavenny and was declared a failure. Rollei Jones, the Ponty fitter, was sent to get the engine back to shed, with his mate Aubry Jones. The side rods were taken off and the driving axle boxes packed up. The big ends wouldn't come off. When at the shed, it was found that the big end bolts had come loose, and had a quarter-inch set in them so they wouldn't hammer out. They had to be sawn off to get them out.

Abergavenny loops

During the war loops were put in at Abergavenny station on the down platform. One train on a Saturday afternoon started from the island platform back road, using a Ponty '64xx' and a 'B set' of coaches, but the loops were normally used by freights to allow passenger trains to pass, when waiting for a path to Little Mill or Ponty. Excursions to Barry Island, Bristol Zoo or London (for the Mother's Union, once a year, using a Ponty 'Grange') also used the back of the island platform.

Three trains could be held in the three down loops at Abergavenny – one in each down road at the back of the island platform, and one in the third down loop in front of the signal box. There was only one loop on the up line at Abergavenny, which is now the only loop still there. In the loop behind the down platform I was once called out to release the brakes on a Stourbridge '68xx', going to Ponty with an extra train of empty wagons bound for Hafodrynys. Mr Morgan was the driver, a Ponty man.

If freights working through Mon Road station had the road from Abergavenny Junction, they came through on the main line, otherwise they were diverted onto the relief line at the back of the platform. A lot of freight, but not all, went through the back of the platform.

I used to go to Abergavenny Mon Road signal box in the evenings when a certain relief signalman was on; I recall watching a train pull into the up loop, but was too long for it! I might have just started at Ponty, and this incident may have occurred in the autumn of 1952. I watched this manoeuvre from the signal box. The train came into the station, backed over the crossover by the signal box end of station onto the down line, and eventually pulled up in to the back of the island platform, to clear the down main. A down train went past, on the main line, and the up train reversed back out onto up main line. The engine was an 'Austerity' tender loco.

In 2017, at Abergavenny Mon Road, the footbridge between the island platform and the bank was removed. This footbridge spanned the main line at Abergavenny Junction until 1958, when it was dismantled and transported by rail for re-use at Abergavenny Mon road.

Penpergwym could hold one freight train in its single down loop.

LMS Ivatt Class 2 2-6-2T memories

Gauging trials were undertaken from Abergavenny (Brecon Road) in LMS days, when these engines were brand new. Abergavenny was the first shed to have any for use; it had the first four after No 1200 (No 1200 went around the country on gauging trials). Trials were undertaken from Abergavenny to Merthyr, and from Tredegar to Newport for passenger trains to Merthyr from Newport or Abergavenny. Of the four engines at Abergavenny, two were based there, and two at Tredegar. The two Tredegar engines would be sent to Abergavenny (Brecon Road) for boiler washouts, and the two Abergavenny engines sent to Tredegar to temporarily replace them; they were all 86K engines.

My interview letter received from District Motive Power Superintendent Charlie Reed of Newport. *Harry Rawlins*

The Medical Examination letter from Charlie Reed. *Harry Rawlins*

Little Mill Yard

Little Mill Yard was there when I was an apprentice, but by the time I had become a fitter it had closed.

Apprenticeship

Harry Rice got me an interview with the Abergavenny shed foreman, Mr Williams, who then got me an interview with Charlie Reed, the District Superintendant, 'Mr 86'. The latter interviewed me

for the job at Ponty in Newport, in Devon Place (86A). A free pass on the train from Abergavenny to Newport was issued. I had a colour blindness test with a box of wool. The medical was at Beechwood Park, Newport, and a free pass was again given.

For my first day at Ponty shed as an apprentice loco fitter, 18 August 1952, I caught the 7.10am train from Abergavenny

An unidentified ex-GWR '57xx' Class 0-6-0PT is seen shunting wagons for Pilkington's glassworks, as seen from Pontypool Road station on 1 September 1953. *L. B. Lapper, Harry Rawlins collection*

to Pontypool Road, hauled by a Hereford
'43xx'; this was the train that would carry me
to work. Sometimes it was hauled by 'Saint'
No 2920 from Hereford to Newport, which
then turned on the Maindee triangle and
brought a train back. It was pouring with
rain during the walk from Pontypool Road
station to the loco shed via the Black Ash
path.

I had to wait until after 9 o'clock for
Chief Clerk Reg Belson. I then started work
with Don Green, and was shown around the
machine shop, situated at the north-west
end corner of the shed, in the round house.
Machines were located along the west wall.

I was with Don for the first week as my
introduction and he showed me how the
machines worked. The second week I worked
with Rollei Jones, who was a senior fitter
when I started, doing valves and pistons
on a '28xx', the third week I was with Jock
Wark doing valves and pistons on a pannier,
and the next I started machining on my
own for about 18 months. My bench was
in the north-west corner of the shed, in
the compound where the machines were
situated.

Pontypool Road station

Pontypool Road North signal box was at
the Abergavenny end of the station and
controlled all roads at
that end of the station.
Both sides of the station
had a main line and
a relief line, with a
diamond crossover in
the middle, controlled
by a little signal box on
the platform, which also
controlled only 'dummy'

Ex-GWR '38xx' Class
2-8-0 No 3816 passes the
East Junction signal box
on the Down Goods Relief
line with a southbound
freight on 3 September
1960. *B. K. Green,
Norman Preedy*

signals. The relief and main lines joined
into a single main line, after which the two
freight lines joined the Up Main line right by
the North Box.

The station booking office was where it is
now, with coal offices on top; the manageress
of the refreshment room had a flat there,
in the red-brick building, and the girls who
worked in the refreshment room had a flat on
top of that.

You accessed the platform by walking
through a subway and up some steps. On the
platform there was the Signal & Telegraph
Inspector's office, waiting rooms, the
refreshment room, and the Middle signal
box, in two halves, with levers on each side
of the platform. Train announcing was done
from the Middle box.

Opposite the bottom of the steps, at the
end of the station subway, was a hydraulic
lift, run off mains tap water; it was a total
loss, and was more often not working
than working. Ponty fitters once had the
connecting rod of a '68xx' stuck in the
lift, which didn't improve it. The rod had
become bent in the frost, so was placed on
the side of an engine, taken to the station,
put on the platform, taken down in the lift,
then by road to Caerphilly Works. When it
came back it was put in the lift and, as it was
going up, the top end of it jammed in the
lift!

Machine and lift repairs were done by an 86A outstation repair gang; one man who did this fairly regularly was Bernard Miles, who later went to work for the Gas Board. Another repair gang from Newport would repair the water columns; prior to British Rail, each Western shed repaired the water columns in its own area.

The South Bay at Pontypool Road was for the Vale of Neath line. Trains from the Vale would arrive and the station pilot would pull the carriages off, then push them into the carriage sidings and the engine would go back to shed. If the train was worked by an Aberdare engine, the loco would propel the train out of the bay, turn it on the triangle and propel it back to the station.

The North Bay was for working to Monmouth. This was an auto-train service, with the engine at the north end of the train; it propelled the train into the bay, and pulled it out. It pushed the auto-coach into the carriage sidings at the end of the day.

Pontypool Road shed fitting staff

To walk to the shed from the station, you went up the road, crossed The Highway, walked down past the old station master's house, past the cattle pen sidings and onto the Black Ash path opposite the South Box. You then passed over the river bridge, past the subway on the right, and along the Black Ash path to the cabins near the East signal box. You then crossed the main line and down and up goods lines into the back of the shed by the water tank and stores.

The shed masters were Jack Rustell (in 1944), followed by Jack Kersley in 1953, then Joe Williams. In 1959 a Scotsman, Mr Watt from Polmadie in Glasgow, arrived, the first mechanical foreman shed master on the Western. He was the foreman when I came back out of the RAF, and when he retired he went to work for Hugh Phillips when the Disney engines were being tested. Mr Watt was ex-LNER, but went straight to the top; he could be awkward. Charlie Hewlett was shed master until 1964, before closure to steam in May 1965, when nine engines remained. Charlie had previously been a driver. Shed foremen on the Western were loco drivers, while on the LMS they were fitters.

The mechanical foreman was Mr Wiltshire, who was keen on keeping the fitters' mates busy by keeping brake screws well lubricated on engines and tenders. He was succeeded by Lesley Norkett, and the chargehand was Theo Leonard. One of the two chief clerks was Reg Belson ('The Beast', but he was honest) – they were

Fitters pose with a Pontypool Road 'ROD' 2-8-0 loco. From left to right they are 'Boot Nose', Aubry Jones, Don Green, unknown and Averyn Walbank ('Wally').
Harry Rawlins collection

From left to right on the back row are Don Green, Ivor Morris, unknown, Aubry Jones and Alf Smith. In the front row are Rollei Jones (alias 'The Camel'), Averyn Walbank ('Wally'), unknown, and Lou Davis. *Harry Rawlins collection*

injured footplate staff. Examining fitters were Dave Fry, Len Drinkwater and Charlie Acker. Fitters were Rollei Jones ('The Camel', as he had a deformed back), Lou Davis, Bert Morgan, A. B. Stafford, who was the NUR Shop Steward, Ron Cox (ex-Navy, nicknamed 'Chiefy'), Cyril Kersley (Jack Kersley's son), Rollei Price, Will Moor ('Jock'), Cyril Marney, Dan Powell (the 'Overtime King'), Danny Davis ('Aberdare'), Haydn Evans, Marcus Hunter and Glyn Morris ('Scratchy'). The coppersmith was Ken Cleavy ('Lovey Dovey'). Fitters' mates were Aubry Jones (who worked with Rollei Jones), examining fitters' mates were Gordon Mills, Ivor Powell, George Hall, Ivor Morris (who worked with Danny 'Aberdare'), Arthur Rolls (who worked with Bert Morgan), Al Smith (an ambulance man, who worked with Cyril Kersley), Bill Spokes (who worked with Jock Wark), Tom Morton (a spare hand), Tom Mathews ('Tom the Dog', who always had an Alsatian, and

worked with Ron Cox), Bill Lewis, Sam Gillett and Melvyn Baker ('Batchy'). The boilersmith chargehand was Mr Bougler, from Cardiff. Marian was the only woman in the shed.

Les Norkett was at Ponty before I started; he had been a chargehand at Aberbeeg. He was a good foreman, and went to Canton to sort out the engines – someone had been signing off repairs that hadn't been undertaken. Aberbeeg was the place to be if you wanted promotion.

Marcus Hunter had started his career in a brewery in London and was there before I started; he had previously worked at Guest Keen. He once nearly fell off the top of the Big Arch at Talywain, when working on a breakdown train in the dark. The train comprised two coaches, and had stopped on top of the Big Arch when he stepped out, only to be held back by Jock Wark, who grabbed his collar. I was an apprentice then. When Ponty was closing down in the

Former Pontypool Road chargehand fitter Marcus Hunter stands beside ex-GWR 0-6-0PT No 7754 at Lower Navigation Colliery water column on the NCB Talywain to Blaenserchan Colliery branch in December 1969. *J. S. Williams*

1960s he left and got a job at Pontypool College as a technician. When I started my apprenticeship, Marcus was a fitter, and by the time I left Pontypool Road he was the chargehand, giving out jobs to fitters and looking at jobs to be undertaken.

Dave Fry and Cyril Kersley had been railway apprentices. Cyril was fast-track promoted. Dave had done his apprenticeship there in the war and didn't go in the forces. He was an examining fitter was I started, and when I came back out of the RAF he was the foreman fitter for a short time. When Les Norkett came back from Canton, Dave went somewhere else. He was the fitter with the most knowledge of the younger group. Rollei Price was the top man, a big friend of Jack Kersley.

Dave Fry once changed the radial wheels on a '41xx' tank; they were jacked out, and one jack started to give way a bit when jacked up high and there was a panic! Valves, pistons, vacuum and gland leaks were the norm. Dave applied for a job with the electricity board in Cwmbran, as a fitter and turner, and passed on the job to Don Green. Dave's father was a driver.

I was finishing my apprenticeship in Swindon, or was in the RAF, when a Ponty pannier failed in service with a sheared wheel. Dave Fry also recalled a story of a pannier with a sheared wheel in Pontnewynydd Yard; a wooden bogie was put under the back of the loco to bring it back to the shed.

Terry Biggs worked with Gerry Smith, the Newport foreman, checking wheel quartering, but had finished his time when I came out of the RAF. His father and his brother were drivers.

Malcolm Hewlett started in 1959 as an apprentice, becoming a fitter and turner at the end of his apprenticeship. Early in 1964 three people transferred to Cardiff Canton – Rollei Price, Malcolm Hewlett and Edgar Davis from Sebastopol.

Brian Ford stayed until the end, then went to Tyseley to work on preserved steam. He had started as an apprentice at Pontypool Road shed in the early 1960s, and attended the craft exam in machine shop engineering at Pontypool College. He was working on the last day on steam on nights, and was the last fitter to leave Ponty.

Dave Hall was an apprentice under me. He was a Bristol boy who lived in Newport, but now lives back in Bristol.

Harry Loveridge was a fitter's mate who came to our first staff reunion in 2004; sadly he had passed away before our second reunion the following year.

Gwyn Lewis was a big rugby player. One day he was talking to me about the day's jobs; we both had jobs changing safety valves on panniers. Gwyn said, 'I bet you I can change it quicker than you.' I was naïve and agreed, putting on a shilling bet.

Two panniers were side by side on the turntable roads. We had both got up and unbolted our safety valves, and I was fitting up chain blocks attached to the roof of the shed to pull the new valve up onto the boiler. Gwyn, however, got hold of his safety valve under his arm and carried it up a ladder, nearly reaching to the top. But he

Averyn Walbank on the left, with John Cross (centre) and Gwyn Lewis, all apprentices. *Harry Rawlins*

lost his grip and threw the valve to the floor. Les Norkett wasn't very pleased.

Gwyn would bet with apprentices that there was an engine called *Dwight D. Eisenhower* (it was an LNER 'A4'). I didn't know. Gwyn said, 'Lend me your ABC book.' He won sixpence for that, although he was hours looking for the loco in the book.

Above: Averyn Walbank (right) with John Garrett. *John Garrett, Harry Rawlins collection*

Averyn Walbank was an apprentice at the same time as me. He became a fitter and left to work at Ebbw Vale steelworks.

The ATC technician was Ernie Stevens, doing repairs and changing batteries. A Newport man, he did the ATCs at Ponty, the tunnel and Aberbeeg. He was a boxing manager in his spare time.

Alec Davis was from Abergavenny Brecon Road shed. He went to Swindon the year before me, then came back to Pontypool Road. He can't get over the modern-day repairs of engines!

Brian Farr undertook his apprenticeship at Ponty at the same time as me, and after finishing it at Swindon he returned to Ponty. He did National Service while there, and is now the last remaining Ponty boilersmith.

Sam Gillett ('Snotty Nose Sam') was a fitter's mate, ex-colliery, and the infamous 'Overtime King'. He always had sandwiches and tea wrapped up in newspaper. When the breakdown crane travelled from the depot, a fitter's mate went with it, to oil the axle boxes, etc. One Friday afternoon at Easter Sam was

Below: Ex-GWR '87xx' Class 0-6-0PT No 8730 resides on the Stores Road on 25 August 1960. *F. A. Blencowe, R. K. Blencowe collection*

sent out to take a crane to Severn Tunnel Junction. There was no relief for him, so he carried on through the tunnel to Bristol, where there was still no relief. He ended up in Somerset in a refuge siding or loop until the Monday after Easter, returning to Ponty on the Tuesday. The train often had an extra brake van, and his train would have been shunted into a siding on Saturday.

Ron Knight was the coal man, and had a coal merchant's business in Panteg station yard. Sam would empty the coal wagons for him, on nights or on the 'monkey shift,' then go straight into work at Ponty. He ended up in St Lawrence's hospital, badly burned – he had emptied a lubricator into a bucket and thrown it into the firebox, without the blower on, and it had blown back all over him. The railway reckoned it caught fire on its own. He had perforated ear drums, which made his nose drip – you wouldn't want him working above you!

There were three store keepers on shifts. Clive Sumner was the top man in the stores; his office was in a tin shed located between the water tank and the Stores Road stop block. There was a fire in there once and he couldn't get out – he was a tiny fellow. After that an emergency door was fitted. Clem Ford was the stores issuer, as well as the first aid man. Brake blocks were kept outside the stores, facing the coal stage. Springs were originally kept between the roads of the round shed, but Dave Fry had them moved and stored on wooden racks outside, near the scrap springs, at the back of the coal stage.

Between the stores and the shed were various buildings. That nearest the stores was the fitters' cabin, then the drivers' and cleaners' cabins nearer the shed. The fitters' cabin was situated beside the Cabin Road. It had a stove, and there was room for four people to sleep in it.

Saturday night saw the main use of the cabin. You would go into work, do the set job, check there was nothing going out before midnight that you had any jobs on, go up the pub, come back, have supper, and go to sleep. You asked the store man to give you a call about 5.15am so you could check

round and finish at 6.00am. Mostly you would have engineering trains at night, so you would have to stop until 7.00am when the day shift came on. Some of the fitters ate out in the shed, others in the cabin.

The lamp room was situated in the coal stage building under the ramp, looking towards the gas works. When I was in the RAF, Abergavenny men went to work in the lamp room. Being the lamp room man was 'easy money', and Mr Welsh, a former Mr Wales body builder who died young, worked there. He got married when he moved to Ponty.

The tool room man was also from Abergavenny, and nicknamed 'The Snake.'

Of the shed's carpenters, Walter Toombes did the wooden footplates, and would fit storm sheets, paint front number plates and shed plates, and paint the shed codes in GW days. He had a collection of Health and Safety photos displayed in the workshop at ground level in the back of the coal stage building, under the coal stage ramp. There was a window in the workshop where he could see the Folly. When he retired his job was taken over by a fitter's mate from Blackwood.

Charlie Reed was the District Superintendant. He would pay occasional visits – they were never unannounced. On one occasion he wanted to see Western piston packing. Ponty had a press into which packing was placed to fabricate piston packing to fit different engines, but it hadn't been used in years. Les Norkett wanted it cleaned up and made to look like it was used regularly, and to make some sets of piston rod packing. There were three different sizes of piston packing on Western engines: the '64xxs', '14xxs' and '16xxs' had the smaller set, with panniers and '28xxs' having different sets of packing. Three sets of packing were made for Charlie's visit.

If someone was in trouble you had to go to Newport to see Charlie. For instance, if a driver ran past a signal or a fitter made a mess of a job, he would receive a verbal caution, or a registered caution. A registered caution would be recorded in a book, and the culprit

Looking south in the round shed on 30 December 1964; the engine roster board is seen on the wall on the left, adjacent to the door leading to the shed office. G. *Vincent*

received a piece of paper. Ponty fitter Glyn Morris reckoned he had his bedroom papered in cautions! His father was the coppersmith at Ponty before I started there. I only ever had two verbal cautions. One was my fault, the other wasn't. On nights, you had a card for a job and would sign it off. Sam Gillard was supposed to have adjusted a brake on a 'Hall' or its tender, but when brake was put on at Hereford station the loco crew couldn't get it off again as it hadn't been adjusted properly. I had a caution over this. I also had a cotter come out of a pannier going down Glyn Neath bank. It was said that the set bolts hadn't been tightened up properly. The heads were probably worn badly, making tightening difficult.

The engine number board was on a wall in the round shed by the main office. Job lists for fitters were clipped to a steel plate, in the order that locos would be going off shed.

The offices of the mechanical foreman and examining fitters were on the west wall of the round shed. The foreman's office was more to the north, while the examining fitters' office was nearly opposite the shortest

road on the west side of the shed. The boilersmith chargehand had an office on the east wall of the round shed, alongside the Lift Road, and the coppersmith had a workshop in the north-east corner.

There was a broken window, which was always taken out, by the coppersmith's forge, which was used to melt whitemetal. This window was in the north end of the shed, on the east side. It was broken to let air into that area of the shed. The coppersmith didn't like it, as he wasn't sociable; people come and sat in the window, and he thought Les Norkett was encouraging people not to work! A whole pane of window glass was taken out – one of the bottom panes, measuring maybe 2 feet by 18 inches. You could sit on the sill, either on the inside or outside of the shed, and look through the window. I spent a lot of Saturday afternoons sitting on the window sill, looking out through the window, passing time away when there was not much on. The window pane was removed in the spring, and replaced in the winter.

Les Norkett's office was built in BR days in the north-west corner of the round shed, where the machines started. One window looked out over No 7 siding; it was the third window from the north wall of the round shed.

The examining fitter's office was the next window down (on the west side of the shed), having been the original foreman's office in the days of the Great Western. It was a little place, the length of two people lying down. The fitter was one side of the doorway and the mate on the other; there was a fire in the middle and room for one person to sleep by the side.

The chargehand boilersmith's office was by the lift on east wall of the round shed, and the boilersmith's forge was situated on the same side behind the shortest road (halfway down the side of the wall), and was used for keeping warm. Sometimes fitters would put cast iron valve heads off locos in the forge and forget to take them out, and they would melt! They were put in the forge to burn off the carbonised oil after the valve was disconnected from the valve spindle. Boilersmiths had separate cabins from the fitters. They would change boiler tubes, which was undertaken all over the shed; big engines had this done in the long shed. One

man changed boiler tubes and inserted and expanded new ones – Mr Churchouse. Only so many tubes were allowed to be changed. Tubes came to order, for a specific job, in a wagon, and were used straight away. Scrap tubes were offered for sale as line posts, and stored behind the coal stage ramp next to the scrap brake blocks. Unsold scrap tubes were loaded into a tube wagon and sent back to Swindon.

Footplate crews signed on in the same office as the fitting staff. This was located in the corner of the round shed/long shed, on the east side, where the two sheds were of different widths. There was a foreman and a running foreman on every shift. The running foreman was boss of the footplate staff, and there were three: Mr Hobbs, Mr Tanner and Mr Bill Selwood (from Newport, who would sign privilege tickets and had retired by 1959).

Bill Selwood was still a foreman in 1952, and had good hand writing and signed most of the privilege tickets for travelling by train. Foremen had no assistants until BR days. Bill Peckham, Les Mathews and Bill Lewis were the foremen's runners.

Ex-GWR '46xx' Class 0-6-0PT No 4639 is seen on the east side of the round shed on 21 September 1964. *Rail-Online*

Loco shed equipment

The equipment for the fitters was situated along the west wall of the round house. There was a radial arm drill from Newport (the most modern equipment the shed had and self-contained, replacing the Cincinnati drilling machine). Overhead shafting powered by a 45hp electric motor (which had to be started up slowly otherwise it would stop) drove an emery wheel (used for sharpening pencils!), a small lathe, a big lathe, a 48-inch sand stone (for sharpening garden shears!), a Cincinnati radial drill, which would only run in bottom gear, and a planing machine (quicker on the cutting stroke than the return due to the white metal inside it). A Tangye pump operated a 20-ton lift via overhead pipework across the end of the shed.

The self-contained air compressor, fitted after nationalisation, was used by the boilersmiths for expanding tubes and drilling out boiler stays. The motor also worked the lift, for lifting the ends of tenders and small locos. If someone stopped the 45hp motor during lifting, the lift would stop and would not go up any more.

Most machine shops have an emergency button to shut down all the machines in case there is an accident. The electric motor had two emergency stop buttons; to start the motor you pressed a button and a rotated a handle at the same time (it was ancient!). When the motor was started, it automatically rotated the overhead line shaft, to which it was connected by a belt. There was a 'clutch system' on the machines, consisting of a series of fast and loose pulleys, to disengage individual machines, such as two lathes, a planing (shaping) machine, emery wheel, drilling machine, plus the hydraulic pump. So to use the lift, the motor would be running, driving the overhead line shaft; if no one was using the machines, these would be disengaged and stand idle. If someone then walked past, they would see lots of machines, the belts running and no one using them, and they would press one of the emergency buttons to stop the motor

(and hence the machines) – but this would also stop the lift! An 'unpolite notice' was then posted on the emergency stop button to stop its unauthorised use!

Starting behind the mechanical foreman's office, the first machine was a 4-foot-diameter sand stone, used for the final finish to lathe and planer tools (and garden shears). The next machine was a Dean Smith & Grace lathe, used to turn axle boxes, inside big ends, eccentric straps, and pistons for '28xx' locos (19-inch diameter by 30-inch stroke). The next machine was a smaller lathe used to turn side rod bushes up to a 4-inch bore, and smaller items like big end bolts, etc. The last machine was a 3-foot emery wheel used for general grinding. All these machines were driven by the overhead line shaft powered by the 45hp motor. About 20 feet from the wall were three other machines: drilling machine, planing machines, and the Tangye pump, which worked the lift. The drilling machine was driven by a line shaft, and was later replaced by a self-contained radial drill.

The lift in the round shed had two controls: a bypass valve and a control to pressurise the ram. The pump was a Worthington-Simpson Ltd vertical triplex power pump, which 'compressed' water via pipework to the other side of the shed. The lift comprised a cylinder on top of a four-legged wooden framing, the framing legs being about a foot square. The piston came out the top of the ram, connecting to a steel bar above. Two steel bars came down the sides, connected to two hooks. A pressure gauge converted pressure into weight. A pannier weighed 18 tons when in the air with two sets of wheels on the ground, and a '94xx' 19 tons. The ram protruded through the roof, into a vertical cover; there was no accumulator for it. The lift could raise a 30-ton load[6].

Measurements were undertaken using a micrometer. In 1952 quite a small set was used, shared with Aberbeeg shed. Later, new micrometers were made with 50 instead of 25 divisions on the thimble. They were easier to read, and were again shared with

Aberbeeg. You would 'mike' the cylinders for valve and piston rings. Engine No 2802 is remembered on No 7 siding out of store with oval cylinder bores – the bore was measured using a micrometer.

Office staff would record engine mileage from the driver's ticket. Long-distance engines recorded accurate mileage, but the mileage of shunting engines was inaccurate, as demonstrated by the use of milometers on the diesels.

Ponty had a hand crane that the permanent way people used for transhipping goods out of crippled wagons. Sometimes it was behind the shed, but the fitters never used it. Abergavenny would use theirs and take it around on the breakdown train; some could pick up about 12 tons! The job of transhipping was overtime for platelayers. One day a wagonload of beer came off the road at Llanvihangel, and the wagon inspector said that it was to go only as far as Pontypool. The platelayers transhipped it there, and we tried hard to shake a barrel off it!

Fitters' mates used a 28lb hammer, known as a 'Mundy'; Edgar Davis was good with one.

I used a 14lb hammer for knocking cotters into crossheads

BRITISH TRANSPORT COMMISSION
BRITISH RAILWAYS

B.R. 19141/1

Your Reference

Our Reference PRO/23.

8th December, 19 64.

Dear Sir,

In accordance with your request, I have been pleased to arrange for your visit(s) to Motive Power Depot(s) as shewn below, and I hope you have an instructive and enjoyable visit.

On arrival at the Depot, this letter should be presented immediately at the Depot office and a responsible member of the staff will conduct you round.

In the interests of safety, no person under 16 years of age will be allowed to visit a Motive Power Depot unless accompanied by an adult, and the visit must finish before dark. The only luggage allowed in the Motive Power Depot will be cameras, and photographs may be taken for private collection only.

Yours faithfully, For T. C. HILTON

L. Chadwick

Motive Power Depot to be visited	Date	Time	No. of Persons
Pontypool Road	30.12.64.	9.30 hours	10
Newport (Ebbw Junction)	30.12.64.	12.00 noon	10
Severn Tunnel Junction	30.12.64.	15.30 hours	10

To :— G. Vincent, Esq.

A shed permit for an enthusiasts' visit to Pontypool Road, Newport (Ebbw Junction) and Severn Tunnel Junction on 30 December 1964. *G. Vincent*

Ex-GWR '57xx' Class 0-6-0PT No 5792 resides on the Stores Road on 16 August 1954. The breakdown train coach is seen behind, with the roof of East Junction signal box in the background. *Reproduced with kind permission of the Railway Correspondence & Travel Society*

and starting gear to get piston rods out of crossheads, and a 28lb hammer to knock cotter pins out of panniers and big end bolts in and out of panniers.

Around the shed

The shed was situated on the east side of the triangle; the west end formed the beginning of the Vale of Neath line, the south end led into the yards at Pontypool Road, and the north end connected to the main line going north.

The coal stage was at the north end of the shed, and the building to the south of it louvres was the toilets. There were three coal hoists; the centre one would lift a few feet and was used all the time. The drum of coal was lifted as the tenders got bigger over the years. The coal stage floor was almost level.

The stores were situated under the water tank, and contained spare parts for engines such as boiler fittings, smoke plates, oil, brass valves, nuts and bolts, and split pins. You'd enter, using the door at the south end, walk up to a counter and ask for what you needed. Spare fittings were booked in and out – you had to put one in to get one out. Nuts and bolts required a chitty from the store man. A cupboard by the pump that worked the shed lift was full

of a ready machined rows of clacks for fitting onto engines.

The water supply at the depot was gravity fed by the canal. The water tank for the water columns in the shed and yards was situated on top of the stores, and had a steel sheeted roof. The short track on the stone wall by the shed stores water tank was the original road where they had kept old-fashioned Great Western breakdown vans. These were replaced by two 70-foot coaches and a packing van, which were then kept behind the coal stage as this road wasn't long enough. Even the conical water tower at the top end of the station, on the freight road, was gravity fed. There were two tanks by the old station house that fed the top end of the station, and possibly parts of the loco depot.

Above right: Ex-GWR '64xx' Class 0-6-0PT No 6400 was a long-term resident, and is seen stored at the end of the Sand House Road at the south end of the shed. The timekeeper's office (for shed staff) is seen to the right of the engine. Derek Saunders recalls that 'we would collect our check and give the boy in the window your payroll number and he would clock you in.'

Right: Ex-GWR '45xx' Class 2-6-2T No 4593 is seen on the Sand House Road at the south end of the shed, with an unidentified ex-GWR '57xx' Class 0-6-0PT behind it, circa 1960. *Kidderminster Railway Museum*

Ex-GWR '28xx' Class 2-8-0 No 2864 is seen on No 4 Road, circa 1952. *Kidderminster Railway Museum*

No 7 siding ran down the side of the shed, and its main purpose was that, if the turntable was out of operation, you could get around the shed without going out on to the main line. Buildings at the side of the shed by this siding were the cabins used by the boilersmiths (and the hairdressers), the boiler-washers and the firelighters; the boiler-washers' cabin was nearest the south end of the shed.

Sidings behind the coal stage included the Sand House Road, which was used for the breakdown train in later years; the sand wagon was kept in the second road next to the stage. The two sidings adjacent to the Sand House Road were used to store trains with sleeping coaches for the Swindon turntable repair gang.

As stated in Chapter 2, there were two sand houses, one by the booking-on office, the other outside the north-west corner of the shed, behind the coal stage. Both sand houses contained a furnace to dry the sand. A fire was kept going all the time; sand was shovelled in and came out dry.

There were eight roads in the shed. No 8 could accommodate 0-6-0s, while No 7 could take 2-6-0s. No 6 was the Through Road from one end of the shed to the other. No 5 was all right for working on the inside of engines, with a greater width between it and adjacent roads. No 4 was wide on one side, but the other roads, Nos 3 to 1, were narrow between.

At the north end of the shed were three roads in a row. The Tap Road started south

BR '84xx' Class 0-6-0 PT No 8493 awaits fire-dropping on 25 May 1960. *F. A. Blencowe, R. K. Blencowe collection*

of the coal stage, and was accessed from the Coal Stage Road (the Through Road), running adjacent to the coal stage and back onto the turntable. The Coal Stage Road (the Centre Road) was a continuation of the fire pit road (where fires were dropped) and went straight on to the turntable. Finally, the Cabin Road came off the turntable, past the cabins outside the shed, and gave access to the East box. Most of the passenger turns went off from the Cabin Road to the East box, while most of the freight engines came off shed from the south end, also via East box. Engines came through the shed at the north end.

Adjacent to the cabin, the Cabin Road had an inspection pit. Most of the passenger engines working south were based on this road, such as the 1.42pm Cardiff (a continuation of an LMS train), and the 2.28pm to Neath. The 4.00pm Bristol is remembered; these engines would leave via the East Junction to get to the station.

The Centre Road was for engines going off the ash pit, through the shed to the turntable, to be stored in the round shed or the long shed.

The Tap Road was so called because there was a tap at the back of the coal stage (at the high end, for drinking water). For example, the engine for the 7.00pm Bristol would be stored here from 9.00am. A 'Hall' Class loco working, the engine would work to Bristol with half a train, and return with a freight. A 'King' or 'Castle' could access the Tap Road via the Coal Stage Road, being bigger than could be turned on the table. All the other engines could come onto the Tap

Road off the turntable, and also by using the Centre Road from the shed, onto the Coal Stage Road and back onto the Tap Road.

By the tap there were two storage locations, one for scrap brake blocks and the other for scrap springs. New springs were stored on racks in between the roads in the round shed, while new brake blocks were stored along the wall of the stores, in piles, with different numbers. Scrap was loaded up and returned to Swindon.

Brake blocks were defined as follows:

No 11 – 4ft 1½in wheels – tenders, '16xx', '44xx'

No 12 – 4ft 7½in wheels – '28xx', panniers, '42xx', '52xx', '72xx', '56xx', '66xx', '15xx', '55xx'

No 13 – 5ft 2in wheels – '14xx', '58xx'. '22xx', '54xx'

No 14 – 5ft 8in wheels – '43xx', '53xx', '63xx', '73xx', '93xx', '41xx', '51xx', '61xx', '47xx', '68xx'

No 15A – 6ft 0in wheels – '49xx', '59xx', '69xx', '79xx'

No 16 – 6ft 2in wheels – '10xx' 'County'

No 20 – narrow 4ft 7½in wheels – leading wheels of '56xx', and trailing wheels of '42xx' and '72xx'

No 21 – narrow 5ft 8in wheels – trailing wheels of '47xx'. These were narrower blocks, as on a '72xx'

No 40 – 6ft 8½in wheels – 'Castle'

Ex-GWR '41xx' Class 2-6-2T No 4138 waits on the ash pit on 23 May 1954. The steel ash shelter constructed during the Second World War is seen in the background.
R. K. Blencowe collection

Looking north, the Tap Road is on the left, the Coal Stage Road (leading to the Through Road) is in the middle, and the Cabin Road on the right. Note the water column by the Coal Stage Road.

Fire bars were stored outside the west side of the incline to the coal stage (where scrap fire bars were also stored). Scrap would be loaded into a wagon, to be sent to Swindon to be melted down to make new brake blocks and fire bars.

Many fire bricks for brick arches were used, as when tubes were being expanded by the boilersmith the old brick arch had to be knocked out. New bricks were stored between the roads, by the boilersmith's forge, inside the shed; they couldn't be stored outside in the wet.

The stationary boiler was inside the round shed between two of the turntable roads on the west side, and was used for hot water for washing and for boiler washouts. It was away for a period and engines were used instead, then later a loco was put on the end of No 1 road for use as a stationary boiler. There was a coal-fired furnace in the wall behind the stationary boiler for lighting fires using hot coals instead of wooden firelighters. Firelighters would put burning coal in the firebox, piling more coal around

it. The shed furnace was used occasionally into the 1960s.

The round shed was wider than the straight shed, or long shed, to its south and between them was the foreman's office. There were eight roads in the straight shed. No 1 was situated against South Sidings and No 7 road. Roads Nos 1-5 could store anything. No 6 was the Through Road from the coal stage and turntable to the south end of the shed. No 7 was used only for 2-6-0s and No 8 for 0-6-0s – the rest would take anything. These roads were about three engine lengths long.

Road clearances inside the straight shed were tight, with limited side room, except for No 5 road, where there was plenty of room on the right-hand side looking south, but still very tight on the other side; you daren't work on that side as it was adjacent to No 6 Through Road, along which engines went south all the time. There was also good clearance on the left-hand side only of No 4 road looking south.

Driver Jimmy Watkins (whose cine films have recently been made available on B&R Videos, courtesy of his fireman Dennis Skinner) is seen at the south end of the turntable in the round shed on 14 August 1963. No 6 Through Road is seen in the foreground.

Pulling a dead engine at the south end of the shed to stable it, using a loco from the fire pit.
Kidderminster Railway Museum

Ex-GWR No 6677 is seen at the south end of the shed on No 3 Road, while a left-hand driving spring is being changed on 4 June 1961. *Kidderminster Railway Museum*

Ex-GWR '28xx' Class 2-8-0 No 2859 rests on No 1 Road at the south end of the shed on 28 July 1963. *Rail-Online*

Ex-GWR '53xx' Class No 5322 is seen on No 7 Road after withdrawal, together with ex-GWR 'Hall' Class 4-6-0 No 6946. The date is 21 September 1964. *Rail-Online*

Ex-GWR No 7230 stands on No 7 Road on 25 May 1960. Wagons of coke are seen on the right. Derek Saunders recalls that 'these may be for the gasworks, and would arrive in a train from Lysaght's in Newport, off the Uskmouth branch (the Orb steelworks)'. *S. V. Blencowe*

Ex-GWR '2885' Class 2-8-0 No 3818 is stored on No 7 Road adjacent to the cabin for lighters-up, boiler-washers and the shed turner, circa 1960. *Kidderminster Railway Museum*

Engines are seen stored on No 7 Road at the back of the shed; the stop block is on No 6 Siding. Ex-GWR '28xx' Class No 2848 is prominent. *Kidderminster Railway Museum*

Another '28xx', No 2857, rests on No 7 siding behind the loco shed on 25 May 1960.
R. K. Blencowe collection

Repaired engines would be at the inside ends of the straight road shed, but there was no guarantee that engines would not run into the back of you on the same line; sometimes they would run onto the same road without brakes due to lack of steam. Panniers and '66xxs' were repaired in the round shed as the road was safe. Big engines were put on four roads for repairs.

Engines with serious failures were stored on the Tap Road near the coal stage.

The lights in the shed were rewired when I was an apprentice, after I'd been there about two years. Until they got dirty it was quite light in there, but before that it was terrible. The conduit was wrapped in Denzo tape.

Flare lamps were used under engines to give light when doing repairs. In the late 1950s miners' lamps were introduced, when I was in the RAF. These were great for examining fitters – just shine them at the job. However, the batteries were quite heavy, and the fitters went back to using flare lamps. These could also be used to warm things, and

the paraffin, tipped out, could be used as a release agent.

The shed floor consisted of bricks laid on sand, and the building was reroofed just after the war, and lifted. In the round shed the 'J' bolts rotted away, and one Thursday afternoon in about 1953 very high winds blew off a lot of sheets. Myself and my mates jumped under a Newport '94xx' tank engine, to be used on the 'Dump' train to ROF Glascoed, until it went off shed. We then found another engine to hide under. It was like an air raid! About 100 sheets blew off and dropped down through the glass. A crew from Abergavenny were there for 12 months renewing the 'J' bolts; the sheets were taken off and the steel work repainted.

The smoke chutes in the roof were originally wooden, but were replaced by asbestos when the shed roof was renewed in 1945.

Engine pits are recalled. They were all of varying depths, and when I first started there they were all too shallow. Turntable pits in the round shed were deeper at the end furthest away from the turntable, their depth varying along their length. These pits were deepened in the late 1950s. The long shed pits were not very deep and remained unmodified. All pits had steps at each end for access.

The round shed and turntable

The turntable was accessed from both ends of the shed by No 6 road, which was the Through Road. Looking north from the south end of the shed, from left to right the lines exiting the shed were the Tap Road, the Through Road and the Cabin Road. The Through Road took you to the coal stage, and the Tap Road joined it at the south end of the coal stage. Inside the shed, to the right of the Cabin Road looking north, was the Plough Road, then the Lift Road. To enter the shed from the north from the Tap Road

you would go onto the turntable, which would be rotated to exit onto any other road.

The Lift Road was the longest road in the round shed. Management didn't like to see tender engines stored on this road in case the hooks on the lift were knocked off – they were difficult to get back on! Tender engines could be stored on six of the turntable roads. These included the Plough Road, the Lift Road, one road at the side of the stationary boiler (the road west of the centre) and the Bell Road (so named by Dave Fry because a bell hung on the shed wall) in the south-east corner, down by the side of the office (the longest southernmost corner road). A '53xx' could be stored in the north-west corner, on one road adjacent to the Tap Road. The adjacent road had machines behind, and could store a smaller tender engine, such as a '22xx' 0-6-0. The largest engines to be turned, 'Halls' and '28xxs', could be stored

Ex-GWR 'Grange' Class 4-6-0 No 6814 is seen on the Plough Road at the north end of the round shed on 4 September 1956. Adjacent to it on the Lift Road (the longest road in the round shed) is ex-GWR '37xx' Class 0-6-0PT No 3717; an engine under repair, a '20xx' 0-6-0PT, is seen behind it. *D. K. Jones*

Here we see the west side of the round shed, looking north on 29 March 1964. Ex-GWR 2-8-2T No 7210 is on the road adjacent to the Tap Road, which could store a '53xx'), and ex-GWR '22xx' Class 0-6-0 No 2287 is in the next road. Behind the latter was a drilling machine, a planing machine, and the hydraulic pump for the lift on the other side. In the background can be seen the overhead shafting coming down to the big lathe; it came down part way and had a three-speed changeover. In the corner was a 4-foot sanding wheel. Les Norkett's office was behind the pannier, ex-GWR '96xx' Class 0-6-0PT No 9650. The stationary boiler was well down the west side of the round shed, past others including the shortest road. Note the asbestos smoke chutes, with a wooden one on the right; most were asbestos. The steam pipe is also seen coming down between the '72xx' and '22xx', fed by the stationary boiler for the washout equipment; there was one pipe between every road, and the cold water supply is seen coming up from the ground. Behind the '22xx' can be seen the belts going across to a countershaft and down to power the unique planing machine. *F. A. Blencowe, R. K. Blencowe collection*

on four of the six roads, but to undertake motion repairs on these engines on those roads was hopeless, as you couldn't move the engine due to the restricted length of track.

The turntable would turn 'Hall', '68xx', '28xx', 'County' ('10xx') and 'Austerity' 2-8-0 locos (a 'Star', 'Castle', 'King', BR 9F and a 'Britannia' couldn't be turned, but all the other GWR engines could, including the 'RODs', while LMS engines always used the triangle to turn, via the West Junction). It had only four roads opposite one another. The Through Road and those at right angles to it were very short. The latter two roads could store a pannier, but you couldn't move the engine to do valves and pistons. The

Ex-GWR '46xx' Class 0-6-0PT No 4639 and ex-GWR '52xx' Class No 5208 rest in the round shed on 30 December 1964. The Lift Road is in the foreground, then the Plough Road, Cabin Road, Through Road and Tap Road. The '52xx' is on the road adjacent to Tap Road in the north-west corner of the round house. G. *Vincent*

snowplough was fitted to a designated snowplough engine on these two short roads.

The turntable wasn't maintained by the shed staff, but was overhauled by a Swindon outstation repair gang, who mainly repaired turntables. It was repaired twice, once possibly in 1953 and again in the early 1960s. The repair gang slept on site in sleeping coaches, kept in one of the two sidings behind the coal stage, where the new breakdown vans were later stored. The first time it was repaired, it was jacked up and the ball in the middle changed. Repairs involved riveting, and the replacement of wood, bits of steel, and finally replacing the track to the steel. Repairs included anything that wanted doing. The second repair took approximately six weeks to complete; the gang worked for a fortnight at a time (working

Fitter John Garrett stands next to ex-GWR 2-8-0 No 2841 at Pontypool Road. He is now in his 80s.
J. S. Williams collection

through one weekend) then have a weekend off. It was one of the most heavily used turntables on the system!

Turning locos on the triangle

A 'Castle' couldn't be turned on the turntable, while LMS engines always used the triangle via the West box. They would be replaced by a '68xx' on the 1.42pm, and the LMS engine would run straight around the triangle, and go onto the front end of the coal stage to be a top priority for coaling when the 2.00pm shift started. This loco would then take the 3.15pm Penzance back to Manchester. It might be a 'Scot', 'Jubilee' or 'Patriot', but a lot of experimental Class 5s with Caprotti valve gear are also recalled. The engine would run south through the shed, on the Through Road, and go back to the station via East Junction.

However, the LMS engines wouldn't take coal at Ponty on the Manchester jobs after electrification, as they then only worked to Crewe. 9Fs were at Ponty when I was in the Army in Malaya, and they were turned on the triangle. Shrewsbury '28xxs' and 'Standard 5s' also used it to turn.

When Cardiff had 'Kings', one of them a train came into Ponty in the morning, and was turned on the triangle, returning to Cardiff with something else. Before then 'Kings' were banned from turning on the triangle. 'Kings' came up daily from Cardiff, but before that that 'Castles' were turned on the triangle.

At dinnertime there was a 'double home' job, Newton Abbot to Shrewsbury. About four engines did this job regularly. The same crew worked up one day, returning the next. One day a Newton Abbot engine would go up with it, the next day a Shrewsbury engine.

'Castle' Class No 5050 *Earl of St Germans*, a Newton Abbot engine, was a regular.

Aberdare passenger trains were turned in their entirety around the triangle, and backed into the bay.

Shed activities

Steam raising would take place anywhere. Smoke didn't worry the fire-raisers, and a cold engine didn't half smoke. The roundhouse had engines raising steam off the turntable roads. I would be working and you couldn't see your hand in front of your face. Most of the lighting up was done on nights, by three night-shift men. There was one man to light up engines on days, and one on afternoons. Most of the locos went off the shed at night.

Quite often engines would blow off inside the shed, bringing the dirt down from the roof down.

One day I and another fellow were on nights, and wandering around, and we got on a '72xx'. As you would do, we blew the gauge frame down but there was no water! So we put one injector on, then the second one. After a bit we realised that the water was over the top of the glass, not below the bottom nut as we had thought! Then we realised it was about time we ought to disappear, as it started to blow off then, and there was no room for any more water – it blew all the muck off the smoke chutes!

Boilers were washed out using hot water from an injector fitted to a water valve

The south end of the shed is seen on 13 September 1955, with steam raising in progress! A test ATC ramp is in the foreground; the railcar diesel tank is on the right, and the diesel fitter's equipment cabin behind it. The column on top of the tank is for filling via an adjacent tanker wagon, using 15 inches of vacuum supplied from a steam loco. *C. N. Fields, Manchester Locomotive Society*

Ex-GWR '38xx' Class 0-6-0PT No 3802 moves south from the turntable on 30 December 1964, with its safety valve blowing. It will exit the shed via the Through Road. *G. Vincent*

on the floor, with steam supplied from the stationary boiler via a steam line in the roof. Great Western stationary boilers were ex-'Dean Goods' loco boilers. In the late 1940s '517' Class 0-4-2T No 3575 was recorded as being used as the stationary boiler at Pontypool Road. The boiler was fed with water by injectors attached to water valves in the floor (between every road). It had a top feed, with a single hole in the boiler, and would blow off in the shed. The fire-lighters lit it up. Many different people would fire the stationary boiler; boiler washers did it to make sure there was enough steam for washing out, and cleaners who were budding firemen – even the foreman cleaner would fire it. It was fired by the men doing boiler washouts, and the fire-lighters lit it up. It was also used to make tea for the urn, and for washing (steam and cold water mixed). It went out after the boiler washers had finished using it, then was lit up for the night-shift boiler washouts. Four sets of men would do boiler washing, and there

were so many engines to wash out in a shift – a 'Castle' would take a shift to wash out. Two or three '57xx' and '77xx' pannier tanks at Pontypool had no top feeds.

The Webb 'Coal Tank' at Pontypool Road was used as a stationary boiler, and the card for this was signed by Albert Evans, a former Abergavenny boilersmith – the 'Dean Goods' boiler was under heavy repair and a loco would be used instead. No 4138 was used, as well as No 6432 and the Webb 'Coal Tank'. The loco would be used for washing out, and was put on the end of No 1 road usually; one of the steam valves was disconnected and it was piped up to

Ex-GWR '56xx' Class 0-6-2T No 6622 rests in the west side of the round shed on 30 December 1964; the stationary boiler is seen in the background. *G. Vincent*

the overhead pipework. The pipework connection to the stationary boiler would be blanked off and the overhead system would be pressurised.

Boilers were washed out seven days a week. Sometimes on a Sunday a cold washout would be undertaken. The Western had injectors that could be screwed to the water main in the floor, via a water valve on a post with the steam pipe hanging down.

Boiler washouts required a pit and were undertaken pretty well anywhere. Every road in the round shed had a steam connection and in the straight shed the only road that didn't was the Through Road. The men tended to do tank engines in the round shed as it was safer; not many engines were washed out in the straight shed.

Education

I started at Abersychan Technical School for north Monmouthshire in 1949, and attended on a Monday, working at Pontypool Road shed the rest of the week.

I lived in Abergavenny, and left for a bus at 8.10am, arriving at Clarence Corner, Pontypool, at 8.30am to change buses and get to Abersychan for 9.00am. If you did one day a week or two nights you got a deferment from the forces, and I did this all the time I worked for the railway. I was sent to Swindon Tech in the final year of my apprenticeship. At Swindon they didn't want me to travel back for one day a week at Abersychan.

D. A. T. Thomas was the metalwork master for machine shop work at Abersychan Tech. The railway didn't have apprentice training schools like the ROF or Girling – you went straight in on the job from day one. I was studying one day a week for five years, the duration of my apprenticeship, studying for City & Guilds, all theory. I attained a first class pass in the intermediate, and a second class in the final. I sat the final exam just weeks before I went into the RAF at the end of May.

To get deferment from the forces you had to show that you attended Tech, either in the day or evening. I had day release, but if you lived nearer the Tech you had to go two nights a week.

I saw '42xxs' on Newport jobs working the Top Line to Blaenavon while attending Abersychan Tech and escaping from the rugby. When part-time at Abersychan I caught a train from Blaenavon to Abergavenny; you caught the train at Abersychan, down to Panteg, then waited for the train from Newport to arrive. This train went to Abergavenny engine-first, returning empty stock as an auto-train. It was the same train I came home from Swindon on, from Newport to Abergavenny: 9.20pm from Newport, 11.20pm at Abergavenny.

The apprenticeship lasted five years, from the age of 16 to 21; however, most apprentices started over the age of 16 and never had the full five years. The first year was on the machines. Time-served fitters were fitters and turners, but they did very little machining after their apprenticeship. I was on the machines for the first year and slightly more; you then undertook fitting work, and did occasional machining, as required. You attended technical school for three years to obtain City & Guilds in machine shop practice, and the final year, the fifth year, was spent at Swindon. You then became a fitter. (Years ago, after finishing your apprenticeship, you spent 12 months working as an Improver, on reduced pay. You then became a fitter. However, the Improver grade had been stopped before I started at Ponty.) There was aggro between upgraded fitters and apprentice fitters; those who served an apprenticeship didn't necessarily appreciate the knowledge of upgraded fitters.

Work and wages

The Foreman's office was in the south corner of the round shed, adjacent to No 8 road in the long shed. This was where the chief clerk resided and where you drew the pay from. In the south-east corner of the round shed was a window with a slot in it through which you pushed your pay check and he pushed your money out. You booked in by using brass checks given out by a man in the foreman's office: 587 was my apprentice number, and 510 was the number given to me when I became a fitter. To clock out, you put the check in, and the clerk noted it in a book.

Money was brought down from a bank in Pontypool via a taxi to Pontypool Road station, then carried from the viaduct to the shed accompanied by a railway policeman. The chief clerk, Mr Belson, another clerk and a policeman from the police office at Ponty station would go to Pontypool to collect this money. They would then sit down for a few hours putting cash into envelopes for pay packets, which were paid out from 12 o'clock to 10.00pm on a Thursday, and from 6.00am on a Friday for the remainder.

Overtime was worked a lot initially, but when the shed started to close down it was only done when needed.

Fitters didn't work afternoons on the Western Region, as Swindon fitters didn't. Afternoon shifts started after 12.00 midday, typically 2.00-10.00pm. To overcome that problem, a 'monkey shift' was used, which started before midday. There was an agreement whereby you started at 11.00am and finished at 9.00pm, but it was normally 8.00am till 5.30pm; sometimes it varied and was 11:30am-9.00pm. The apprentices were on a five-day, 45-hour week: four 9-hour days and an 8-hour day on Friday. Most started at 7.00am but as I lived in Abergavenny and caught the train to work I started at 8.00am and worked till 5.30pm. On Fridays I started at 9.00am. Les Norkett would take a check and go home at 3.30pm with the rest of them.

Fitters worked 7.00am-3.30pm on the day shift, 11.00am-9.00pm on the 'monkey shift' (so-called as you weren't supposed to work afternoons), with two different weeks, and at night one shift started at 10.00pm on Sunday, and 9.30pm Monday-Friday, 10 till 7 on Sunday, 9.30-7.00 all the rest. On a Sunday at 10.00-12.00pm you were the only ones there, as the drivers didn't book on till

after midnight.

The other week of nights you started 8.30pm on Monday till 6.00am, including Sunday morning.

The night and 'monkey shifts' were reserved for running repairs for engines going off shed.

All jobs required two men, and you always had a mate. There were one-man jobs, but two people were used. Two men were required to remove side rods. Eddie Stephens was a fitter's mate and worked with me for years. Three-men jobs involved valves and pistons; an apprentice was the third person, and had to be trained.

The coppersmith produced the new white metal and give the job to the machinist. He also repaired any lamps or oil feeders in his spare time, and softened and put new ends on copper pipes and patches on steam pipes. He was the only person at Ponty allowed to burn off seized parts. If you wanted anything burned off, you had to get a note from Les Norkett – 'The gas costs money.' It didn't matter if it took you hours to undo something – to burn it off was the last resort.

I remember spring hanger brackets (shaped like a dog-leg). For a single spring, there were two – one was bolted to the frame, the other riveted to the frame. The end of the spring was supported by a spring hanger bolt passing into the spring hanger bracket, with two nuts at the end of the bolt. When changing a spring these nuts could seize to the bolt, making spring changing prolonged; these bolts were the worst for becoming seized, and you could mess about for 4 or 5 hours to release them. We used to stick oily waste on the bolts and light it – all sorts of methods were used to get them free.

If the spring hanger bolt was totally seized up, you got the spring off by removing the bolted-on bracket, allowing the bracket, bolt and spring to be released. The spring would then have the bracket and bolt at one end. The nut end of the spring hanger bolt was then put in the fire and, when hot, the nut and bolt could be undone, the bracket refitted to the frame and the spring changed.

Smaller nuts were cut off with a hammer

and chisel. The nuts weren't the quality they are today.

About halfway through my apprenticeship they started using penetrating oil, which was quite successful. It was put on the spring hangers and the intermediate middle coupling between the engine and tender – anything that had seized – before you started splitting it.

Certain repairs required the engine to be uncoupled from its tender – for instance to change intermediate buffer springs on the front of a tender, or to swop tender wheels, the tender needed to be lifted; swopped wheels might need to be sent to Swindon for turning. An engine would be uncoupled from its tender otherwise you couldn't get at whatever part of the tender needed to be repaired. There were three couplings, all of the same design, one big one in the centre, and two smaller ones, one each side. The centre coupling was done up tight, to give a gap of 8½ inches between the engine and tender; the smaller outer couplings were not done up tight, but were there in case the bigger coupling failed.

The coupling comprised of a jaw with a spindle and thread. Between the jaw and nut was a series of rubber washers enclosed in a cup, then a thick piece of plate. Penetrating oil was put on a rag and left on the middle coupling thread overnight. This coupling had a jaw at one end, and a 4-inch-diameter, 11 threads-per-inch thread for the nut. The big nut on the tender coupling would work loose; when uncoupled from the engine we'd have to release it to tighten it back up to stop any end play. If we couldn't release it, we would split the nut on the thread using a long bar and a sledge.

Typical daily machining repairs in June 1953

Monday 1st: engine No 6424 (task not recorded)
Tuesday 2nd: Abersychan Technical School
Wednesday 3rd: engines Nos 6424, 4597 (tasks not recorded)

Thursday 4th: engines Nos 6472, 6400 (tasks not recorded)
Friday 5th: engines Nos 3040, 3730, 6675 (tasks not recorded)
Monday 8th: Abersychan Technical School
Tuesday 9th: engine No 6432 (right-hand big end), No 6871 (two eccentrics, R1, L2, straps)
Wednesday 10th: engine No 6432 (right-hand crosshead)
Thursday 11th: engine No 6432 (left-hand crosshead), No 3692 (left-hand big end)
Friday 12th: engine No 6432 (left-hand big end and two right-hand eccentrics (straps))
Tuesday 16th: engine No 3717 (right-hand leading, driving, trailing side rod bushes)
Wednesday 17th: engine No 2884 (right-hand crosshead), No 6432 (left-hand leading side rod bush), Nos 6653/6429 (valves and pistons)
Thursday 18th: engines Nos 6653, 6429 (valves and pistons)
Friday 19th: engine No 6653 (task not recorded), No 6403 (big end bolts), No 5756 (big end set bolts).
Tuesday 23rd June 1953; engine No 6653 (left-hand big end and two left-hand eccentrics (straps))
Wednesday 24th: engine No 3862 (right-hand crosshead); to Aberbeeg (side rod bushes)*
Thursday 25th: engine No 6653 (right-hand big end), No 3040 (left-hand crosshead)
Friday 26th: engine No 3040 (left-hand side rod bushes)

* An Aberbeeg repair undertaken at Ponty rather than Newport, as Ponty would turn the job around more quickly. Les Norkett was ex-Aberbeeg, and would help out Aberbeeg with repair requests. Eccentrics on the axle are in pairs, one pair on the right, one pair on the left, referred to as R1 and L2.

This record was kept when I was machining; I had only previously undertaken machining at the Tech. The lathe had a faceplate chuck, and jobs weighed a hundredweight or so. The jobs were all white metal, and it cut easy when being machined. Bushes would wear due to lack of lubrication. Sometimes you had to do all the bushes, other times you would do just one side. Bushes were repaired under the 24,000 mileage exam. Bushes were re-metalled, re-machined and refitted to the side rods. I worked for 18 months on the machines, I then worked with fitters on valves and pistons.

1950s loco memories

After the war, in the early 1950s, the railways were carrying too much freight, and the Up Goods Relief line between Pontypool Road South and North signal boxes was full of freight trains; it would take one freight train two shifts to get from Pontypool Road to Hereford. It was common for a crew to book on and spend an entire 8-hour shift waiting to move north, stationary between the South and North boxes at Ponty, only to be relieved by another crew at the end of the shift without going anywhere. At this time 'ROD' 2-8-0s were used on such freights.

I started on the breakdown gang when I was 24 or 25. Les Norkett didn't consider me to be available, but if I had a phone call I was there before half of them.

The auto-train was kept in the station sidings opposite the platform at Pontypool Road station; these sidings were between the goods loops, the Up Main and the Down Relief. DMU sets were also kept here in the late 1950s. The auto-train was used for the Blaenavon to Newport, Pontypool Road to Monmouth, and Pontypool Road to Nelson turns. On a Saturday it worked to Newport, the Eastern Valley, then to Abergavenny at 1.00pm.

Ponty also had ex-GWR railcar No W14, then No W30. Steam railmotors were stored in the wagon repair shed in earlier days. Railcars Nos W23, W30 and W11 worked Pontypool to Bristol, Pontypool to Swansea, and Pontypool to Shrewsbury all day long. Nos W30 and W23 ran with auto-coaches,

but No W11 couldn't. No W30 was kept in the loco shed at the viaduct end, by way of a siding from the loco side, as was the steam motor.

A diesel fuel tank was located on a stand by the Carriage & Wagon shed for fuelling the railcars; it was round, small in diameter and 10 to 15 feet long, supported on two stanchions – the standard type issued by the Great Western. The tank was covered in, and had a lid in the top. A rail tanker was brought underneath it, then the diesel tank lid was opened, revealing a miniature water column-type fitting. This was swung around and placed into the rail tank wagon below. Further up the track there was a 2-inch pipe connection in the middle of the rail with a blank end; the blank was removed, a piece of 2-inch-diameter pipe was screwed into the connection, with a flexible bag on the end, and connected to the vacuum system of a steam loco placed at the door of the shed, and the vacuum connected to a hole in the floor. This sucked 15 inches of vacuum to create vacuum in the tank on the stand, thereby sucking the diesel out of the rail tank wagon and into the elevated tank. (This tank was replaced by a different one when the canteen was turned into a mess room and wash rooms for footplate staff in the early 1960s.) An electric pump was installed to supply fuel oil for the new rest rooms.

If more than 15 inches of vacuum was pulled on the steam engine, diesel would be pulled through to the steam loco. I did this once – you could smell the diesel, so I eased the vacuum back a bit!

Railcars Nos W30, W11 and W3 were stored in the wagon repair shed during the 1955 strike. They used more diesels in the strike than they had for years. No W14 was used on the Newport-Brynmawr service. It couldn't have been put on a worse route – the low-numbered railcars had Ferodo brakes, and the brake shoes were being changed at an alarming rate! The railcars left after the Monmouth branch closed, at the start of the summer service.

The 1955 ASLEF strike

The Abergavenny fitters were Sid Burr, a fitter's mate, and Eddie Stevens, fitter's mate to Buster Williams (who broke everything). I picked them up in a Bradford van – they travelled by train normally – and took them back in the afternoon. There was a 'Super D' in the shed at Ponty with a broken tender spring. On one of the days I went to Abergavenny shed first to pick up a tender spring and take it to Ponty to put it on.

The big thing about the strike was having the three railcars with us. No W30 had always been here, and W23 had been here for a few months on the Monmouth branch, trying to make it look good when it was totally uneconomic. No W11 was sent here. Nos W23 and W30 were coupled to auto-coaches, and No 11 worked on its own. They worked to Swansea, Bristol and Shrewsbury, all day long, in different patterns, covering more miles during the strike than ever before. Normally railcars weren't allowed through the Severn Tunnel, but they were during the strike.

Railcars weren't used on the Vale of Neath – Ponty used '68xxs', '41xxs' or panniers on that route. In the 1930s railcars had been used to Blaenavon and on to Brynmawr, and No W14 was used on these turns. The only other train running during the strike was a '52xx' working from Hafodrynys to Uskmouth Power Station, with a driver called Alf Batley. He did this on the first day of the strike, and as there was so little traffic about he was doing the journey so quickly that two trips a day were being made by the end of the two-week strike – he didn't go into any loops and went straight through. Only this '52xx' and the diesel railcars were running. All the diesel drivers during the strike were NUR. Alf Batley was an ASLEF man, but chose to work through the strike.

The shed was full of engines – you couldn't move there. There was no overtime and the fitters were not too pleased. I worked refuelling the diesels, and refilling the diesel tank, which passed my time during the strike. It was then that the first engines started to go into store.

Swindon Works, 1957

All railway apprentices did 12 months at Swindon, virtually the last 12 months. I stayed in Ashford Road, lodging with a fellow who became the Mayor of Swindon and handed over *King George V* to Bulmers. He was Alf Bown, who used to work on the bogie gang and had one eye. You went to work with him in the morning, and in the afternoon he would be in a council meeting!

Swindon loco shed would fill in a big form pointing out any engine faults. This was based on mileage. Most engines were repaired after 100,000 miles; 'Kings' were every 40,000 miles, but 'Castles' would do 100,000, as would '28xxs' and tank engines. Someone decided whether the engine went to Caerphilly, Wolverhampton, Newton Abbot or Swindon. There were few '66xxs' or '42xxs' in Swindon. The '1363' Class were repaired at Newton Abbot, and the boiler sent in a wagon to Swindon. Engines from South Wales for repair at Swindon Works never went through the Severn Tunnel in case they broke down, instead travelling via Gloucester.

The repairs varied depending on the class and type of repair. 'Castles' and 'Halls' were repaired in about six weeks.

There was no separate Paint Shop, and engines were painted as they went through the works. If you left your tools on the engine where they were painting, the tools would be painted over, or your hand if it was on the frame! Paint was tested outside on the Gloucester Road for carriages; painted blocks of wood were attached at an angle to a low-level fence, facing south to catch the maximum amount of sun.

The front sections of locomotive frames were often cut off and replaced. The rear section of the frame was never touched, and the cabs were left in place during repairs.

Name and number plates were stored in an office in A Shop, situated above ground level. Older plates were stored there also. Also in A Shop was the replica broad gauge loco *North Star* together with a set of 'Castle' valve gear on display.

When stripping an engine the same motion went back on it as originally fitted. An inspector went through the parts and painted them blue, green or red. Red was scrap, green was for repair, blue was for minor repair. When an engine was scrapped, all the bits and pieces were taken off and marked. Two asterisks meant that the part was to be scrapped. My mate used to put all the scrap boiler cleating back on. A massive pile of parts was located outside in the yard where a couple of men were cleaning them and painting them with bitumastic. My mate went through the bits, and if he found a scrap part he would be over the moon and put it to one side, as it might come in useful for the engine he was working on. The men cleaning the parts were into greyhound racing, as there was a big greyhound track in Swindon. They would tell you tales of the dogs while you were looking for parts in the parts pile.

Brass fittings, which were maybe changed, went to the Brass Shop, while wheels went to the AW at the bottom of A Shop, where they were re-tyred, skimmed, crank-pins changed and the wheels balanced. Crank-pins could be refaced if not below a certain size. Big end pins on crank shafts were re-machined, and wheels dynamically balanced. They had calculations for the amount of lead. When completed, the engine went to the weighbridge for weighing. Adjustments for springs were written down.

The overhead crane in the Works would lift 100 tons. On the big engine side you could lift any engine over the top of any other – you could lift a 'King' over the top of a 'King'. The two bays on the big engine side had two Ransome & Rapier cranes in each bay. Engines would be lifted under the buffer beam. A 'King' was like an LMS engine – the shackles were put in the front, while most Western engines had two hooks placed under the buffer beam. There were holes for

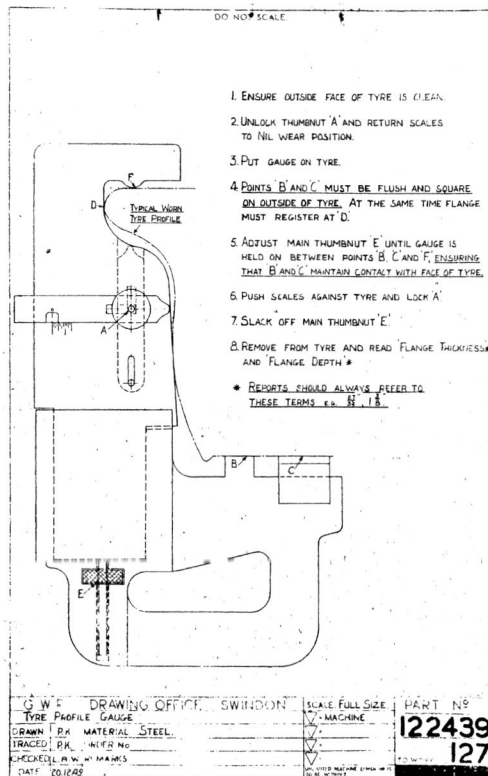

A tyre profile gauge. *Harry Rawlins*

the hook to go into.

When lifting boilers, the hooks went in the firehole door at the back end, and two cladding plates were left on the back of the boiler for the hooks to rest against. Wire ropes were put around the smokebox. A man on the ground told the crane driver what to do.

For valve setting a rolling road was available, but was all very secret. Only big engines were put on it; small engines had the side rods left off and a roller was used to rotate the axle on the small engine side. Only certain people did valve setting.

Big engines started on the end of the bay fully assembled, then got stripped and cleaned and went on to the frame gang. There was a machine for horn grinding, then Comley's gang would start refitting, i.e. slide bars, re-wheeling, boiler in, and boiler cleating on. They were then sent to Lewington's gang for connecting rods,

DO NOT SCALE

8 DIA: PIN, RIVETED OVER.

To fit 1" SPANNER

▽ ALL OVER.

DIAGRAM SHOWING JACK IN POSITION

G. W. R. DRAWING OFFICE, SWINDON.	SCALE: FULL SIZE	PART No
SCREW JACK FOR LOCKING REGULATOR HANDLE	▽ - MACHINE	122439
DRAWN. F.A.Y.	MATERIAL. STEEL.		148
TRACED. F.A.Y.	ORDER No. ~	▽ .
CHECKED. L.A.W	REMARKS. Superseding D&CNo 106368	▽.
DATE. 30.4.48		TO W.O.

Drawings for a screw jacking for locking a regulator handle during in-steam maintenance. *Harry Rawlins*

82

83

Piston crosshead shifters for a '56xx' Class (above) and 'Wolverhampton' Class.

eccentrics, motion, pistons and bogie to be added. Finally, they were sent for valve setting, then weighed, being painted on the way through.

P1 was the boiler fitting shop. I was there for four months, facing up gauge frame faces, ejector box faces and blowdown cock faces. You drilled and tapped the holes for brackets to hold the back end of the boilers – 31 studs, 7/8 fine thread 10 thou oversize, took some pulling in! 'Kings' were 12 thou oversize – everything on a 'King' was bigger and more awkward!

Men behind me in P1 worked on superheater flue tubes, cutting off the old ends and butt-welding new ends and odd pieces back on. The middles were still good and were reused.

In the P1 Shop the regulator rod had to be set, or a new end fitted to it. In the latter case the regulator rod was placed on a two-wheel trolley, and you went from the shop down a slope under Rodburn Road (alongside which the Works shunter would push locos) and up the slope on the other side to V Shop (the Boiler Shop, where you couldn't hear yourself think). You can still see the brickwork of the tunnels between P1 and the Boiler Shop through which the regulator rods were pushed. After V Shop was WS, where they burned the frames out and machined the liners for cylinders. Beyond the door there you would be looking at seven chimney stacks, made from the boiler barrels of 'Dean Goods' locos. Turn right, go round the back of there and into the blacksmiths. You then sat down while the blacksmiths fitted a new end and set the regulator rod. Then you took it all the way back and put it back in the boiler.

The inspector would then come along and open the regulator to the first valve; he would put his hand in the valve to feel if it was set correctly – don't let the handle go! It was then put into second valve to check that it was working properly. During the steam test, the valves were checked again, opened fully at one point with full boiler pressure. A second steam test was done with the superheaters in.

Boilers were repaired in V Shop and passed down underneath the Rodburn Road to P1 Shop, where all the fitting and testing was done. The boilers would go down in a lift, under the road on rails and up the other side on a lift. That's where the spare 'County' boiler was, on a frame in the shop; it would be swopped for the next one. Next door was where oxygen was bottled. This came in on a lorry, and was compressed; Swindon made its own bottles. It also made its own acetylene, which was piped around the works.

While I was there the boiler off 'Britannia' *Polar Star* was in the shop for repair after the engine had run down the bank at Milton, near Didcot. It was there most of the time I was in P1 Shop, then all of a sudden it had a steam test and the engine was back together in a couple of weeks. I never saw the frames, as they were in A Shop. (A 'Britannia' without a tender could be pushed by hand by three men.)

P1 Shop was in two parts, one bay for the work, the other for fitting the superheaters. I had the pleasure of fitting the superheaters into the first 9F 2-10-0 to be built in Swindon. They were fitted on a Friday morning, all 35. The superheater was a Millesco type, where the header was bolted to the front tubeplate of the boiler, and the regulator valve was in a housing in the header. Every row of superheater flues was further below the header. Each superheater element had a vertical section coming out of the header, before going through a 90-degree bend to go into the superheater flue; lower rows of superheater elements became heavier as the vertical section was getting longer, the further each flue was below the header.

I went into Swindon running shed once when I was working in P1. One of the fitters in P1 wanted to put a bet on with somebody in the running shed and took me with him to see it.

For the final eight months at Swindon I worked in A Shop. Two days were spent with the stripping gang on pannier tank No 7740, a Pontypool Road engine. It was totally stripped, and they took the back covers off the cylinders; this was the first time I realised the back covers were not full size on a pannier. No 7740 was stripped in two days using six men. Everything came off it – cab roof, chimney, tanks, and boiler cleating. The motion was stripped at the same time. Two fitters were directing the strip-down. The parts were put in caustic soda to clean them, while the frames were cleaned by hand by a gang of men.

Smaller engines were sent to the small engine frame gang. An inspector checked the frames for jobs to be undertaken. Horns were ground by hand, the horn ties refitted and the horns realigned. Frame welding was also undertaken. The frame gang was the longest part of the rebuild.

The Tender Shop used to be the small engine place. I went in there once; it was located where Swindon Museum is now. The cranes on the small engine side were hydraulically operated.

I next worked on the big engine frame gang for two days, then the rest of my time at Swindon was spent on the re-wheeling gang. This was led by Mr Comley, the chargehand. Engines were re-wheeled, the boiler fitted, side rods refitted, boiler cleating applied, and the slide bars set.

I never went to the scrap shed; I remember that 'Star' Class loco *Glastonbury Abbey* was being scrapped when I was at Swindon. One man I worked with on Comley's gang went everywhere except there. He was a socialite, and on a Friday afternoon would go everywhere to see people, including O Shop where the toolmakers were located. Swindon bought in jointing from James Walker, but made its own taps in O Shop, as well as its own gauges.

At that time 30 or 40 'Castles' were out of service waiting for a certain casting to be machined, for the valve quadrants. These brackets on a 'Castle' and a 'King' would crack, and Swindon bought a new milling machine so all the milling for the brackets could be done on one machine. There was a labour dispute with the men about how much money they were to be paid to use this machine. The 'Castles' were stripped with parts all over the place waiting for this new machined casting; *Abergavenny Castle* was attended to on the small engine gang because the big engine gang were so busy.

I saw the famous test bed at Swindon, but was not encouraged to go and have a look. I saw a 'King' and a couple of 'Castles' on it. All the diesel shunters (later Class 08) that were rebuilt and tested were tried out on this test bed; you had figures to work against. I also went into the Foundry for a look, but not to work.

I re-wheeled and re-sprung a '47xx' loco undergoing an intermediate exam – they hadn't taken the boiler out – as well as refitting the piston in the vacuum cylinder. I worked on every eight-wheeled class of Great Western engine, including the 'RODs'.

Locomotive frames were prone to cracking, and the front of the frame would be cut off. The frames of '45xx's cracked, and I also remember 'Castle' frame renewals. When changing cylinders, the frame would be changed as well. The frame was cut at the rear of the outside motion bracket using a burning torch, then ground straight. A complete new frame section with cylinders and motion bracket, saddle and the inside bracket for most of the inside motion was then fitted. A 3/8-inch weld gap was allowed for, and it was welded on each side of the V-shaped weld prep. When finished, the frame was then the right length. The four cylinders, the saddle and the big valve casting (already assembled), with the outside motion brackets, were already attached to the new frame. You could never see the join. The same repair was done with the 'Kings', when the engines were re-boilered. I did a '42xx' on the small engine frame gang, and new cylinders were fitted; the frame was cut off and a new section welded back in.

One day I was putting new cylinders on a '42xx' tank engine with the small engine frame gang, and the main finishing gang were getting ready to put the pony truck into another '42xx' tank engine, which was suspended about 4 feet off the track. Suddenly there was a big bang and the main frames bent underneath the back steps.

The engine was lowered rather quickly, but the trailing wheels were 2 inches above the rails. The engine was sent to the small engine frame gang, who took off the cab roof and bunker and removed the trailing and intermediate wheels. They burned out two sections of frame under the steps, then warmed and straightened the frames and welded two new pieces of steel about a foot deep and 3 feet long into the frames. The engine was then reassembled and away it went. These were the only two '42xxs' I saw in Swindon, as they usually went to Caerphilly for repairs.

Engines for test were put on the Works turntable. A repaired tender engine would run slowly in reverse to Chippenham, then return to Swindon at a certain speed and be taken back to the turntable to be examined. If needed, repairs were undertaken on the turntable roads.

I remember *City of Truro* coming into Swindon for overhaul as No 3717, from York Museum. Repairs were undertaken by the wrongly named light repair gang, who did some of the biggest jobs done in Swindon. The light repair gang repaired 'Britannias' and '90xx' 4-4-0s, changed outside cylinders on 'Castles' without taking the boiler out, and undertook any awkward, out of the ordinary job. If they knew an engine was coming in, there were rows and rows of castings stored for possible use.

Engines from other regions sometimes arrived. Ivatt '2s' from the Southern Region were once repaired, and I worked on the frame of one of them.

My last jobs were working on the slide bars of 'Castles' and 'Granges' for a couple of months.

The whole Works was paid out in 10 minutes. The process started 10 minutes before the Works shut down; little benches were set up and you had a coloured pay cheque. You all got in line and zoomed through. Cash was fetched using a truck built from ¾-inch thick plate, towed by a little tractor that could only go at 5mph. It was taken into Swindon town and reversed against the back doors of the bank, then returned into the pay office in the Works. This office is still there, up through the tunnel; up the steps by the drawing office is a big arch where the truck used to reverse, and in front of which was the yard where they did the crane testing and repairs.

The main offices in Swindon were the first place that I saw double-glazing; you go by them to go into the Swindon Museum. It has two lots of sash windows about a foot apart. Mr Prodler, the chief clerk of Swindon, used to work in this office.

I was entitled to privilege tickets but you couldn't buy them on Swindon station. There was a ticket office in the tunnel under the railway to the Works, on the right-hand side when entering from the main road. It was open at certain times; I would come out at 3.20pm on some Fridays and hand in a piece of paper to get a ticket back home. I then had 10 minutes to get to the station for 3.30pm – the next train stopping in South Wales was at 7.29pm. If I had to get that I would be in Newport at 8.40pm if I was lucky, getting off the 'Red Dragon', which was rarely on time. I could then catch the 9.20pm auto to Blaenavon, from Newport, which travelled to Caerleon, Ponthir, Cwmbran, Lower Pontnewydd, Upper Pontnewydd, Sebastopol, then Panteg. I then had to get to Abergavenny by a down Blaenavon auto, which would arrive at Panteg, reverse, go through the yard and pass the east side of the shed and the East box, to be in Abergavenny by 11.20pm at night. It took 2 hours to get from Newport to Abergavenny at night. The loco would be a '64xx', which would go back to Ponty from Abergavenny light engine.

I was sent back to Ponty in April 1957, and made a fitter in May.

Pontypool Road loco repair memories

As an apprentice, I worked on No 1422 undertaking a valve and piston exam, working with Glyn Morris (who was nicknamed 'Scratchy' – when serving in the RAF he had contracted dermatitis

from contact with high octane fuel). I also remember in the early 1950s, before I went to Swindon, a Cambrian 0-6-0 tender loco that had been to Caerphilly Works for repair, had failed with 12 hot axle boxes (all wheels). It arrived at Ponty shed and myself and Rollei Jones worked on it. Rollei eased the tender axle boxes, and oiled everything up, and it was sent to Hereford very slowly! Rollei was not there when I came back from Swindon as he had by then retired.

'Star' Class locos were still coming onto the shed when I started at Ponty. I remember one coming in for repair with leaking steam pipes in the smokebox. There were three different types of outside steam pipe on these engines. It was repaired inside the long shed by a fitter called Mr Mahoney, who later went to work for South Wales Switchgear as an apprentice instructor.

The 'Saints' had nearly all gone when I started at Ponty, and I never saw one on shed. I recall No 2920 *Saint David* working the Hereford to Newport train that left Abergavenny at 7.10am. It ended its days as the station pilot at Hereford.

One day I promised to take a girl friend to meet a train in Newport on a Saturday morning, and changed shifts to do so, from a 7 o'clock start to 6 o'clock. However, I found out that she was going to London for a reason I didn't approve of, and told her I wasn't going to take her to Newport. But I had still changed shifts, so had to start at 6 o'clock.

The first hour was spent doing running repairs, which went all right. Les Norkett arrived and asked me to take the left-hand valve out of '28xx' No 2896. The covers were taken off, but the next bit was tricky. The valve pin needed to be removed, and this required putting your fingers at the back of the pin, and hit the outer part of the rod with a hammer. You could then release the pin with your fingers.

I hit the rod so hard that the pin jumped straight out, taking a layer of skin off my nose. Then my finger followed it through the hole, and the rod dropped down and took a sliver of skin off my finger. The extracted pin hit the engine next door, and bounced back onto the lace-holes of my boot. When I took with boot off, the eyelets were imprinted on my foot. My mate then said it was time for tea!

At one time a bridge was being repaired at Shrewsbury, and engines were changed at Ponty instead of there. As a result 'Castle' Class No 5076 *Gladiator* was at Ponty for three months. It was in reasonably good nick, and I did the piston glands and the odd steam valve on it. It was washed out on a Monday morning, as they wouldn't pay anyone on a Sunday to do it, and they would rush like hell to get it ready to be out for its allotted turn. Examining fitters booked jobs on the engine; it wasn't clean, and wasn't the best of the 'Castles'. It worked a 4.00pm-5.00pm to Bristol only, returning with the 7.15pm from Bristol. It would leave for the station via the East Junction. The Ponty 7.00pm turn to Bristol came back with a freight train. A Shrewsbury 'Castle' might come on shed if it broke down, but that was not often. [Author's note: the bridge repair in question took place in March 1962, on Castle Foregate bridge, Shrewsbury.]

I never saw *Abergavenny Castle* coming through Ponty, but *Lockheed Hudson* would come through. We used to get 'Castles' from Bristol, Cardiff and Shrewsbury, as well as from Newton Abbot. *Earl of St Germans* was used a lot of the time. They were mainly Cardiff and Shrewsbury engines – you wouldn't get 'Castles' from Swansea.

One day a 'Castle' spectacle window glass needed to be changed in the station, when someone threw a bottle of beer from a passing train, smashing the driver's window. Three or four different glasses were taken to the station to fit to the engine. Windscreen wipers were also present on these window

'Class' Castle 4-6-0 No 7000 *Viscount Portal* passes the East signal box with a Manchester-Plymouth passenger working on an unknown date. This engine was based at Newton Abbot, and was a regular on this turn from 1946 until the early 1950s.

glasses.

Likewise, 'Kings' visited the shed only when they failed. No 6003 is remembered as having a split blower pipe in the smokebox, and was repaired in the shed. No 6018 had a valve disconnected and was stored on the Tap Road for a few weeks while the valve was repaired at Swindon. These were both Cardiff Canton engines, and had both failed on southbound workings.

Of the pannier tanks, No 3628 was a long-time Ponty engine. Another was No 7724, and one Saturday afternoon I was working on a piston gland in a place I shouldn't be. I was just finishing underneath when I heard the safety chain drop off the handbrake. I dropped into the pit, and away went the loco, with the flare lamp left in the motion. My mate was next to the footplate

Ex-GWR '87xx' Class 0-6-0PT No 8716 raises steam on the Tap Road on 25 May 1960. This was the 1955 Branches Fork runaway engine. *R. K. Blencowe collection*

and didn't see anyone get on, as he was reading about the horses in the newspaper! That was my closest ever shave with death.

I recall drilling out a broken stud in the steam chest cover of No 4600, and the drilling gear came apart. Glenn Ford went with me to Panteg Hospital to have two stitches in my head.

No 8716 was in on a Sunday night for brake adjustment. A piece of steel was inserted to push down the steam brake cylinder and allow brake adjustments to be made. As my mate was doing this, I heard the vacuum pump tick, and I was underneath. I jumped out of the pit, and the loco was rolling towards the turntable hole. I had a hammer in my hand with which to knock out the brake rod pins, and I threw it under the front wheel. The engine then started to move back towards the shed wall, so I shouted to my mate to put the steam brake on. I found out that the drain cocks were shut, and my mate should have chocked the engine while brake adjustments were being made, and checked that the drain cocks were open.

On another occasion I was putting the snowplough on No 3779. I took over from Marcus Hunter, who wanted to go home. He had got the buffers off and was going to move the engine up to the snowplough. I got on the footplate, and wound the hand brake off. Suddenly away it went – the regulator was blowing through and Marcus had shut the cocks to stop the steam blowing on him. I rammed the steam brake on quick – I didn't want to derail the snowplough!

The snowplough had been fitted to 'Dean Goods' No 2385, then No 7426 and finally No 3779. I'd fitted it on a few times, but it never got used in anger. It

was kept on the shortest turntable road on the west side of the round shed. To fit the plough, the front buffers and the coupling of the loco removed, and the plough was packed up so that it hopefully aligned with the buffer beam – you'd jack and bar it if it was down an inch or two. In the middle of the plough was a long bolt, which was inserted into the coupling hole; you then put a nut on this bolt to pull it onto the buffer beam. There were four bolts in each buffer to attach the plough; 7/8-inch-diameter bolts were used, but sometimes you had to put a few three-quarter-inch bolts in as the holes didn't line up properly. A fitter travelled with the snowplough to tighten up these bolts, which would loosen when the plough was being propelled into snowdrifts. When used with No 2385 the plough was stored inside the round shed, on the plough road adjacent to the lift road, but that loco had been scrapped before I started at Ponty.

The kidney-shaped cover on the smokebox of a tender engine was where copper pipes from the footplate exited from underneath the boiler cladding into the smokebox to supply oil to the regulator, and to each steam pipe after the superheaters. Sometimes it was necessary to fit a replacement external pipe along the outside

The snowplough is seen in action in 1947 at an unknown location using No 7426, with a Pontypool Road footplate crew. Driver Harry Robins is seen second from the right, in the back row. *J. S. Williams collection*

A triple-header for the snowplough in 1947 – No 7426 is the leading engine. *J. S. Williams collection*

of the boiler, which was a particular occurrence on pannier tank engines. This repair was undertaken by the coppersmith.

Only pannier tank axle boxes were repaired, while crossheads, side rod bushes, small ends and eccentrics were other routine repairs. The shed lift could only pick up 20 tons; a '57xx' pannier when picked up at one end weighed 18 tons, and a '94xx' pannier 19 tons. Tenders could be picked up so that the middle pair of wheels could be swapped to the back if the back flanges were getting sharp, or sent to Swindon to be machined. Near the end of steam Swindon transferred work elsewhere, and 'Castles' were going to Caerphilly at the end. Wolverhampton was also used for steam repairs prior to closure of Ponty; No 2859 went there as the last loco to be repaired there. It came back, but drivers were booking the valve timing as being out. In 1957 Harold Good drove class-mate No 2857 into a tree from a landslide at Nantyderry; I went to the road bridge at Llanfair Grange to have a look down on it. The pony wheels were derailed.

At the same place a 'Castle' working a continuation of an LMS train had a branch pipe break off the vacuum pump going down the bank, bringing the engine to a stand. The driver put a cork in the end of the pipe and carried on.

Fireman Dennis Mathews (left) and Driver Harold Williams are seen on No 3779, which was used on snowplough duties after No 7426 was transferred away from Pontypool Road. *Phil Williams collection*

I can recall two cranes going to Branches Fork to re-rail No 8716 on Tuesday 8 March 1955, when I was an apprentice. The first day they went up with the Newport crane and failed, so booked two cranes the following day, but one was from Cardiff.

When I was in the RAF a pannier sheared a wheel off. Terry Biggs knows the story. Gerry Smith came up from Newport to check that the driving wheels hadn't moved on it.

After I came out of the RAF, the only time I was sent out to examine an engine was to Hafodrynys Colliery (the deep mine, not the New Mine), to examine an NCB engine to give it a certificate to travel over BR. That was in the 1960s. It was a '20xx', No 2034. It had good tyres, but the buffer springs were broken. I mentioned this to Les Norkett, and he said, 'That's all right.' It was inspected to allow it to travel to the NCB workshop in Blacnavon for repairs, where it arrived sometime between August 1962 and April 1963.

[Author's note: From the diaries of Austin Jones, the Blaenserchan Colliery Engineer, and railway enthusiast, which are in my late father's possession, the following information on No 2021, a Pontypool Road '20xx', is available. GWR No 2021 ended its life while on hire to Blaenserchan Colliery, on the middle run at the back of the washery, on Thursday 30 May 1951, while going to Target End: '2021 on hire. Breaks small end bolts, piston gland, cylinder cover and piston, and cracks cylinder flange at stud – all in left-hand cylinder. Occurred at 9.15am going to Target End. Driver is L. Jones.' Rollei Price had undertaken repairs on it at Pontypool Road the previous weekend. Rollei had started his carrier at Tirpentwys Colliery.]

One '54xx' came on loan from Taunton, and was on shed for a month.

Of the shed's '41xxs' and '51xxs', Nos 4135, 4138 and 4121 were the station pilots, available to pilot a train. The low-number '51' arrived, No 5103. Levelling pipes never cracked on these like on the '42xxs' and '72xxs'.

Ponty had two '42xxs', Nos 4229 and 4230, as well as an occasional '52xx', which were used on the Hafodrynys to Uskmouth turn. There was one '42xx' at Ponty when the shed was down to nine engines at the end of the summer service in 1964.

Ponty had a '22xx' for six months. I worked on one sent down from Hereford, as they had too much work. It was sent down for valves and pistons in late 1963 or early 1964. They were easier to work on than a pannier. I remember that one had a 2,500-gallon tender, with a steam brake.

In the 1950s there were probably only four '43xxs', and Ponty had one of them, No 4303, which was scrapped before I started. It used to break springs all the time. No 4358 of Gloucester survived nearly to the end of steam. We had No 5318 for a long time, and No 5322. No 5318 had a crack in the main frame, which never got any longer; it was later shedded at Tyseley and finally Swindon, being withdrawn from there in September 1961. No 6300 was also based at Ponty and scrapped at Swindon, but I can't remember it.

I recall watching a '53xx' working a northbound banana train, which had stopped at signals by the East box in the cutting. It was a train of ordinary vans with steam heat. When the signal changed, it struggled to get going; it slipped a lot and took a long time to go a couple of yards. It would be routed onto the relief line (up main) through Pontypool Road station – the up main was used fairly often for vacuum-fitted trains at night and the banana train.

I changed a few sets of piston valves on '43xx' No 5322. Superheaters and steam pipes were also changed, as it wouldn't steam. It wouldn't get past Hereford on a train for Shrewsbury, and would be taken off the train and sent back to Pontypool Road. It had the boiler changed, and was out on No 7 siding when it was lit up without any water in the boiler. It had another boiler and still wouldn't steam. The engine record states that the boiler swop took place at Wolverhampton Stafford Road Works, the replacement boiler being from No 7218, and

No 5322 was released back into traffic on 26 May 1961. No 5322 – no more needs to be said about it!

Nos 6370 and 7325 are also recalled. The latter was the updated version with screw reverse and ATC on the bogie. Taking the ATC off the main frame was a big improvement, as the equipment on the frame would be knocked off as the main springs settled. I did the piston valves on this loco at least once, and an ATC wearing piece on the pony truck (there's more about ATC equipment later).

Hot axle boxes are recalled; if panniers were derailed the bolts holding the oil pad would shear off. I recall this happening to No 6848, and 'Castles' suffered a bit. 'Super Ds' suffered hot boxes at Abergavenny.

On the '56xxs' the lance cock was on the left-hand side when built, but was then moved to the right-hand side. On a '66xx' valve/piston ring changing, big ends, brake blocks and springs were typical tasks. Mr Collett is said to have locked his staff in the drawing office to come up with a solution, as valve spindles were bending when the first loco was tested at Swindon. They were big heavy engines to work on, and had massive crossheads. The smokebox overhang was deadly when opening the smokebox door.

The '56xxs' had springs with curled-up ends, but the '66xxs' had continental spring hangers, which were easier to change. '64xxs', some '72xxs', high-numbered '52xxs', '14xxs' and '54xxs' also had continental hangers.

On one occasion '57xx' No 4616 came back from the Southern Region with Southern lamp brackets and no brake whistle. This was put back on as soon as it arrived at Ponty, using one from a scrapped engine.

Levelling pipes leaked worse on the '72xxs'. Compared to a '28xx', the trailing wheel was right behind the steps and the coupling rods came off a bit quicker. Just after I started on the railway the '72xxs' had 4-inch rubber bags fitted to cure the problem of levelling pipes cracking, but that doubled the filling time. The levelling pipes on the '72xxs' were always being worked on when I was an apprentice; leaks occurred where 7/8-inch bolts were attached; and a tar band grommet was used to prevent this. But after one trip it would be leaking again the next day. '72xxs' were mighty heavy to lift. No 7246 in particular was a rough loco – its boiler jumped about in the frame.

Class 37 diesels saw the '72xxs' off mainline jobs. The first of the '37s' arrived at Ponty in 1963, and were stored on No 7 siding. Jack Drayton was driving a pair of them at Miskin, on driver training with Graeme Evans. He told Graeme he knew the road, but he ran off the end of the loop with the locos, walked off and left Graeme Evans there!

I remember a '74xx' working from Hereford to Ponty, and running a hot box. Ponty coppersmiths made strips of white metal, and I jacked up the loco and put three strips over the axle. Les Norkett said let him go on his journey. The loco had been in store at Hereford.

A '94xx' pannier from Newport came in off the Glascoed ('Dump') train and stay on shed all day long. It would bring it back to Panteg, for Newport. A normal pannier would take three or four coaches from Panteg back to Blaenavon.

The Rhymney engine off one of the 'Dump' train double-headers would go back to Ponty for the day, while the other one took the crews back. 'Dump' trains worked from two places in Merthyr to Glascoed double-headed. '94xxs' had a problem – the water would run off the tank straight into the sand box; whereas the older engines had lipped-over sand boxes, the '94xxs' had straight lips and the water went in more easily.

No 9710, the condenser pannier, had one injector on the left-hand side and a Weir pump on the right-hand side. There was a lever allowing you to shut the blast pipe, and exhaust steam returned via two pipes, one into each tank; there was a pipe joining them with a vent on top. Oil in the exhaust wasn't removed before the steam entered the tank. I saw the loco at Ponty on its way to

Caerphilly Works for repair, and on its way back. It was parked out where the breakdown van was stored, so we went out and gave it a good looking over. It was at Ponty in 1963 when Swindon wasn't doing many engines. When it came back, it stopped at Ponty. There was a 6-inch water valve under the bunker on the left-hand side so you could release the water and fill it back up with cold water, so you can use the injector. It also had a water tank under the bunker, fed by pipes under the steps; the pannier tanks extended to footplate level. The plated-in part of the tank was for extra water, and it also contained the big valve for draining the tanks. I also saw the loco in Swindon during my apprenticeship.

The 'Granges' were the easiest engines to work on, as lifting the valves out of the cylinders was easier than on a 'Hall'. I fitted a cab side window to engine No 6872 the morning before it had an accident with Jack Drayton.

One day there was a problem with the brake on a 'Grange' tender; it had come from Stourbridge Junction, working to Hafodrynys, and the train was stopped on the Down Relief loop on the island platform at Abergavenny (Mon Road). I went on a light engine from Pontypool to Abergavenny, and a pannier was coupled to back of the '68xx'. I rode back on the 'Grange' to Pontypool Road and the loco was banked around the triangle then back to the West box to turn.

No 6800 *Arlington Grange* was based at Ponty before it was scrapped. I remember it when I was an apprentice with Haydn Evans. It was a standby engine at Ponty station. During the week the station pilot was used as the standby engine; at bank holidays and times of heavy traffic a tender engine was used at the station in this role, while the station

pilot was used on its rostered duties. The standby engine was kept on the engine spur at the South Bay, and if it was the wrong way round it could be turned on the triangle. One bank holiday the train engine on a northbound train failed when the big end run out; No 6800 was the rostered standby engine and took the train onwards.

No 6802 was a rough engine. Les Norkett had somebody change six springs on it to see if it would ride better, but it was getting old, due for a factory repair and surplus to requirements.

I cut my finger on No 6849 *Walton Grange* when I was 17. I was changing a gauge glass with Dave Fry, but he had gone home; he was the 'monkey shift' examining fitter and would go home for tea unofficially. I was being clever and broke all the rules of changing a gauge glass: you should smash it all out. I pulled the bottom up and went against what was left in the top, and cut my finger. When Dave returned he thought I hadn't changed the gauge glass as it was so dirty – but it was all my blood! He took the top off and felt the new glass inside! You would put a 5/16in square steel rod, about

Ex-GWR 'County' Class 4-6-0 No 1000 *County of Middlesex* is seen at the south end of the shed in the early 1960s, on No 7 Siding adjacent to the three-way point. The footplate staff are unknown, but the apprentice fitters from left to right are Malcolm Hewlett, David Venn and Brian Ford. *Malcolm Hewlett, Harry Rawlins collection*

18 inches long with a handle bent through 90 degrees, through the top and bottom water ways of a gauge frame before changing a gauge glass. It was 18 inches long as you didn't want your hand to touch the gauge frame if it was blocked and the rod suddenly cleared the blockage!

I remember No 6848 one Christmas. A driver said, 'I have an eccentric run out.' I went underneath to look and it was the left driving axle box. I said, 'You'll have to take it out of service.' The foreman came and said we just want it to go to Abergavenny and back; it had just got a full firebox of coal. I was persuaded to let it go, and never heard any more about it.

The odd 'County' 4-6-0 was seen on shed, but there were not many on the main line to Shrewsbury. They came in on specials and excursion trains on summer Saturdays. I saw more 'Counties' on Ponty shed than 'Manors'. In the 1960s the 'Counties' were on the North and West route frequently. I recall once watching a 'County' go past the front of the shed on the up Goods Relief line heading to Shrewsbury with a passenger train, following the 4.09pm Bristol, the 6.00pm at Abergavenny. The first 'King' worked this through Abergavenny in around 1951. 'Saint' Class *Lady of Lynn* had worked the train before the 'County'. I once put a steam heat bag on a 'County' between engine and tender when the steam heat was put on at Ponty station; I did this job in the station, then went to the refreshment room for a rum and blackcurrant.

'Manors' would sometimes run on the Vale of Neath to Ponty shed, but were based at Neath shed. Nos 7828 and 7829 both appeared. No 7828 had a tender vacuum cylinder Hyab band (India rubber) changed at Ponty by fitter Glyn Morris ('Scratchy'); this

was before I started there. Glyn later went to work as a fitter on the locos at Panteg steelworks.

I only ever saw one 'Dukedog' at Ponty. It come down on a freight train from Shrewsbury, and went back on another freight. We had a good look at it!

The tenders that were the worst of the lot to fit brake blocks were Hawksworth's. You needed two people to put them. As you went to put the block up, your hand came against the bottom of the frame and you needed help to put them up a bit higher.

'ROD' tenders were steam braked. I put brake blocks on one when I was an apprentice, with another boy helping me. The blocks were 3/4cwt each. They had the same pins as the engine blocks, but the nuts were on the outside, which made them much easier to undo. I also examined the valves and pistons on these engines; they were the only engines where you see the crosshead turned upside down to knock the cotter pin out. When this was done to one particular engine a joggle was seen in the cotter pin, as it had been fitted using a hydraulic jack. The piston had been pushed further in the crosshead than it should have been, and the job was sent to Swindon to be redone. Pistons were pushed out just enough to change the rings; they were never taken out

Ex-GWR 'ROD' 2-8-0 No 3040 moves on or off the south end of the shed, circa 1953. *Kidderminster Railway Museum*

of the cylinder. The internal pipe from the steam brake exhaust under the dome was a copper pipe with a wall a quarter of an inch thick. If it needed to be cut it took a long time in a restricted area.

A. B. Stafford attempted to drill the firehole door stud on an ROD on No 7 road when it was still in steam. I got the boilersmiths to do this.

I also did valves and pistons on the 'RODs', the valves at 12,000 miles and the valves and pistons at 24,000 miles. This was a favourite job for Les Norkett to leave for the Saturday night shift; the valves came out from the inside. I re-metalled the big ends, side rod bushes and eccentrics, and crossheads. The valve heads were right close together. Liners were used for the eccentric straps, specially made, which you hammered in; if you weren't careful you'd break them. You fitted the liner, and machined them to suit the eccentric, in a four-jaw chuck; it was measured with callipers and a telescope gauge. If you put them on and they were a bit tight, you hit the eccentric strap with a sledge, hoping to get the strap to turn; it's surprising how you could get the liners to go in that extra couple of thou, and the strap would then rotate.

One Christmas Day I worked from 6.00am to 2.00pm. Les Norkett had left four eccentric straps to take off a '56xx', and every nut had to be split with a chisel as they had been over-tightened and had strained the threads. No 6820 or 6821 was standing on the turntable, and a set of brake blocks was booked on it. After the eccentric straps had been taken down, the brake blocks were changed on the Through Road. I finished at 1.00pm and got home in time for Christmas dinner. When working on Christmas day there was a lot of hanging around, as there was nobody there. (I remember that on New Year's Eve the cleaners would go around hanging monkey wrenches on the whistle chains to welcome in the New Year.)

Oil or blower pipes were repaired at the shed, depending on the engine. It was done to avoid taking the cleating off the boiler. A Ponty '77xx' pannier ran around a long time

with this type of repair, which goes down the outside, as well as the lubrication pipes.

Rods were removed from engines to save paying tax. For a steam loco, if a connecting rod was removed tax could be saved against the earning capacity of that loco.

An ex-LMS 'Duchess' Class engine, *Queen Mary*, was on shed at Ponty one weekend.

Royal Train engines

Four or five engines were done up for the Royal Train. In 1963 three were prepared – a 'Hall' and two 'Granges', fresh from Swindon. I had the 'Hall' to repair. These engines would be tested for Royal Train duty by acting as the Abergavenny banker for a week following repairs. A fourth was supplied to stand on the Royal Train all night at Portskewitt; this would be a 'Hall', as Severn Tunnel Junction didn't have one of them available.

I did up No 6928 *Underlay Hall* for the Royal Train, as it was getting on a bit. I had to take the side rods off; the ends were crack-tested for the bushes and also the connecting rod small and little ends. The rods were cleaned, painted and covered in oil to check for cracks. Valve and piston rings were changed, but the back right-hand cylinder cover failed on raising steam for the first time after repairs. I was on nights so I didn't have to repair it. It went to Portskewitt to supply the steam heating for the Royal Train. It was also a standby engine for 'Castle' breakdowns on the main line.

Two '68xxs' were done up as spares, fresh out of Swindon. No 6836 was cleaned up, and the Royal Train was hauled by one of them.

BR Standards

'Britannias' were on shed occasionally. The Cardiff examples slipped a lot until they found out that they needed a different sort of sand. I once had a girlfriend from Abergavenny who would visit me when

BR 'Britannia' Class 4-6-2 No 70051 *Forth of Firth* resides on the Tap Road on 29 March 1964. *R. K. Blencowe collection*

BR '73xxx' Class No 73096 takes water having reversed off the coal stage. *Harry Rawlins collection*

I worked at Swindon; one day her train was stuck in Patchway Tunnel, hauled by a 'Britannia' that had slipped to a stand.

One of the '73xxxs' was stored at Ponty shed for three months waiting for firebars; it had been steamed with a bad fire, which had burned the bars through. It was kept on the end of No 5 road.

The '80xxxs' hardly ever came on shed. Neath engines went to Ponty shed only as failures.

9Fs were on shed regularly. There was one on shed on nights working a train to Soho in Birmingham, having injector trouble. Nos 92234 and 92235 arrived on 6 September 1953 and Nos 92231, 92232 and 92233 on 9 August 1958. These engines moved to 86E on 24 January 1959.

DMUs

These were refuelled at Newport. The North Bay at Pontypool Road station was used to keep the Blaenavon DMU, and another in the South Bay. Marcus Hunter started at 3.00am on a Monday morning to fill up the DMU and top up the antifreeze when he was chargehand. Antifreeze was kept at the station. When he was on holiday I covered for him once. The batteries used to be switched off, and the first thing you were supposed to do was to start them; I was still trying to start it when the driver arrived and showed me how to do it. I nipped up to the North Bay and got that going. The DMUs saw off the '64xxs'.

The breakdown train

The track by the shed stores water tank was the original road where the old-fashioned Great Western breakdown vans were kept, but these were scrapped in early 1952 before I started. They are shown in early photos of Ponty, carrying the words 'Loco Carriage and Wagon Department'. The original GWR breakdown train was taken out of service when it became beyond economic repair. A 'fish' bolster and 'Toad' van were used as a temporary measure until replaced by two 70-foot coaches and a packing van, which were kept behind the coal stage as the original Stores Road wasn't long enough. These coaches went to Cardiff Canton when Ponty closed.

One of the new coaches was set out with

Ex-GWR '36xx' Class 0-6-0PT No 3651 is seen attached to the Pontypool Road breakdown train, date unknown. *Kidderminster Railway Museum*

Ex-GWR '66xx' Class 0-6-2T No 6677 rests on the road used to store the breakdown train, with the water tank in the background.

a kitchen in the middle, with a stove with a hot water bottle. One end was where two foremen went, and there were two plush beds. The other end was for the breakdown crew, with a table and two benches down each side. There was a toilet at each end of the coach. The tool van was a modified coach, with sliding doors in the middle, and little gantries carrying rope blocks to get the heavy gear out. Then came a van with blocks of packing in, packed right up to the roof. There were 20-ton and 40-ton jacks; the latter went to Newton Abbot when the diesels came in.

Further information has since come to light, as a result of correspondence from Brian Penney to Harry Rawlins. Brian worked for British Railways, and moved from Birmingham to the Cardiff Divisional Office in August 1963. The Pontypool Road breakdown train comprised of three vehicles: staff riding coach DW.150062, bogie tool vehicle DW.150056, and packing van DW.150069. Brian remembers Les Norkett

being present at a derailment at Talywain in December 1963, when a Type 3 diesel-electric locomotive come off the road.

Nearby cranes in the late 1950s were Ransome & Rapier 45-ton No 18 at Canton, and 25-ton No 14 at Radyr. In 1961 the Canton crane was replaced by Cowans Sheldon 75-ton No 142, and Ebbw Junction received the new Cowans Sheldon 30-ton crane No 139.

Les Norkett was sent to Cardiff Divisional office when Ponty closed to steam in 1965, to monitor the condition of the remaining steam locos and ensure that better ones were kept at the bottom of the scrapping list, with no major repairs prior to withdrawal. Les toured the remaining steam depots to inspect locos and record their condition.

ATC ramps

The ATC wearing piece on a pannier was fitted to the front axle boxes, making the fitting of the piston gland packing awkward to undertake. The piece was a solid tray with the ATC placed on it. A 'King' had the ATC on the back end of the frame, as it couldn't be fitted to the bogie. Later 'Castles' had the ATC fitted to the bogie, while '28xxs' had it at the back end of the frame. '93xxs' had the ATC fitted to the pony, while the earlier 'Halls' had it fitted right at the front, as was the case with '42xxs' and '56xxs'. When leaving the pit beneath one of these engines, if you stood up too soon you rubbed your back against the ATC wearing piece, but the shoe never went up to activate the ATC bell! I have seen people walk into them. Older panniers had the ATC fitted to the back of the frame, as did '55xxs'.

The ramp was never square to the sleeper and rail – it was obliquely angled to minimise wear when the engine passed over it. The wear was also evened out on the shoe – some would be all shapes. Going off the shed there were two short ramps, one live and the other dead, to test the ATC and ring the bell. The brake was put on with the second ramp. There was also an ATC ramp on the road going onto the fire pit, so they could test it coming back on shed. If there was a fault a spring-loaded red plate stating 'ATC out of use' would pop up; a key ring was needed to hook the trigger up.

The ATC was tested every time you went off shed. Some drivers placed a cork under the trigger when leaving. One day Driver Harry Crump was coming down with a passenger train, ran through a Distant signal at Nantyderry and ran through the station with the signals against him; he was stopped at Little Mill by a detonator. He had been running the loco with the ATC

pegged up. He reckoned he was changing a gauge glass.

ATC failures were very rare, but a few incidents are recalled. The LMS men at Abergavenny, when they started driving Western engines from Ponty, were full of praise for the ATC – you didn't have to look out in the fog. The AWS came about as a result of the Harrow & Wealdstone rail crash – the driver missed a Distant signal.

Ernie Stephens was the ATC battery changer, and also a boxing manager. He always had to have an apprentice with him. To change a bell was the end of the world – he lacked confidence! It consisted of four bolts, a bit of conduit, and three or four wires, all black with eyelets and labelled. The ATC was designed to a high standard.

Main-line failures

The regulator rod on No 2800 broke when coming on shed. The two pieces were dragged from the shed, up to the station and sent to Caerphilly for repair.

One Saturday night I was taken to the station to take a look at an express train, maybe a lubricator, and to the New Sidings to put a screw in a vacuum gauge. One Christmas Eve I went to the station to fill a lubricator on No 5900, with a Ponty crew on it, double-heading in front of a 'Castle'. I had just finished filling the lubricator when the driver of the 'Castle' blew up and was away. The Ponty driver put the brake back on,

Ex-GWR 'Castle' Class No 5073 *Blenheim* is seen on the Tap Road with a blowing safety valve joint, some time between 1957 and 1960. *Malcolm Hewlett, Harry Rawlins collection*

otherwise it would have been first stop Shrewsbury!

'Castles' were also dealt with. *Blenheim* arrived on shed one day with the safety valve joint blowing, and *Earl St Aldwyn* is recalled being at Ponty with the front cover knocked off. It was stripped down inside the shed on No 1 road, ready to go back to Swindon for repairs. Alf Smith took the inside connecting rods down.

Rollei Jones went out to fetch a 'Castle' whose crew

Ex-GWR 'Grange' Class 4-6-0 No 6872 *Crawley Grange* resides on the Cabin Road at Pontypool Road on 29 March 1964. This was the engine that ran into the back of a freight train at Hereford in 1959 when driven by Jack Drayton; the guard was Ron Petty of Griffithstown.
F. A. Blencowe, R. K. Blencowe collection

had felt the gudgeon pin come out when coming over the top of Llanvihangel, but they decided to just let it run and didn't put any more steam on. They put the note out at Abergavenny for a breakdown and stopped coming up into Nantyderry. The gudgeon pin had come out of an inside connecting rod, which was disconnected on the flat, without a pit – not an easy task. The gudgeon pin was found the next day.

A 'Castle' going up through Llanvihangel once dropped all the firebars out.

A '64xx' tank going to Newport broke the reversing rod, forcing it into forward gear. It was tied up and taken to shed.

Vacuum cylinders would fail with India rubber (IR) joints. On one occasion Marcus Hunter was doing an IR band on a locomotive vacuum brake cylinder while working on No 5 Road alongside the Through Road. Around the top cover is a joint like catapult elastic, quarter-inch rubber, and the joint had fallen out of this cover. I went in and sat on top of the cylinder, which was right up the front behind the bogie, right under the boiler. Marcus Hunter's mate, Harry Loveridge, a

tall man, was passing the joint, soaked in rubber solution, up the inside of the vacuum cylinder so I could go round pushing it up in the groove.

On the floor in the pit was a 7lb tin of rubber solution, but also a naked flare lamp. Harry Loveridge dropped the rubber band into the flame of the flare, then dropped the band into the tin of rubber solution, and burned his arms. Imagine the smoke off that! I was out of there quicker than I got in! Luckily we were on No 5 road, against the wide road.

On pannier No 7740 Marcus had the valve gear apart outside Les Norkett's office. It was put into full gear to go onto the turntable, but the engine went backwards instead!

One day No 3826 was coupled inside another '28xx' and ran off the end of the up loop at Maindee Junction, Newport, by the Glebeland's Road bridge. No 3826 was on its way back from Swindon, and only its front coupling was damaged, but the '28xx' in front tipped right over, and was there for a few days until the weekend. The '28xx' was No 2848, a Ponty engine. It was sent to

Ebbw and never repaired. It was then used for re-railing exercises (see Terry Biggs's notes).

Driver Jack Drayton on No 6872 once ran into the back of the 9.42pm Pontypool Road to Crewe freight train, in fog, north of the River Wye bridge at Hereford (the freight line crossed the Wye south of Barton loco depot.) The front end was badly damaged and the cylinders dislodged by the impact. Ron Petty from Griffithstown was the guard and Jack Ford the fireman. The loco was taken to the works for repair, and subsequently returned to Ponty shed.

This incident occurred between Hereford loco shed and Redhill Junction, on the freight bypass. All the Western freight trains turned off at Red Hill Junction, south of Hereford (Barr's Court) station, using the Up Goods line to bypass the shed and rejoining the main line north of Hereford station, at Barr's Court Junction, south of Shelwick Junction. Jack was following the passenger train and ran into the back of it.

On the Vale of Neath I worked on breakdowns at Pontllanfraith, Fleur-de-lys, Markham Colliery and Oakdale Colliery. We went to Marham Colliery a couple of times in the middle of the night. There was a pub next door to where the water column was situated at Oakdale Colliery; when we stopped there the engine took on water and somebody got a couple of flagons of beer. You could see them doing that today!

Repair tasks

Examples of the various repair jobs undertaken are described here, to record the work and time involved. Ponty work was mainly brake blocks and springs.

Spring changing

This was a simple but heavy job. The packing used was timber baulks stored between the roads of the round shed. Officially, to change a spring you jacked up the two sides nearest to the spring until the spring came loose, let it drop into the pit, put on the new spring, then release the jack. The jacks were kept in the round shed between the roads and were 20-ton hydraulic examples, the same as used on breakdowns, but not in such good condition. Packing was put under the jacks.

BR Standards had preset springs. Older '28xxs' had compensating gear, with a pin through, while '47xxs' had a roller underneath the frame, with a bar across the springs; the other end had springs with 1.75-inch-diameter Whitworth spring bolts. The easiest ones were the continental hangers on '14xxs', '54xxs', '64xxs', low-numbered '72xxs' and '66xxs, and high-numbered '52xxs'. The weight came on the end of two springs – take the centre pin out and it would fall off.

It would take two or three hours, sometimes longer, depending how seized up it was. The old spring was put into a compound by the coal stage for removal to Caerphilly for repair. Springs were changed when a leaf broke, as booked by a driver or examining fitter.

Pony trucks had no springs, but reacted to the leading springs of the engine; a '55xx' had a trailing pony that was sprung off the rear loco springs. The '44xxs', '45xxs' and '55xxs' were the only Western locos with a trailing pony; the '56xxs', '72xxs' and '41xxs' used radial wheels with a spring above. Radial springs were never replaced at Ponty as they didn't break.

Two people were needed to lift and replace a spring.

Springs were classified as follows in the GWR Loco and Tender Springs Book, as supplied by Edward Freeman:

103 – '60xx' trailing spring, 34 leaves 5 inches wide, 33 leaves 3/8 inch thick, 1 leaf ½ inch thick, 5cwt.

134 – '57xx' and '64xx', 4.5 inches wide, 10 leaves 5/8 inch thick.

147 –'41xx', '43xx', '49xx', '68xx', '4073'/'50xx'/'70xx' 'Castle' driving springs, 18 leaves, 17 at 7/16 inch thick, 1 at ½ inch thick, 5 inches wide.

G.W.R. ENGINES.

70A	Crosshead Drawer Outside Cylinder Engines 18 to 19" x 30".
70B	40's
70C	44's and 45's.
70D	P.T. 17.18.19
70E	P.T. 20.21.
70F	103, 104.
70G	Rail Motors
70H	King Class.
71A	Crosshead Drawer Inside Cylinder Engines 2 Bar Motion.
71B	Nos 4169 to 4172.
72	Superheater Unit Drawer.
73	Valve Spindle Crosshead Shifter.
74	New pattern leading Crank Pin, Washer, Nut and Bolt 44xx & 45xx Class
75	
76	Valve Spindle Crosshead Shifter 28xx Class Engines.
77	Reseating Tool for Steam Lance Valve.
78	Crank Pin Washer, Set Bolt Tube Spanner.
79	Tyre Flange Turning Attachment.
80	Crosshead Lifter 56xx Class (With Driving Wheels removed.)
81	Reseating Tool for 1" Spherical Injector Steam Valves.
82	Piston Crosshead Shifter - 5600 Class.
83	Wolverhampton Class.
84	Tool for Inserting Intermediate Buffers fitted with Cotter.
85	Support for Valves when Removing Pins in Head. (Injector, Ejector & Blower)
86	Punch for Valves with 3/8" Pins.
87	
88	Support for Valves when Removing Pins in Head. (Steam Heating)
89	(No 4 Blower & Steam Lance)
90	(Old Injectors)
91	Smoke Box Door Lifter.
92	Hook for Lifting Trailing Ends (Engines with Extended Bunker)
93	Lifting Clips for Changing Pony Truck Springs (43xx Class)
94	Gudgeon Pin Nut Spanner. (4 Cyl. Engines)
95	Lifter for Vacuum Cylinder for new 4000 Gall. Tenders and Transverse Reservoir
96	Spring Compressor for self contained Intermediate Buffers

DIVISIONAL SUPT. NEWTON ABBOT.

96

INDEX OF SPECIAL TOOLS USED IN ERECTING SHOPS SWINDON.
G.W.R. ENGINES.

1	Coupling Rod Pin Drawer.
2	Old Man Drilling Post.
3	Axlebox and Horn Block Stretcher.
4	Coupling Rod Washer Spanner (Large)
5	Motion Bar Gauge
6	Piston Crosshead Shifter (Bulldog Class).
7	Box Spanner Cylinder Relief Valve Adapter.
8	Stud Drawer (Various Sizes).
9.9A	Piston Crosshead Gudgeon Pin Drawer (9-4000,4400 and 4500 Classes).
10	Spanners. Cylinder Relief Valve. (9A - King Class)
11	Valve Spindle Crosshead Drawer (Outside Cylinders).
12	Piston Cotter Drawer with Hydraulic Jack.
13	Valve Spindle Crosshead Drawer. (Inside Cylinders).
14	Eccentric Sheave Bent Chisel.
15	Piston Crosshead Gudgeon Pin Drawer (18 x 30 Cylinders).
16	Reversing Arm Drawer and Spanner. (Outside Cylinders)
17	Cylinder Cover Drawer. (4 Cylinder)
18	Shackle for drawing Pony Truck Centre Pin.
19	Cylinder Cover Drawer (18 x 30 Cylinders).
20	Packing Drawers. (Screw and Hook)
21	Reversing Arm Drawer for Starting.
22	Buffer Lifter.
23	Crank Pin Washer Drawer. (4 Pins)
24	(5 Pins)
25	Tender Vacuum Cylinder Lifter.
26	Tender Spring Lifter.
27	Jig for holding Brass (O.K. Type) whilst scraping. (Fixed to Wheels)
28	Eye Bolt and Shackle for lifting Trailing End (2301 and Std. Goods)
29	Steam Brake Cylinder Lifter.
30	Jack for revolving Crank Shaft when cutting Keyways.
31	Regulator Stuffing Box Drawer.
32	Crankpin Washer Spanners (4 and 5 Pins)
33	Piston Crosshead Drawers. (Steam Motors)
34	3/4 Bent Spanner and Bar. (Regulator in Dome)
35	Piston Lifter. (16 to 17 1/2 Inside Cylinders)
36	Valve Spindle Drawer. (Bulldog and 2600 Class)
37	Valve Spindle Drawers. (2301 class etc.)
38	Front Cylinder Cover Lifter. (16 to 17 1/2 Inside Cylinders)
39	
40	
41	Piston Ring Compressor. (16 to 17 1/2 Dia.)
42	3 1/2 Piston Crosshead Nut Spanner.
43	4 1/2

149 – 'King', front four springs.
201 – '68xx', '49xx' bogie spring.
252 – '66xx' loco springs.

The 201 was the inverted bogie spring. Alf Smith at Ponty once changed one of these without removing the bogie, possibly on a 'Hall' or a 'Grange'.

Tender springs required lifting up into position, as they were above the wheel.

On '28xx' Class locos, the front coupled wheel and intermediate wheel had compensated springing, as did the trailing wheel and driving wheel. Both sides of the engine would be jacked up to change a main spring, after which all the parts became 'loose'. Jacks were put under the footplate at the rear end, making it awkward to jack up.

Panniers suffered from hot axle boxes. The trailing axle boxes would shear the axle box keep bolts if they derailed – this saw off pannier No 4616. I never saw a hot box on a '28xx', but I recall one on No 6848, which I stopped, and had to let go to Abergavenny on a mail train, where it again ran hot. Axle box oil pads were changed very occasionally, when you had a hot axle box.

1/8, 1/16 and 1/32-inch feeler gauges (long ones) were used to check axle box horn clearances and crosshead wear between slide bars.

Crosshead repairs

Crossheads would wear rather than run hot. They were checked during the mileage exams. Crossheads were white metalled and machined to fit the existing distance between

Left and overleaf top left: Tools of the trade: the steam locomotive is a complex, precision-made hand-built machine, and a list of tools to aid dismantling are shown here. Harry Rawlins

G.W.R. ENGINES.

71A	CROSSHEAD DRAWER. INSIDE CYLINDER ENGINES. 2 BAR MOTION.
71B	
72	SUPERHEATER UNIT DRAWER.
73	VALVE SPINDLE CROSSHEAD SHIFTER.
74	LEADING CRANKPIN WASHER SPANNER.
75	" " " 4400 & 4500 CLASS.
76	VALVE SPINDLE CROSSHEAD SHIFTER. 2800 CLASS.
77	RESEATING TOOL FOR STEAM LANCE VALVE.
78	CRANK PIN WASHER SET BOLT TUBE SPANNER.
79	TYRE FLANGE TURNING ATTACHMENT.
80	CROSSHEAD LIFTER. 5600 CLASS. (WITH DRIVING WHEELS REMOVED.)
81	RESEATING TOOL FOR 1" SPHERICAL INJECTOR STEAM VALVES.
82	PISTON CROSSHEAD SHIFTER. 5600 CLASS.
83	" " " WOLVERHAMPTON CLASS.
84	TOOL FOR INSERTING INTERMEDIATE BUFFERS FITTED WITH COTTER.
85-90	
91	SMOKEBOX DOOR LIFTER.
92	HOOK FOR LIFTING TRAILING ENDS. (ENGINES WITH EXTENDED BUNKERS.)
93	LIFTING CLIPS FOR CHANGING PONY TRUCK SPRINGS (4300 CLASS)
94	GUDGEON PIN NUT SPANNER. (4 CYLINDER ENGINES)
95	LIFTER FOR VACUUM CYLINDER. (4000 GALLON TENDERS) & TRANSVERSE RESERV
96	SPRING COMPRESSOR FOR SELF CONTAINED INTERMEDIATE BUFFERS.
97	GUDGEON PIN DRAWER (18"x30" CYLINDERS WITH TAPER GUDGEON PIN.)
98-99	
100	CROSSHEAD COTTER SHIFTER 4900, 5300, 2900 CLASS. C.S. CR SHP.
101	VALVE SPINDLE CROSSHEAD SHIFTER. 5700 CLASS
102	GUDGEON PIN DRAWER 5700. 4400.4500 & 4 CYLINDER ENGINES.
103	CONING TOOL FOR ⅜" BORE COPPER PIPES (HAND OPERATED.)
104	SPANNER FOR SPECIAL CRANK PIN WASHER 4500 CLASS
105	LIFTER FOR PONY TRUCK.
106	A.T.C. SHOE DRAWER.
107	FOR CLEANING STEEL STAYS ⅝" TO 1⅜"
108	PISTON VALVE SPANNER.
109	LIFTER FOR A.T.C. SHOE. (PLUNGER TYPE ONLY)
110	VALVE SPINDLE SPANNER. RACK NUT ADJUSTER. 4 CYL. ENGINES.

INDEX OF SPECIAL TOOLS. G.W.R. ENGINES.

111	LIFTER FOR A.T.C. SHOE (TYPES A & B.)
112	VALVE SPINDLE STARTING TOOL. 2884 CLASS ENGINES.
113	VALVE SPINDLE DRAWER. 3300 3400 & 2600 CLASS ENGINE
114-124	

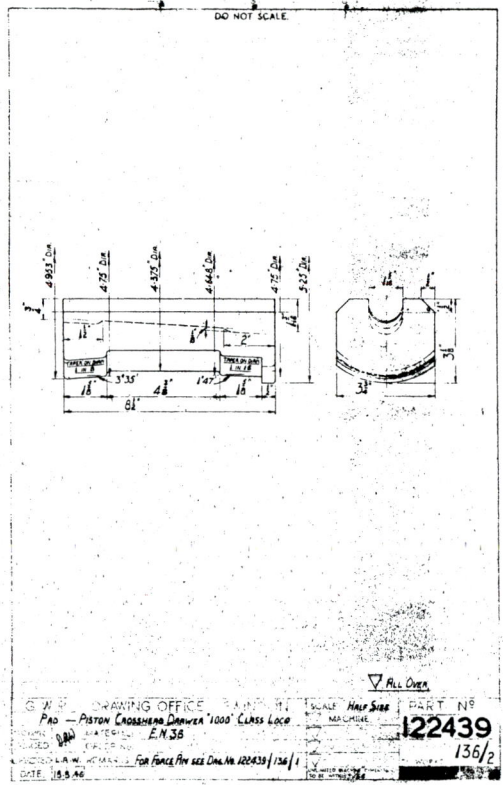

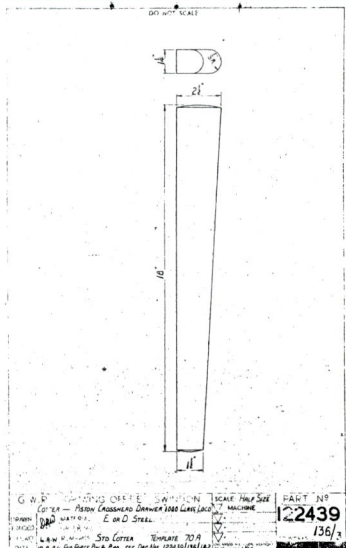

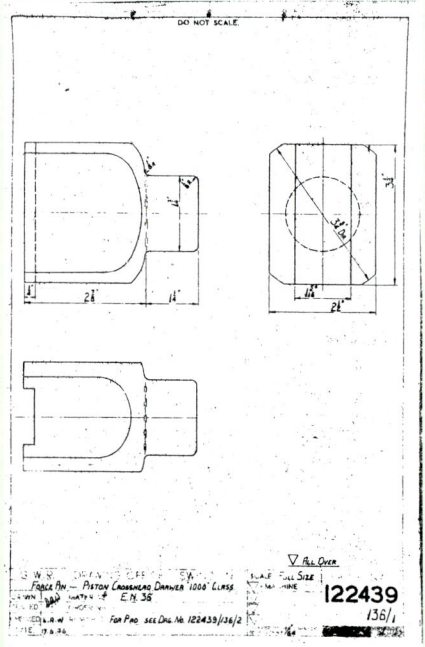

Drawings for a crosshead drawer (splitter) for a
GWR 'County' Class 4-6-0. *Harry Rawlins*

the slide bars, using the planing machine. This would usually be undertaken during the valve and piston exam.

There are centre punch marks on the boss of the crosshead for you to measure off the centre of the crosshead to the bottom of the crosshead slipper grooves. You usually only metalled and machined the bottom slipper. The slide bar width was measured using outside callipers, and the dimension transferred to inside callipers. Inside callipers were used to measure between the slide bars, and outside callipers used to measure the depth between the base of the top and bottom slippers during and after machining. The lower slipper was re-metalled by the coppersmith, white metal covering the base and sides of the slipper groove, and the crosshead was put onto the table of the planing (shaping) machine; the upper slipper was supported on two 2-inch parallel bars, with a bar through the gudgeon pin hole, and clamped to the bed, after being aligned axially. Axial alignment required the crosshead to be aligned so that the groove in the slipper would be machined parallel to the piston rod. The top slipper groove (as well as the lower slipper groove) was already machined at the bottom and its sides; we aligned the inside edge of the top slipper on the machine, above the white metal; we probably aligned it using the tool of the shaping machine at varying positions of its stroke, before clamping the crosshead to the table of the machine. The outside face of the crosshead was a rough cast surface, which was of no use for alignment purposes. The lower slipper was then planed to the correct width and depth using the calliper-measured slide bar measurements (width and depth between slide bars).

Crosshead cotters were easily removed. We had a special tool for this, a crosshead splitter (kept in a cupboard by Les Norkett's office, where all the special tools were kept). There was one for engines with a 19-inch by 30-inch stroke, one for a pannier, one for a '64xx'/'14xx', one for '66xxs' and one for 'RODs'. First of all we removed the little cotter at the back of the crosshead, then fitted the special tool – it was shaped like

a big pein pin with a large bulb on it. The tool straddled the cotter and clipped in position – it had a semicircular pin in lieu of the gudgeon pin – and a tapered wedge was driven through this assembly to split the piston from the crosshead. The LMS didn't have this method.

On a '45xx' we went into the pit and, after removing the little cotter at the back of the crosshead, hit the small end of the cotter with a bar and a sledge, to break the tapered fit between the cotter and crosshead (because the starting gear to remove the crosshead cotter at Ponty never fitted properly). We did the same thing for LMS engines.

Other repairs

Side rods and eccentric straps were worked on occasionally. On side rod knuckle joints we replaced the bush, but the pins were left untouched as they were case-hardened and we had no means of repairing them. Side rod bushes were removed by placing a round disc over the bush, and hitting the disc with a sledge; in later years we pressed the bushes out.

Connecting rod big end failures occurred sometimes on panniers and '56xxs' if an oil cork came out. One bank holiday, as an apprentice, I went up to the station with Haydn Evans on a '68xx' standby engine and took a 'Hall' off a train going north, which had run a big end out. We brought it back to the shed, and it was repaired the next day.

Pony trucks are recalled. Beneath the bell-shaped cover on the front of the engine was a 2-inch bolt that would sometimes break; it was used for adjusting the balance of the compensating beam connecting the pony truck to the beam between the front end of the leading springs (there was no leading spring hanger bracket to the frame; the load was reacted at a pivot pin beneath the cylinders). The front end of the beam would drop onto the pony axle and wear a small groove in it; but it wasn't enough to change a wheelset. Drivers and Examining Fitters would report these faults, which would arise on engines with pony trucks such as '28xxs', '38xxs', '42xxs', '52xxs', '72xxs', and '41xxs', '51xxs' and '45xxs'.

Packing outside piston glands was easy, but '64xxs', panniers and '56xxs' were the worst, being inside. The bigger the wheel, the easier they were to get at. These were half-hour jobs.

Valve glands on slide valve engines were a fireman's job. In the 1930s the footplate staff fought the fitting staff for the privilege of doing this, as well as the steam brake glands. Piston valve glands were the fitter's responsibility, but being on the exhaust steam side they were rarely replaced.

Vacuum pumps were repaired on pannier tank engines. We would check the packing was OK, change metallic glands, grind in valves, put in rubber gaskets and maybe change rings. The left handrail was used to lift the vacuum pump out of the frames for repair and would often bend during this process. Sometimes we repaired vacuum pumps on bigger engines.

Brake blocks were changed fairly often on trains carrying the H headcode lamp arrangement. On a Western engine, split pins and clips were used on the brake block pins. The fitter removed the split pins and the brake block pin clips (these were not on LMS engines), and on a '28xx' the fitter's mate would slack out the brake screw or screws. You then took the brake blocks down, and put the new ones up. The most difficult ones were the leaders on '43xxs', '41xxs' and their derivative engines, as they were very low down on these engines.

A terrific amount of adjusting was done on shift work, as every freight train engine leaving shed would require brake adjustments to be made. Fitters' mates would do this on engines fitted with brake screws. It was different on panniers and '14xxs', which used rods; these could only be adjusted when the screw was rotated a certain number of turns – for a '14xx' and a '64xx' it was 10 turns, and for a '57xx' pannier it was 3½ turns.

On a 'monkey shift', if you were unlucky, you could do two sets of '28xx' brake blocks, but on nights it might be three sets. You would try not to do an engine and tender at the same time, as it would make the braking poor. Nearly every time a '28xx' went off

the shed, its brakes would be adjusted. The worst part of this was adjusting the brakes on the tender; if you were asked to do this before the tender had been filled you were OK, otherwise on the older Churchward tenders, if they had just been filled you would be underneath trying to avoid the leaks from the tank!

'RODs' wouldn't have their brake blocks replaced on a normal shift, as the job took longer than the shift due to complications with fitting them.

Ponty was renowned for a lot of sand box maintenance, due to the gradients worked by its engines. Wet sand would be removed by the fitters (footplate staff didn't have the time or equipment), but the footplate staff would put clean dry sand back in. I scooped out the sand using a baked bean tin. Probably a hundredweight would be removed from all the loco and tender sand boxes. A '14xx' sand box was the same as the trailing sand box on a 'Castle'. The sand valve was changed in 1920s from a lifting plunger to a rotating valve.

Examining fitters used to change water gauge glasses during the 3-5-week exam with engines above 200psi, and during the 7-9-week exam with engines of 200psi and below.

Injectors were examined regularly under BR, and very rarely went wrong. Exhaust steam injectors had the cones replaced. There was a grease box halfway along the 4-inch pipe; coming back from under the smokebox and down, the grease box was located between the frames, approximately under the safety valve. I never did much with this, possibly when it let the grease run out. LMS Class 8s used a 6-inch pipe.

No work was undertaken on safety valves except to replace the entire item. A lightly blowing safety valve would be replaced by a new unit. In Swindon, the P1 Shop had a board for steam fittings to be tested and set. If a joint blew, the safety valve would be removed and the joint renewed. They wouldn't allow it today – one man would stand on the round part of the boiler, the other on the firebox, and the safety valve would be removed and placed on top of the firebox. It would be lifted by placing two steel bars 2 inches by ¼ inch between the springs of the valve beneath the clamping bars.

Both clack valves would be removed beforehand. The left-hand clack had enough room between the handrail for it to clear the studs on the safety valve, but the right-hand clack required the cone joint to be undone at the bottom, and the clack box removed, otherwise if you just pulled it off you would bend the clack pipe and it would never go back on properly, as the four-cone ejector was close by. The cone joint was a conical bronze washer between the pipe and clack.

Regarding smokeboxes, the odd superheater, steam pipe or regulator valve was attended to. It was found that superheater elements failed as they had copper joints in them, until BR changed the joints to cones. The copper joint was a hat-shaped copper washer with an asbestos insert; the asbestos was between the copper, just like car gaskets are today with different materials. When I was an apprentice I was repairing superheaters all the time. LMS superheaters were more robust; the Western ones were too thin, too close to the firebox and had the wrong sort of joints. BR changed the Western design to that of the Manchester Superheater Company, which had a more robust return end in the firebox. The Western superheater had three tubes per element, while the BR ones only had two tubes per element. On a No 1 boiler, for a '28xx', '38xx', 'Hall' and 'Grange', two superheaters per flue tube were used; a bridging piece connected these together in the smokebox, for attachment to the header. There were six tubes per flue. On BR, the element pipe was heavier and thicker; these were then put on the Western Region engines, reducing the number of tubes in each flue to four. The 'Counties' and 'Modified Halls' had three-row superheaters, the 'Castles' went to four, and the 'Kings' to five.

The engine was tested when in steam, so you knew if a joint or a return end had failed. Sometimes superheater elements would

come out easily, sometimes they wouldn't. You would undo the 1-inch Whitworth nut on the header and pull the elements out; they were attached to an end plate that was attached to the front of the header (see the drawing in one of the photos). I never had to resort to pulling it out with a chain block, like Terry Biggs, or Malcolm Hewlett. I had a steel bar, with a 90-degree end, which I inserted between the superheater tubes, above the bridging plate, rotating it so the end was behind a tube, and pulled the superheater out. The Millesco superheaters were worse, because all the ends were floppy; luckily I never did many of those.

Steam joints tended to leak – we did them all at one time or other.

Lubricators were repaired by the fitters.

If a clack or steam valve was booked for repair, you would do both as you couldn't be 100% sure it was one or the other that needed attention.

Examining fitters would book work to be done on regulator stuffing boxes, which was done fairly regularly. If squeezed up a bit, they booked them as two rounds of packing, a rubber ring and another three rounds of packing.

There were six ex-LMS 8F 2-8-0s at Ponty at varying times, having replaced the 9Fs. Springs, brake blocks and injectors are recalled, the latter giving a lot of trouble – they wouldn't pick up. We never did much with the valve gear; the engines were here a long time but never seemed to get through the mileage. I never saw a valve or a cylinder cover out – once off the shed, the engines worked OK.

Spindle valves on slide valve and piston valve engines and the gland on a steam brake piston were the responsibility of firemen, who had pinched the job from the fitting staff in the 1920s, and a fitter's job was lost at Ponty. I won't do these two jobs on preserved engines. Fitters were responsible for the regulator gland, as tools were needed to remove the regulator handle, so it wasn't suitable for footplate staff to do it.

Adjustable packing was used on spindle glands – these were nipped up tight most days. Fitters had to unpack these glands to take the valves out. At the end of steam, the foreman would put a card in for the running shed man to get footplate staff to repack them. Firemen used to shove extra packing in all the time, and when it was time to remove a piston valve the first rings were like concrete. The valve would wear, and wouldn't come clear until the last piece of packing was taken out. Packing drawers weren't available as they are now – only home-made equipment. These would be left-handed.

On a pannier, as you pulled away at the packing you hit your head on the leading axle. If the loco was in steam, some firemen would open the regulator to blow the packing out.

Piston glands were non-adjustable, and were repacked by fitting staff. '14xx' Class tanks were awkward – the gland had steps in it, and you couldn't get sockets on them, as the nuts are set back into the gland. At Ponty, claw foot spanners were used to tighten the nuts on these glands, rotated by means of a bar. '64xxs', '74xxs', '14xxs' and '54xxs' all had these glands with the nut set back. Pannier piston glands were bad enough to pack. '56xx' piston gland packing was different from every other Western engine, being half an inch square instead of three-quarters of an inch square. If this blew out you really had a blow. Management was very keen on checking that the piston glands were all right on the '56xx' tanks used on the ammonia train; these engines were worked hard with a very heavy train (to Billingham-on-Tees, near Stockton, where explosives were made). A '56xx' used half-inch-square instead of three-eighths-of-an-inch-square packing, because, we think, they used to use secondhand piston rods from bigger engines, machined down to get a second use out of them.

Loco examinations

The 24,000-mile exam was undertaken for changing valve and piston rings, as well as examining all the motion, side rod bushes, crossheads and big ends. I was lucky in that I was examining all the outside-cylinder engines. Tenders were not examined on this task. When British Railways took over, procedure MP11 for all British Rail engines was used for this examination, having been formerly used by the LMS.

Brake gear was examined every day if the loco was on a passenger train, and every week if on freight trains, based on the requirements of MP11.

The 24,000-mile exams were undertaken by one fitter and a mate, and an apprentice would examine each engine. This would take five days. You would start it on a Monday morning and finish it on a Friday, and occasionally into Saturday.

The daily exams were undertaken once a day on each passenger engine. Sometimes the same engine came back on the shed a second time, but was not examined again. The daily exam was a general look at everything, and was undertaken by three examining fitters and their mates.

In the summer on a Friday and Saturday a lot of special trains were worked, which had to be examined as they were passenger trains. In the absence of an examining fitter, if he was on holiday, a card would be left for an ordinary fitter to do this work. On the daily exam, one fitter would exam the engine and his mate would exam the footplate, making sure that the engine wasn't moved. This exam would take officially 30 minutes, but you could do it in 10 minutes with experience.

Brake exams covered the engine and tender. When brake blocks were changed, nine times out of ten you changed all of them. The trailing wheels of '72xxs' had narrower brake blocks, which wore a bit quicker, so occasionally an odd block would be changed. You could only change an odd block for engines with compensated brake gear, so panniers and '14xxs', and the older tenders, required all brake blocks to be changed in one go. This would take, say, 2 hours for a '28xx' or a '72xx', while a pannier would take 1 to 1½ hours. The satisfaction was seeing the job complete. At breakfast time most of the younger fitters would say what jobs they had, and if somebody had a set of brake blocks they would say what time the brakes would be ready for changing, and the younger fitters would arrive and help put the blocks up. Older fitters disapproved of this method of working – these were men upgraded from fitters' mates.

The big thing for an examining fitter was the X exam, undertaken before a washout. This was a card designed to exam an engine's condition when coming in for a washout. Someone was on top of the pit examining the loco while still in steam, then after the washout the engine was examined mechanically. However, in practice, the in-steam exam was undertaken after the washout had taken place.

Examining fitters would write what jobs they had found on brown repair cards, and these were given to Les Norkett to be recorded in a book. This applied to daily exams and X exams. These jobs were given out the same day, for a daily exam, or if serious would stop the engine, for example for a broken spring. On nights Les Norkett would give the booked jobs to fitters, and the night fitter would have to decide whether to stop the engine. For example, No 5818 came down from Pontrilas in the evening, went through Abergavenny at 4.00pm, and went on the pit at Ponty at 5.00pm to be washed out as the first engine on the night shift at 10.00pm. The driver and fireman from Pontrilas brought it down and went back as passengers on overtime. A Ponty driver and fireman then took it to Pontrilas at 6.00am the following day, and came back on the passenger train. Only once did it not go back at 6.00am, as it had something wrong with it. It came down about once a

British Railways 'Repairs Required' cards; those shown are for an ex-LMS 'Duchess' Class locomotive, based at Carlisle Kingmoor loco depot, on the Midland Region of British Railways. *Phil Williams* month for a washout on a Thursday afternoon.

No 1422 was the standby for the diesel on the Monmouth line, and would do a job to Nelson early in the morning, as an auto. The diesel didn't fail very often – rarely in the summer, and only in the winter with the heater.

Derailments

No 8716 was the Branches Fork runaway engine from Graiggdu Brickworks to the Jack Pitt at Pontnewynydd. It was sent to Ponty for examination, but was not badly damaged.

A pannier with a 'Noah's Ark' brake van is recalled derailing at Pontnewynydd Yard below the bottom end of Branches Fork loco shed.

No 4616 came off the road on the day I put my notice in, between the end of the platform at Pontypool Road station and the South box. I was working the 'monkey shift' on that Monday in the second week of October 1964 and had gone to see Les Norkett to hand in my notice, to finish in three weeks. He said, 'Send your mates up the station for a spring for a 9F on No 4616.' The 9F was the only engine in the shed at this time, on No 4 road. Les said, 'Go up to the station to pass the time.'

Three fitters got on the '46xx' to go to the station, but the lift wasn't working, and as the spring was 2½cwt it was walked up the steps to the platform, chipping all the steps, and put on the front of No 4616. The backing board at the end of the platform came off and away we went. After a few minutes there was a massive bang, and I thought the spring had fallen into the motion. We got off and found that the front of the engine was in the air and the back on the ground, but the spring hadn't moved. Somebody walked to the signal box to ring for the breakdown van, and No 4616 was

An X exam card, as used for an ex-LMS 'Duchess' Class locomotive. *Phil Williams*

put back on the road. The trailing axle boxes hadn't been checked; those on panniers had bolts in them to keep them up as the spring was on top, and they would very often shear off in a derailment. No one checked this. Later that same week the engine ran a hot box and was scrapped.

Returning from the Vale of Neath one day, No 6151 came off the road twice in the same week by the South Sidings signal box (goods line) by the viaduct. The first time it happened, I missed it. The pony wheels had come off. To re-rail the loco, you put hooks in the pony, through the circular plate in the running board, to hold the wheels up. I was standing on the side step tightening the nut down when it came off; a fitter's mate bent down behind me and I accidentally walked over the top of him. A track inspector asked me to check the bubble on his track gauge – I told him what to do with it!

One night in early 1953 No 6963 *Throwley Hall*, a Chester 'Hall', was in the up loop at Abergavenny when the crew fell asleep. They were woken by the sound of the signal arm dropping off (for the main line), and without checking the signal they moved the loco forward and through the catch point at the end of the loop. The loco was re-railed by the Abergavenny Brecon Road shed (86K) breakdown gang and the Newport Ebbw Junction (86A) 60-ton steam crane. The loco was taken back to Pontypool Road shed, where damage to the brake gear and springs was repaired by myself and Haydn Evans. The bent spring and brake gear were taken to the blacksmith in the carriage & wagon shed at Pontypool Road to be straightened. He was the only blacksmith at Pontypool Road, and his work was shared by the carriage & wagon and loco shed, although more blacksmithing work was undertaken on wagons. A few other jobs were undertaken on the engine while we were waiting for the parts to be straightened out, then it was reassembled in the long shed and away it went. Photos were taken by Albert Lyons, a former LMS fireman based at Abergavenny, who ended up as the shed labourer.

Nearly all the men who re-railed the loco ended up at Pontypool. They were Edgar Williams (alias 'Buster', as he broke things), Bert Chapley, Sid James (with whom I worked when I came back

Ex-GWR 'Hall' Class 4-6-0 No 6963 *Throwley Hall* is seen having derailed through catch points in the up loop at Abergavenny (Mon Road), due to driver error, in early 1953. Left to right are Sid Burr (fitter's mate, who moved to Ponty just after), Trevor Knight (fitter, who never moved to Ponty), Mr Bartlett (Station Master, Abergavenny Brecon Road), Albert Evans (boilersmith, who moved to Ponty and stayed there until it finished), Sid James (Brecon Road chargehand fitter), Bert Chapley (fitter) and Edgar Williams (fitter, alias 'Buster'). The photo was taken by Albert Lyons before Abergavenny shed became a sub-shed. *S. Brown, D. K. Jones collection*

Looking west out of Panteg & Coedygric Junction signal box, ex-GWR '14xx' Class 0-4-2T No 1422 heads north with an auto-train for Blaenavon Low Level. The Ballast Siding is seen in the background, and houses on Station Road, Griffithstown. The down loop is just visible below the railings.

from Swindon for a few weeks before going in the RAF), Albert Evans (boilersmith), Trevor Knight (who didn't go to Ponty), and Sid Burr. The biggest part of the job was carting the parts from the loco shed to the carriage & wagon blacksmith to be straightened – not an easy route over which to move parts!

Abergavenny men covered Penpergwym to Pontrilas, while Ponty men covered Penpergwym to Llantarnam. When Abergavenny shed closed, Ponty covered Llantarnam to Pontrilas for breakdowns.

One summer No 6675 derailed above Blaenavon High Level station on the double track part on a Thursday afternoon while running engine and van to Talywain. The breakdown gang left the shed at 3.00pm, near finishing time, and we got up there at about 4.30-5.00pm. I got to Blaenavon with a pannier hauling the breakdown train. It was still light when the brake van was re-railed, but as the ground was soft it was about 3.00am before the engine was re-railed. I got back to Ponty about 7.00am. They put the brake van off in the cripple siding at Talywain on the way back to Ponty, and crawled on down. I fell asleep on the way back. I had breakfast, then examined No 6675. There was damage to the spring and brake gear, and it went to Ebbw for repairs.

A '72xx' derailment is recalled becoming derailed on the line from Crumlin Junction to Llanilleth, on a controlled catch point halfway down the 'muck hole'. The signalman didn't tell the driver of No 7251, with a brake van in front, that he didn't have the road. The loco, driven by Graeme Evans, was off all wheels. It propelled the van going down, and I had done a brake test on it a few hours before. Another brake test was undertaken after the derailment, and the engine stopped as required. '42xxs' and '72xxs' had slow-acting brakes; a ball bearing was fitted in part of the pipework for the Welsh valleys workings, which slowed the brake application to avoid the wheels being picked up (this was not fitted on '28xxs'). Another '72xx' is recalled coming off all wheels near the site of the old

Coedygric loco shed at Panteg, on the line from Coedygric signal box to Panteg Sidings (possibly where the line from the Old Yard and the two lines off the Goods Relief line converged opposite Coedygric loco shed), while another came off the road outside Furnace Sidings signal box at Blaenavon.

The tender of a '28xx', backing on to one of the Birkenhead Sidings by the side of the shed, became derailed after a Sunday telegraph and signalling repair gang had misconnected the signal and point connections. Fitters uncoupled the loco and re-railed the tender – this was the only tender engine I saw being driven away without its tender. The driver was Harold Good, whose son was a diesel driver. The boiler was filled up, and I and someone else went underneath to disconnect the feed bags and the vacuum and reservoir bags. The centre pin and two side pins were knocked out and the engine driven forward. The tender was re-railed and the engine was driven back. The tender went on straight away; its wheels didn't gauge well, but Les Norkett decided to let it run.

'Hall' Class No 4949 came off at the same place, and was back on the shed afterwards. I helped to re-rail it, but had another call to re-rail a Wolverton car-carrying bogie wagon up at the north end of the station; another one had come off a few weeks earlier, at the other side of the station.

In 1959, when Mr Watt was the shed master, I remember a BR '73xxx' Standard working on a banana train, being banked by an '84xx' tank loco, dropping a fusible plug going up Llanvihangel bank. The train was pulled back into the refuge siding by the tank, and a 'Hall' was sent out from Ponty to pull the 4-6-0 off the train. But as the 'Hall' was backing on to the front, the engine came off all wheels. Meanwhile the '84xx' tank loco at the back had run out of water and the fire was thrown out. I remember seeing the three engines coming back to Ponty, the 'Hall', the '73xxx' with the dropped plug and the '84xx' with the fire thrown out.

A 'D67xx' diesel (later Class 37) came off the road at Station Road, Griffithstown, with a couple of wagons by the garage on the road.

Four Class 37 derailments are also recalled in the sidings at Talywain, at the back of the signal box. Two of the engines came off at the same place on different occasions, due to poor track. One derailment cut a slot through the flange of the wheel on one of the bogies of the diesel. One Christmas Eve at 11.00am another Class 37 came off the road at Talywain siding, and I arrived to find one bogie off the track. The breakdown gang isolated the derailed bogie, and it was re-railed using rails to guide the bogie back on; a bit of bullhead rail track was laid on its side, and the isolated derailed bogie was pulled back on with the other bogie. This was something new to us.

The only crane job at Talywain occurred when a wagon came off and dropped down over the bank in the yard, where the NCB engines worked up from the Big Arch. Marcus Hunter was in charge of the breakdown gang, and his first thought was to call out the Newport 60-ton steam crane. There was a 4-hour wait, so everyone retired to the local pub, the Globe. (A few weeks later the steam crane driver was killed at Rhiwderin, near Newport, while driving the same crane.)

On another occasion we also had one or two wagonloads of pit props off at Talywain. Our men tried to shake these off the wagon for use as firewood! So I've been to Talywain Sidings on at least four occasions with derailments!

My biggest job was when either No 8493 or No 8495 dropped a gudgeon pin at Hafodrynys while working a freight train on the Vale of Neath. I went out there to take a connecting rod off it on the flat section of track where it had been brought to a stand, and brought it back with a '28xx'. Charlie Evans, who had a red nose, helped me with that job. I never touched this engine when it came back to Ponty. The engine was dismantled at Pontypool Road, knowing that the crosshead and piston would have to go to Swindon to have a new gudgeon pin made; it had ripped the side out of the

valve guide box, so this was taken off. When it was being put back together, the motion plate was found to be bent, as a replacement valve guide box did not line up with the steam chest. Les Norkett said, 'Take the front wheels out under the hoist' – Clive Morgan did that job. So they took out the leading wheels, all the slide bars, knocked out the fitted bolts of the motion plate, and took it up the station to go to Caerphilly to be straightened out, then brought back to Ponty shed to be refitted. This was a repair that lasted a while as more repairs were required than initially thought.

Nos 8493 and 8495 were based at Pontypool Road in the early 1960s. They were not well-built locos and required a lot of maintenance. Both of them fell to bits. No 8461 was also there at one time.

Another '84xx' incident is recalled. One night, I was at the side of the railway at Llanvihangel bank, sitting in my car with a girl. An '84xx' went past, acting as the Abergavenny banker, and sounding rough. Sometime later it was booked for a valve repair, but when the cylinder cover was removed it was found that the no piston was present, as it had failed. It was running on one cylinder! This was after I returned from the RAF, in 1959 or 1960.

One Saturday afternoon, a '28xx' travelling light engine by Panteg & Coedygric signal box became derailed. Les Norkett was away, and Jock Wark was in charge. It was driven back on; I can't remember which way it was travelling.

During the 'big freeze' of 1963 I was living in Abergavenny and, unlike these days, we had no central heating or phones in the bedroom. Coal fires were the norm, and the lucky ones had just one phone in the hallway. On Monday 7 January, fast asleep and tucked in bed, at about 2.00am I woke to hear the phone ringing. I struggled downstairs in the cold, wondering what was wrong. Would it be a problem at Ponty? Yes, as anticipated, it was the foreman from the shed on the phone: 'The 1.30am Saltney's off the road in the North sidings. Can you come as soon as possible please?' Saltney was the yard outside Chester, and Ponty had workings there right to the end.

I got dressed, managed to start the car, and struggled through the snow to Ponty, arriving at about 3.00am. We had the Stanier 8F back on the road in about 30 minutes – it had ridden up over the snow and there was no damage – then got back home by 4.30am, minus my best 2-foot rule, which foreman Les Norkett had borrowed and left on the front buffer beam of the Class 8! Oh well, at least I should get an extra 7s 6d call-out allowance!

There was no time to go back to bed, as I was back out again in time to be on duty for my day shift at 7.00am, picking up my mate on the way. As we booked on we were greeted with, 'Don't bother to start work – get the breakdown vans and we're off to Crumlin Junction. A snow clearing train is off the road. There's an engine waiting.'

Apparently the train of two brake vans and three opens wagons, manned by one of our crews but with Army men to dig the snow, had parked by Glyn Tunnel, Hafodrynys, and the loco, No 5218, had left the train to go to Crumlin Junction for water. The brakes on the train had not held, and the wagons had followed and crashed into the front of No 5218, badly injuring someone fast asleep in one of the vans. No 5218 suffered smashed buffers and one pair of wheels off; it was at the Hafodrynys end of the viaduct by the water column, near which there was a siding coming down by the signal box.

We set off in the vans, hauled by one of Ponty's panniers. With a backlog of freights waiting to pass, we 'dug ourselves in' at a siding at Crumlin to allow four of them to pass, then went back out onto the main to set about re-railing No 5218. We then loaded the smashed buffers into the vans, ran round the vans and buffered up to the rear of No 5218 before propelling it back to Pontypool Road at about 2.30pm – it was put on the front of the breakdown train to save running back as light engine. We were stopped outside the Station South box at Pontypool

Road, where there were two routes onto the shed – we found that we and the signalman had different views on which route to take! Charlie Hewlett had a row with him in what in polite circles would be described as a 'frank and full exchange of views'. Charlie wanted the vans to drop down the back of the coal stage and the '52xx' to go onto the coal stage, but the signalman wanted them to go on through the East Junction, and he won the argument. We eventually proceeded through East Junction, stopping at the crossing at the East box, at the side of the shed, for us to leave, as the foreman had told us to get ready to book off and go home.

But back in the cabin there was a call, '5218 is off again!' The pony wheels were on a tight curve, caused by the bent front frames. Back out we went, and it was re-railed in half an hour. There was an extra 4s 8d for that! At least we could now go home, getting back about 5.30pm. No 5218 remained on the Tap Road at Pontypool Road for a few weeks, then went to Caerphilly Works for repair.

No one worked on Christmas Day in the early 1960s, and the kitchen in the breakdown coach froze up; it was away for months at Swindon. An old Great Western travelling van – with square wheels! – from Duffryn Yard replaced it for six or seven months until the coach returned from Swindon.

Hereford shed failed to operate as a working outfit in 1963 due to the snow, and shed staff were off sick. A few days were spent bring half a dozen engines at a time from Hereford to Ponty, to have their fires thrown out, recoaled and repairs undertaken before going back into service.

There was a catch point at the bottom of the line from the New Sidings down to Panteg Junction, and a 'Hall' went through it one day. I was on shift work and never saw it.

A big derailment occurred at Llantarnam Junction, and they had to burn the wagons to clear the wreckage.

Loco rides

My first ride on an engine was at Ilminster to Ashbeecham in Somerset on a '45xx'. I rode on a '72xx' to Llanvihangel with Driver Albert Wyatt after returning from the RAF; I was at the station and was asked to ride with him to Llanvihangel to demonstrate the loco's inefficiency. On the return journey he had great pleasure in closing the regulator coming to a standstill on a 1 in 80 gradient. I had numerous rides on railcar No W30 back and forth on the Monmouth line in the winter when the heater was broke down.

One day I went to Newport to a friend's house for dinner, and upon returning to work found that my mate had got the tools ready to change the gauge glass on the water gauge of a 'Britannia'. It was changed between the shed and the station. We rode up on the loco, and got off when it had backed onto the train. We then went in the refreshment room for a rum and blackcurrant, and walked back to the shed. This engine was a replacement for the rostered LMS engine, but there were no LMS gauge glasses stored at the shed.

I went from Pontypool to Hereford on a Brush Type 4 diesel (later Class 47) to sort out a fuel leak, and back on another on a parcels train to Pontypool to book off. When at Hereford sorting this out, I met the Hereford foreman who offered me a job in a fortnight. I was sent to Hereford loco depot on the last week of work there, travelling by DMU back to Abergavenny.

Engine working over Crumlin Viaduct

Normal working

The speed limit of 8mph had not to be exceeded.

The following engines in the 'Red' classification were permitted to work over the viaduct: '68xx', '56xx', '15xx' and '94xx'. All other 'Red' engines were prohibited, except in cases of emergency (see below).

The following engines in the 'Blue' classification were permitted to work over the viaduct: BR Standard 9F 2-10-0s (except Nos 92163 to 92167 inclusive).

For double heading, not more than two 'Yellow' or 'Uncoloured' engines could be coupled. Tender engines when assisted had to work chimney leading, and tank engines were not allowed to be coupled to the chimney end of tender engines. 'Blue' and permitted 'Red' engines could not be coupled to any other engines.

Emergency working

In cases of emergency, all other 'Red' engines except BR Standard 'Britannia' 4-6-2s and D10xx, D6xx and D8xx diesel-hydraulics, were permitted to work over the viaduct at a speed not exceeding 5mph, but they must not be coupled to any other engine.

Drivers

I knew Phil Williams – 'Full Load Phil' – when I was a fitter. He used to say, 'Come and have a look at the brake, I've got a full load.' I have been taken out into the yard and seen him take off with about two wagons. Mr Jackson, one of the foremen, said, 'Phil booked a brake didn't he? Come and have a look at this.' But he could have picked up more going across to the Yard.

Ted Preece, known as 'Presto', was one of the younger drivers and used to do the Saltney run and booked the brake every night until the Friday, but you would never see him on a Friday – he would be off as quick as he could to get back to watch the rugby. The engine would usually be a '28xx'.

Ted Hounslow recalled working double-home to Newton Abbot using 'Aberdares' ('26xxs'). They would go down on an 'Aberdare' and stop at his mate's mother's house overnight before working a train back. Ted's mate was Ernie Milverton, who was later made a driver, but was taken off the footplate in the early 1950s as he was always full of cider. Ernie would fill up the axle boxes, but fitter Rollei Jones reckoned he used to just tip the oil in the pit. He would sit by the fire by the shed lift the worse for drink.

Arthur Garrett requested that the leading sanders with attended to for going through Ledbury Tunnel; both his sons were fitters. Fitters on nights would moan about Driver Oliver Payne, and Fred Reason was a Salvation Army man (he played the big drum) and a driver on the branch passenger link. I recall Driver Edgar Charles moaning one day that when handing over his engine to the next driver he had left his coat in the locker on the tender! He was working long-distance jobs when I knew him.

A driver nicknamed 'Popeye' once worked a train right through one of the sand drags and out the other end. He was taken off the footplate. Fireman Henry Williams used to drive back from Ebbw Vale because 'Popeye' was sozzled.

One day in the early 1950s Driver Arthur Hathaway backed on to the TPO train heavily, putting some people in hospital. A coach from this train was put into the wagon repair shed at Ponty for repairs. Allan Foster was the fireman. The next day I was working with the people on the railcar, and when we walked back into the carriage shed to store it the mail train coach was in there. I bet it cost the railway some money for every minute it was late, as it was a guaranteed train. They didn't have the proper coach to use and half the Post Office staff were in hospital!

Harold Good's son was one of first diesel drivers. Ted Kilby was a steam loco man in the top link, then went onto diesels. Melvyn Shorthouse was a top fireman with Ted; he was steam engine mad, but went to Cardiff as a diesel driver. One day Ted and Melvin were working the 7.00pm Bristol with a 'Hall' when, going towards the Severn Tunnel, a manhole dropped out of the bottom of the tender. Ted didn't know the road to Severn Tunnel engine shed and wouldn't move the engine. Melvyn was a passed fireman and knew the road, so he drove the engine on shed.

A typical day

You went to work and returned home in your ordinary clothes. When I first started you took your overalls home and took them to the dry cleaners. When the first group of Abergavenny Brecon Road men came to Pontypool in about 1953, they had been running an overall scheme there, which they brought with them and ran it at Ponty for some time until someone stole the money and put them on the black list. You had three sets of overalls kept in a cupboard with drawers; one pair was away being cleaned, one was being worn, and there was a clean pair in case you needed it.

You got into a state working on the engines and there were no real washing facilities. The engines were mostly dirty, and sometimes you could get one cleaned if you had a big job on it. Les Norkett would talk to the foreman cleaner to allocate a cleaner and maybe get some of the muck off it. Most of the cleaning of the inside was done with fitters' overalls!

Valves and pistons were my typical job. I would change the valve rings and piston rings, which would take five days. If it was a 'Grange' you might have side rod bushes or big end bushes as well, but it was usually the crossheads that needed work. This was all part of the mileage exam.

The first valve and piston exam was at 24,000 miles, the next at 48,000 miles. Long-distance freight engines did 24,000 miles quite soon. Mileage was all calculated in the office.

One of the few faults on Western engines was on the outside-cylinder engines, where the valve rings wore out more quickly than other regions' engines; this was more expensive in terms of replacing valves and reboring valve bores in cylinders.

By the time I was a fitter I had other interests besides engine numbers, but I was lucky – I did '68xxs', 'Halls', the odd '41xx', '72xx' and occasionally a '56xx'. I dodged the panniers – they were difficult to work on and would take a week. A pannier would have the valve cover removed the same day, to see if it wanted new valves. I was lucky and didn't do many '56xxs', as they had a very heavy big end, and 18-inch pistons. They were one of the few Western engines to have large port openings at the top of the cylinder, requiring a piece of tin to stop the piston rings going up into the port. They had 8-inch valves – it was joked that the step at the front of the smokebox was there to rest your chin on when pulling the valves out! The crossheads on a '66xx' were enormous, between 1 and 1½cwt.

When undertaking a valve and piston exam, you took the valves out first, then the pistons. The valves were taken out on the first day by breakfast, then after breakfast I used a micrometer to measure the valve bores. The cylinder covers were then taken off and the pistons removed, and the piston bores measured with a micrometer. You would give these measurements to Les Norkett to order new valve and piston rings – he didn't trust the man in the stores! They were ordered from Newport Ebbw Junction; if they didn't have any, they were ordered from Swindon. The new piston rings were pre-cut, and peened over on the inside to make them springy.

If you were doing both valves and pistons, the replacement rings would arrive on the Tuesday afternoon by train to Ponty station. The fitter's mate would walk to the station and pick them up, aided by an apprentice. If you were an apprentice this was regarded as a skive; if you were lucky you would carry the piston rings, and your mate would carry the valve rings, as they were a lot heavier. If you were really lucky, there would be an engine going back to shed and you could put the parts on the engine at the station and ride back. Valve rings were a standard size, in 1/64-inch sizes. On '28xxs' the valves needed re-boring after 48,000 miles. Pistons went from factory to factory.

The motion would be taken down during the 36,000-mile exam, requiring eccentric straps to be repaired, as per MP11, as with all the mileage exams.

To undertake valve and piston exams the engine had to be in the right position. All sorts of things had to be in the right position to come off, such as the gudgeon pin locking bolts. That's why a rolling road would have been ideal! If you were on a straight road, you'd have to move to two or three engines. You'd have your engine at one end of the road, and sometimes the engine moving you would be outside the shed. With all the slack between the engine moving you and the engine you were working on, you'd shout before the engine started to move – it was guesswork sometimes.

For interest, I shall describe the Valve and Piston Exam for a '45xx' ('bigger engine' refers to 30-inch-stroke larger engines).

The piston valve was removed first. You took the nut off the taper pin in the valve crosshead and hit the taper pin with a lead hammer to remove it. The valve link hung down, supported by the pin in the rocker arm. The valve spindle crosshead was rotated, the split pin at the end of the cotter removed, and the cotter knocked out. The valve rod crosshead was held onto the valve spindle on a taper. Inside the valve crosshead was a hole, into which you placed a button, and a couple of pieces of plate; you then put a wedge through the middle and pushed the valve spindle out. You then removed the front cover, and grabbed and pulled the valve spindle; the front valve head was pulled clear of the front valve chest bush. You placed a spanner in the front exhaust chamber to support the valve spindle between the front and back valve heads. As you pulled the valve spindle forward, the back valve head would slide through the back valve chest bush. Between the back and front valve chest bushes was the steam chest, into which the back valve head could drop. As the valve spindle was resting on the spanner, this kept the back valve head in alignment with the front valve chest bush. Once it had entered the front valve chest bush, you removed the spanner from the front exhaust chamber and pulled the valve spindle clear of the cylinder, placing it on the floor. The valve bore was then measured using the micrometer. This process was repeated for the other cylinder.

The piston was removed next. On the

outside of the crosshead was the gudgeon pin locking bolt, on the end of which was a hexagon nut with a split pin through it. You took the split pin out, and took the nut off. To get the gudgeon pin out, the wheels had to be in the correct position for the gudgeon pin to clear the spokes when the pin was knocked out. On '45xxs', there was a nut and a spring washer on the back of the gudgeon pin, which was absent on the 'bigger engines'. You positioned a starting gear into the crosshead to pull the tapered pin out of the crosshead. You could now move the crosshead free of the connecting rod.

The front cover would be removed next, using a starting gear, but I used the piston to do this, as follows. You took the nuts off the front cover, unpacked the piston gland, and barred the crosshead forward (using a 4- or 5-foot-long bar against one of the spokes of the wheel) to push the front cover off; the back face of the piston would just overhang the end of the cylinder studs at the front of the cylinder. Piston rings would need to be changed and piston grooves cleaned.

You then disconnected the crosshead from the piston rod. You knocked out the crosshead cotter; on a '45xx' the starting gear at Ponty never fitted properly, so you got into the pit with a bar and a sledge to hit the cotter out from underneath the engine. The 'big engines' had a starting gear to pull the cotter out. After the cotter was out, another starting gear went into the gudgeon pin hole of the crosshead and a wedge was used to start the piston rod out of the taper in the crosshead. The crosshead would then be removed, and the bottom slipper remetalled and machined as described elsewhere in my notes.

The piston rod would remain in the rear cover to support the piston. The piston would then overhang the studs just enough to change the rings. The back ring groove in the piston was over the end of the studs, so you could get the piston rings off.

On a '28xx' the two rings would drop out together eight times out of ten, as these engines had smaller wheels and the pistons moved back and forth far more; and the piston groove would be full of carbon.

After taking the rings out, we'd push the piston back into the bore, and insert big feeler gauges between the top of the piston and bore to check the gap. There were limits of fit between the piston and the cylinder. Occasionally, if the clearance was too big, we used to change the piston. If that was the case, the piston would then be pushed out of the front of the cylinder and lowered into the pit, using a block and chain attached to the handrail of the smokebox. We'd send it to Swindon and, after a while, the piston rod would come back with a new piston head.

Once the piston was removed from the bore, we would measure the cylinder bore using a micrometer so that the new rings could be ordered. This process was repeated for the other cylinder.

To clean the grooves, two pieces of pipe were placed over the ends of two studs near the bottom of the cylinder cover, and the piston eased forward to sit on these pipes. The piston was then rotated to allow the grooves to be cleaned. On '28xxs' the lubrication wasn't brilliant, and the grooves would be full of carbon, which you had to chip out before you put the ring back in. I have seen a '28xx' piston put in a lathe, the piston ring dowels removed, and the groove cleaned by machining; that was unique among the dozens of pistons I cleaned. On '68xxs' the rings would easily come off the piston – they would spring out – and you could virtually put the same rings back in.

New rings were gapped as follows. The piston was put in the cylinder by about 6 inches, and the piston ring put in the cylinder bore. It would overlap, so you drew a line down with a pencil indicating a complete circumference, then added five-eighths or half an inch, as it was a half-inch screw, add an eighth of an inch for expansion, cut the ring with a chisel and fit it to the piston. You cleaned the piston groove next, and made sure that the new ring would go in backwards. You tried the ring in backwards and rolled it around the groove before fitting, making sure the ring fitted below the surface of the piston, around its circumference, otherwise you couldn't get it back in. It had to be inserted so that it stayed beneath the surface of the groove in the piston when finally fitted. There was no need to compress the ring to go into the cylinder, as the end of the cylinder bore had a taper so the ring self-compressed when the piston was pushed into the cylinder.

There were two half-inch brass screws in each piston ring groove, fitted radially at the bottom of the piston, to stop the ring rotating. Occasionally one fell out and you would put a new one in. We didn't like '45xxs', they were small and you had to undertake a lot more moves to get parts off, compared with the 'bigger engines'.

For the 48,000-miles exam on the older low-numbered '28xx' the whole valve would have to go away because the spindles would be badly worn. The '38xxs' and No 2884 onwards had sleeves fitted to the valves, which lasted the engine right out. There were special boxes to carry the valve in, and they were trundled up to Pontypool Road station. Fitters' mates would take them down to Newport, and put them on a train that carried Enparts – station staff wouldn't handle loco parts.

The Enparts train was a special train that ran out of Swindon carrying just loco parts. If Les Norkett wanted to get the parts back fairly quick he would arrange for them to be carried to Swindon on the Enparts train, which had special vans with 'Enpart' marked on them. There might have been other goods on it, like a parcel train. The South Wales one went down from Swindon, stopping at Severn Tunnel, Newport, Cardiff, and all the sheds down to Carmarthen. It would drop parts off and pick parts up. It was a regular train, possibly daily – I'm not sure.

Abergavenny had a van that came from Crewe weekly on a double-home job on a Wednesday morning, and went back on the 9.10am train that took the ammonia tanks to Crewe. It was a long-wheelbase four-wheel van, a bit like a GWR 'Fruit D' van, was vacuum-fitted, and went next to the engine.

Swindon also had special open wagons for wheels, which were attached to the back of passenger trains. There was a 'library' of wooden boards at Swindon, one of which had 'Pontypool Road' on one side and 'Swindon' on the other; you could slip it out and turn it around. They'd go back with a stopping passenger.

'Austerity' 2-8-0s were at Ponty long enough to have the valves and the piston rings done. These went for so long, but we didn't have the technique of extracting the piston valves. When Abergavenny Brecon Road shut, the chargehand was transferred to Ponty (he wasn't a foreman, as they didn't have enough engines), and I did valves and pistons on an 'Austerity' 2-8-0 with him.

I never did the valves and pistons on ex-LMS 8Fs, as they would go 36,000 miles before a valve exam, whereas a '28xx' would only do 12,000 miles. You could see why BR went for LMS-type engines. And the BR Standards were similar. '73xxs' came in from Shrewsbury, some with Caprotti valve gear. One Shrewsbury engine was in Ponty shed for months, waiting for firebars; it was stored in the shed on the end of No 5 road. Eventually its tender was derailed on the flat ground between the two sheds, as it had been bumped by other engines. The engine required tiny bars for the rocking grate,

Ex-LMS 'Royal Scot' Class 4-6-0 No 46129 *The Scottish Horse* is seen on No 4 road at the south end of the shed on 18 August 1962.
M. Dart, *Transport Treasury*

which Ponty didn't have in stock.

I did a spring on a '73xxx' with Haydn Evans. I can't recall seeing a '75xxx' on shed, although occasionally the Neath '80xxx' tank would come on shed.

The 9Fs came on shed occasionally, and had to through the shed – you couldn't turn them on the turntable, so they had to be turned on the triangle; it was awkward getting paths on and off, due to other traffic using the yards and the triangle. They came to Ponty brand new and lasted six months before being sent to Severn Tunnel Junction. I missed the Ponty ones. I was in the RAF in Malaya on National Service when they were being transferred away. (I was still entitled to the British Railways magazine, issued to employees, and my mother would send them to Malaya.)

There was a special trolley for taking the grease trap out of the exhaust steam injector of a 9F. They were never there long enough to get the piston valves out. I would struggle getting the piston valves down out of a 'Hall'.

The odd 'Britannia' came on shed from Longsight in Manchester for coal, but the number of failures on this daily train was remarkably low.

An ex-LMS 'Jubilee' passed through Ponty shed when its tender derailed, having run a hot box. The axle box was repaired using the shed lift to raise the tender. A 'Royal Scot' once ran a hot box, but was sent to Hereford for repair. The lift at Hereford was never the same after!

The '69xx' 'Modified Halls' were mostly Oxford engines in BR days. The number plate once fell off one of them, and landed up on the floor by the first signal box north of Hereford; it was kept in the signal box coal bunker for a long time, and now Gordon Watts owns it. None of our engines lost name or number plates. We never took them off, but they started to be removed in 1964. We lost all of our named engines at Ponty that year, and they all went away with name and number plates on.

Talking of Oxford, there was a through train in the morning to Yarnton via Worcester – it worked right through, with a Ponty '28xx', 'Hall' or 'ROD', or occasionally an LMS 8F – the 'ROD' was used in earlier times. After the engine had worked to Yarnton it worked to a yard at the bottom side of Oxford station, then back into the shed. It wouldn't get into Oxford until 2 or 3 o'clock in the afternoon, depending what loops it had been in. Ponty men took it to Worcester, where Oxford men took it forward. Then at 3.30pm the following day there was a Pontypool train from Yarnton to bring the Ponty engine back home.

A similar train ran at night; we called it the 'Worcester', and it returned an Oxford engine to Oxford; Ponty men worked it as far as Worcester.

The only time we got London engines at Pontypool Road was when they turned up on the Yarnton turn. Sometimes it would be an Old Oak Common engine, a 'Hall', 'Modified Hall' or maybe a 'Grange'. They worked back on a Ponty train to Worcester, and another train from Worcester to Yarnton.

Shed fatalities and accidents

No fitters or shed staff were killed in the shed when I worked there. However, a fireman was killed on No 8 road when he was squashed between the wall and his engine. They were going off shed, and No 8 road was hellish close to the wall. It may have occurred when they were going out through the doors at the south end of the shed – the fireman was on the engine looking out.

The worst fitters' accident in my time was when Aubry Jones fell backwards out of a smokebox on the Through Road, where they shouldn't have been working; he was pulling superheaters out. Aubry would go at things like a bull at a gate. He fell right out of the smokebox, right down into the pit, and broke both his ankles. He also broke an arm when lifting the side rods of a 'Super D' out at Little Mill, before I started at Ponty; he was on nights with fitter Glyn Morris (who usually worked with Edgar Davis – if holidays were different, you might work with a different person for a few weeks).

There were lots of minor accidents. I don't know about the war or anything, although it was the sort of thing they would have talked about. No 6840 saw three people off, one of them out at Little Mill – I don't know where the other two were.

Scrap engines

When we scrapped engines we removed the connecting rods, but some went as they were; Hereford burned the valve rods off. Engines were stored on No 7 road, and some by the Stores on the little wall where the original breakdown train was kept.

Special tools

I was looking in the cupboard in the round part of the shed, next door to the examining fitters' cabin, when I found a ring spanner with two eyes on it. I asked Glyn Morris what it was for, and he told me it was used to take the nut off the front of the piston on a '26xx', known as an 'Aberdare', but they had all been withdrawn by then. The 'Aberdares' used a piston rod that was part of the crosshead, like on Southern locos. They were the only Great Western loco I know that you had to take the piston head off to get at the piston to change the piston rings. Single-ended knocking ring spanners would bounce due to wear in the spanner, and lose a lot of the shock of being hit, so you would put a pinch bar against the buffer beam, the other end against the end of the double-ended ring spanner to keep it tight on the nut, and give the end of the spanner a clout.

Final thoughts

The fitters, fitters' mates and carpenters were employees of the railway, and all the rest were railwaymen, whose conditions of employment were different from ours. We were treated as a necessary evil – we were considered to be the rabble! We were given very little information about failures and incidents – it was like the secret service. You only heard about engine faults or failures if you were involved in that incident.

Working on the railway was a way of life, backward compared to a lot of industries. When British Railways took over it changed a lot and improved, but not in the eyes of die-hard Great Western men. I was not a true Great Western man, or other company man, as all the railway companies had good and bad points.

2. Loco Fitter Terry Biggs

My father, Wesley Biggs, was from Radstock in Somerset. He started on the Great Western at Bristol, and was made a fireman at Pontypool Road. He had a chance to go back to Bristol, so did so, and was made a driver for Neyland. However, a Neyland man had gone to Aberbeeg, and wanted to go back to Neyland, so father transferred to Aberbeeg, thinking that it was nearer Radstock than Neyland, and he stayed there. That's where I was born, on 6 March 1940. Father fired over Crumlin Viaduct when it was still double-track, and he knew Les Norkett when he was foreman at Aberbeeg loco depot.

When I was a boy I can remember walking past the site of Aberbeeg Colliery (the name given on old postcards). It opened in 1861 and in its later years was part of Llanilleth Colliery. It closed in 1926, and was known locally as Bud's Colliery). It was later demolished, but the footings of old buildings could be seen. It was on the left-hand side of the railway line, just above Aberbeeg station on the line to Ebbw Vale. It had a pump down the shaft, to pump out old workings and protect Llanilleth Colliery and Crumlin Navigation Colliery from flooding; water was discharged into the river. A red-brick building on the right-hand side of the road, looking towards Cwm, was the pumping station. On the left-hand side of the road is the River Ebbw. [Author's note: it was later used to pump Marine Colliery, until that closed in 1989. This site is described in photographs[5]; there is a photo of the inside of the red-brick building showing a set of steps in the side of the shaft wall to walk onto the concrete cap between the walls of the shaft.]

If you continued along the road and went over the road bridge over the railway line to join the road to Cwm, on the left was Ivor Wright's pub, where there was later a petrol station. You turned left, and went some distance up the road, maybe 100 yards up from the pumping station, then turned left again, down a lane to access the other side of the valley; you went over a level crossing and across a wooden river bridge with two handrails and a ladder across; you then went past a farm and in front of you was a fenced-off mine shaft. Further on, up on the bank, were the remains of an engine house, on what we called the tip wood. The shaft was round, and fenced off, and we'd throw stones down it; someone nearly fell down there. They dug the bank out to fill the shaft, using a Fordson tractor with a small blade. Today the path leading from the road to the Cwm, down over the bank, would probably be at the south end of the reinforced concrete wall, recently installed to support the road to the Cwm, just north of the old petrol station on the right.

The River Ebbw is recalled. Trains of coal from Rose Heyworth Colliery and Six Bells Colliery would go to Aberbeeg, then to Marine Colliery for the coal to be washed. The river changed colour depending on what time of year it was. Normally it was black, from the discharge from Marine Colliery washery; when the miners were on their annual holiday in August the river changed to orange from the discharge from Ebbw Vale steelworks. On the odd occasion when neither Ebbw Steelworks nor Marine Colliery Washery was working, the river would be clear.

Coming from the Ivor Wright pub, there was a 3-foot-diameter pipe for water from the Aberbeeg Dingle further up the valley. It was piped into the river. Ryan's of Cardiff bulldozed a road across the river to collect washery water that contained coal dust. A drag line worked there 12 hours a day, producing a pile of coal the height of a two-storey building.

BR 9Fs working iron ore trains to Ebbw Vale are recalled. One day I looked out of my bedroom window, which was level with the track, to watch a 9F working an iron ore train; it had stopped, awaiting a banker to go on the back. All of a sudden there were about five lots of wheel slip, the wheels spinning around like Catherine wheels! My brother-in-law worked in Ebbw shed, and I asked him, 'What's all that about?' When starting, you would open the regulator, get the train moving and adjust the regulator. But there was a design fault on the regulator so that, if the boiler was full, water was carried over, rather than steam, so the regulator couldn't be closed – it would jam open. The wheels started to cut into the rails. At River Row, Aberbeeg, there were two railway bridges that crossed the road,

Friends reunited: fitter Harry Rawlins with ex-GWR 2-6-0 No 5322 at Didcot Railway Centre. *Harry Rawlins*

with a gap between them. One bridge was for the relief line for freight, the other was the passenger line. These bridges were reinforced with the damaged rails on which the 9F slipped. The banker was put on the train to act as a brake, in case the tender coupling on the front engine broke.

Coaches were always parked opposite the big water tank at Aberbeeg station and the junction signal box, and two engines would take this train from Aberbeeg to the 'Dump', ROF Glascoed. The Ebbw Vale engine came off shed first, to go on the front end of the train for carriage warming; it then took this portion to Ebbw Vale. The other loco went Brynmawr. Both trains returned to Aberbeeg later. The Ebbw Vale train came back down and the loco dropped down over the points. Then the Brynmawr train came down, the Ebbw Vale engine coupled on the front, and the train was pushed back on to the Ebbw Vale portion. It then travelled to Glascoed as a double-header.

I have some documents from the Great Western, including a letter when my father was made a fireman at Pontypool, a driver for Neyland, and rescinded to Aberbeeg. One card is signed by G. J. Churchward, telling him that he didn't have to go into the forces. I also retain my father's food box, with 'W. S. Biggs' on it.

My father once failed on a train, the Newport to Brynmawr train at Abertillery, with No 4593. It lost all the steam after leaving the station, having blown a hole about 2 inches in diameter in the top of the steam pipe. It went to Ebbw where a patch was welded on it. Some years later that engine was at Ponty, after an overhaul. I got in the smokebox and the patch was still there on the steam pipe.

I gave up train spotting after a week. I remember seeing 'Castle' No 5080 *Defiant* coming into Newport station on the 'Red Dragon'. It arrived in the old Platform 3 or

4. The sun was shining off the chimney, and it entered the station with a bit of steam on. It was my favourite engine as a spotter. That was the first time I went to London.

I started at Ponty in March 1956 and finished on 28 February 1961.

Apprenticeship

When I walked in Les Norkett, the loco foreman, said, 'Are you any relation to Wesley Biggs?' I said yes, and he asked me how he was.

I started at Ponty with an examining fitter to learn the various parts of a loco. I then transferred to valves and pistons.

I studied for the City & Guilds certificate in machine shop practice; it took three years of part-time study. I started the course in 1958 at the newly opened Pontypool College of Further Education. The final two years were spent at Alt-yr-yn Technical College in Newport. Mr Gunter was the lecturer, and had previously worked for Girling – you were OK if you were a Girling apprentice. He used to ask, 'How long is an engineer's flat file?' I said, 'Sixteen inches,' and everyone laughed, but I was serious. However, Girling's files were shorter! We were asked to write out how to make a set of callipers, then make them. Girling's apprentices went to the stores for a chitty, and withdrew a piece of thick steel 1 inch by one-sixteenth of an

Ex-GWR '45xx' Class 2-6-2T No 4593 takes water at the south end of the shed, on the point leading to Nos 5 and 6 Roads. *Phil Williams collection*

inch and 1 foot long. They marked it off, went to the shear to shear it, and made the nut and bolt. Then it was our turn. I said to my mate Dave, a fellow apprentice, 'Go up the coaling stage and get a shovel.' He said, 'What do you want that for?' I said, 'It's the only place we can get a piece of one-sixteenth steel plate.' We had to draw-file it and put it on the sandstone to polish it. Dave told the Girling apprentices that we had belt-driven machines to make parts to an accuracy of thousandths of an inch.

My first job was to work with examining fitter Charlie Acker. He was good, as he told you about the job. There were the X exams, daily exams, and 3-5 and 7-9 weekly exams. On different weeks you did a different exam. I worked with Charlie for a month.

The daily exam was undertaken on any passenger engine or vacuum-fitted freight engine. All other engines were examined weekly, although on half of ours this was never done.

The 3-5-week exam had to be done by the fifth week or the engine had to be stopped. It was governed by washouts, being the next exam after a boiler washout. Charlie Acker was the injector man.

During that period I went under *Hazeley Grange*, a loco that had killed a man between Abergavenny Junction and Pontypool. It later killed two other people at different times. Charlie Acker said to me: 'You don't want to go under there and see that.' I went under it at Ponty and there were bits of skin and blood – a mess. There was a lot of grease, and a pair of false teeth on the brake spreader beam. This engine worked the train down in the morning, and went back with the 1.42pm to Cardiff; this was a continuation of the Crewe to Cardiff.

Injectors came under the 7-9-week exam. You could have three engines on the same week, or you could go a week without examining any injectors. You generally did a couple a week. You took the injector apart and examined the cones, checking if the insert in the nozzle needed to be changed, as they would wear.

Ponty fitters

Once trained you did everything – examinations, fitting, machining. I had six months at Ebbw Junction while at Ponty.

There were three top fitters at Ponty: Bill Wark (whose mate was Alf Smith), Dave Fry (mate Edgar Davis) and Marcus Hunter (mate Harry Loveridge). Bill Wark was a good fitter; if you were prepared to listen, he was all right, but he could be abrupt.

The first loco I worked on was with Marcus Hunter; it was No 5516, on a valve and piston exam. On another occasion I was worked with Marcus and Harry Loveridge on a 'tanky' on one of the short roads in the shed. We had to refit a steam chest cover, into which we had fitted a new bush for the valve spindle. We had to rotate the cover, but it was a tight fit on the valve spindle. So we decided to rotate the cover by holding a bar against it and hitting the bar with a sledge. I was holding the bar and Harry was hitting the end, but he missed and caught me! Marcus had a go at Harry. Harry had his own way of doing things. If you mentioned a different way of doing things, or Bill Wark's way of doing things, Harry would go mad.

When we heard on the grapevine that Charlie Reed, the District Superintendent, was making a visit, out would come the whitewash to paint the edge of the turntable! On one such occasion Bob Garrett and I looked out through the broken window in the north-east corner of the round shed, near the coppersmith's forge, to watch a 'Castle' on the main line, hauling a banana train from Barry or Avonmouth Docks. It was struggling, and blowing steam from an inside piston gland. Bob said, 'Some poor bastard's got a job on there.' Then we felt a hand on our shoulders, and Les Norkett said, 'I've got news for you two boys,' and we were given the job!

The engine came on shed, and was yellow with grease inside the frames. We had a toss up to see who was going underneath, and who was going on top. I won, so was on top with Bob underneath. We were busy trying to sort things out when Bill Lewis came along, with his posh voice. Bob had got the packing out and I asked him if he wanted a rest; he said, 'No, let's get on with it.'

A little later, someone came up and said, 'Packing a piston gland are we?' Bob shouted up, 'You can **** off!' The next thing I knew Les Norkett came up and said, 'Who's the prize bastard who told Reed to **** off?' He later saw the funny side. Everything was hot and Bob's arm was burned.

There was a derailment at Blaenavon Low Level in 1958 or 1959, and I worked on it with Les Norkett. A two-coach 'B set' had gone to Blaenavon, the engine had uncoupled and run round, then pushed the train over the level crossing at the top of the station. Coming back down through the points the engine and bogie of the first coach stayed on, but the last bogie of the first coach and the rest of the train was across the track! I used a claw chain to tie the bogies up. The bogie on the first coach was jacked up and traversed across on to the track, and the second coach was re-railed.

Les bought an Austin A40 car and was learning to drive. This was during rationing, and you had fuel coupons. At that time they would allow learner drivers to drive, and he drove me to Blaenavon to examine an engine where the NCB had welded up the tyre flange to avoid fitting new tyres. You couldn't see where it was welded.

Les went around with 'Scratchy' (Glyn Morris), who built Les a new part for his exhaust, using a piece of copper pipe from the coppersmiths. It was polished too!

I went with 'Scratchy' to examine an engine at Hafodrynys Colliery and to put an inspection plate on it. We got to Hafodrynys, and hitched a ride on a '66xx' coming down from Hafodrynys New Mine with 40 wagons of coal. Coming down, the driver eased on the brake and 'Scratchy', who was on the bottom step, jumped off. I was on the top step, looking for somewhere safe to jump off; by the time I found somewhere 'Scratchy' was further up the track! We had to examine the engine in the tin loco shed at the Old Furnace, but when we got there it was locked up, so we went home.

I went to Tirpentwys once with Scratchy, to sort out a runaway. We spent three parts of the day emptying wagons before we could lift them back on the track.

Dave Fry was a past master at using a sledge. He would spit on his hands before picking one up. One day we were working outside on a '68xx' and had to remove the gudgeon pin. Dave said, 'We'll have a Mundy on this,' a Mundy being a 28lb hammer. I was on the bar, which I held against the pin. Dave picked up the sledge, and as he swung it, it would slide through his hands until he hit the pin. He was an expert.

He had a '66xx' in the shed once to get the valves out. To put them back in took two or three people. Dave Fry would check tyre flange depths using his fingers; he could tell what it was by feel. I used the tyre gauge and Dave would be spot on.

On another occasion a 'Castle' came on shed, having failed between Hereford and Abergavenny, or between Ponty and Newport. The inside cylinder cover was hanging on by two studs, the others having broken off. The old studs were removed and renewed. The worst studs to get at were the two by the dished part of the frame. These were replaced by Dave Fry. The stay studs were those that went through the ports. The ends were threaded with a plain middle piece. You were supposed to remove these by drilling them out at each end, but Swindon would unofficially burn the middle piece out. Bob Garrett and I replaced the plate work at the front of the loco, then it went back to Ebbw on 26 February 1959. On Saturday 28th, Bob and I caught a train to Shrewsbury for the Wales v Scotland match, and the engine hauling the train was the 'Castle' we had just repaired. The rugby match was the first Welsh cap for Cliff Ashton from Newport.

Rollei Price was the first person to show me how to use the lathe. He got a micrometer, and I was using the 6-inch lathe. He measured the work and told me the measurement, then asked me to measure the work in the chuck. He was spot on every time. He machined gun barrels in Cardiff ROF during the war.

One day a fitter from Abergavenny had to fit repaired side rod bushes off a '68xx'

'Grange' loco that Rollei had machined. They were fitted to the side rods and offered up to the engine, but wouldn't fit. He got a pair of callipers, and they wouldn't fit onto the crankpins, having been squeezed oval in the vice. They had to be put in the lathe and a skim taken out.

Bevan Price, Rollei's brother, was a machinist at Panteg Steelworks, and Rollei had a daughter who greatly resembled Elizabeth Taylor.

I was working with Rollei Price one day taking down the eccentric straps on a loco by the stationary boiler. The pit was shallow, and Rollei got a few straps down, hitting out the strap bolts. All of a sudden he hit his thumb with the hammer just as Marian, the shed's only woman employee, was walking past. Later we got out of the pit for a cup of tea, and there was Les Norkett looking over his glasses, beckoning me and Rollei into his office. 'Rollei, you've been using your prize language again. Apologise to Marian.' She stuck her head around the corner and Rollei said, 'I'm sorry, I wouldn't have done it if I'd known you were there,' then he turned to me and said, 'She shouldn't have ****** been there.'

One day a 'Hall' Class with an eight-wheel tender came on shed requiring new tender brake blocks. Sam Gillett was given the job and he obtained eight brake blocks from the stores, when only six were required! The tender was only braked on six of the eight wheels.

Sam had a drum of smoke-stack black paint with a hole in the top. It was like treacle. Sam had the bright idea of sticking it on the fire to thin it down. He was stirring it up through the hole, then took the stick out and poked the fire. He then put the stick back in the tin. The paint come out of the top like a volcano!

Sam was keen on lubricators. He would run paraffin through the lubricator, run it all in a bucket and throw it in the smokebox. I told him to throw the paraffin into the tender, on the coal. Jack Davis later worked with Sam, who would throw paraffin in the firebox. He worked the night shift.

When the shed was being rewired around the work benches, Sam was running down some nuts and bolts at the work bench and asked the electrician if he could have some wire for a lead light in his garage. 'How much do you want then?' 'About 20 yards will do.' It was chopped off, rolled up and put it in the bottom of my cupboard. The bloke went off, then came back and asked about the brand-new roll of electric cable that had gone missing. I opened Sam's cupboard and found the rest of the roll. Sam had put it there safe.

I remember pannier No 4600 from the mileage exams – no one ever did any work on it and you could see 'GWR' through the fading paintwork. I was in the round shed with Sam Gillett fitting a crosshead on the loco. A bar was placed over the top of the

Fitter Rollei Price (right) with Arthur Rolls (fitter's mate), next to ex-GWR 'Castle' Class *Blenheim*.
Malcolm Hewlett, Harry Rawlins collection

leading splasher, against the cotter pin, with the end resting against the curved part of the tank. We used to lie on the footplate to hold a shaped bar against the cotter, and someone would hit the bar with a sledge. Sam was standing on a trestle we used for pulling off side rods, and was swinging a 14lb hammer. He wouldn't stop – I shouted, 'Stop, Sam!' Holding the bar your hand would go. The first two swings were all right, then the bar moved. I used to wear a cap when working, and Sam missed the bar, hit the round part of the tank and caught my cap, which landed in the pit!

Ken Cleavy ('Kiddo') was the apprentice coppersmith and worked alongside Bob Garrett as an apprentice. He was always hanging out of the missing window in the loco shed. By our bench was a tin of detonators, and when 'Kiddo' was cooking Bob rolled a pair of wheels over a detonator, and all the muck off the roof came down over where he was cooking.

Me and Bob Garrett had cupboards on the east wall of the shed, by the coppersmith. My bench had belonged to Dave Fry. On the floor against the wall was a 6-inch gas main from the days when the shed was gas-lit. The bench was cut to cover the pipe, but a gap existed. On nights Dave Fry came across and said, 'Give the bench a good bang – I won't tell you why,' and walked away. One night, about 12.00am, Bob and I went to the benches and Bob bent down to unlock his cupboard, ready to start. He opened the door and a big rat jumped out over his shoulder! Due to the gap, rats could run from one cupboard to the other. 'Scratchy' come in one morning to open his cupboard and put on his overalls. He left his keys, and went to find Les Norkett for a job. Someone had put a dead pigeon on his tool box in his cupboard. He went berserk when he opened his cupboard, as he didn't like feathers! I later years I had Ted Jenkins's cupboard (he was ex-Abergavenny and had spent the war years at Swansea Victoria shed, then became an Examining Fitter).

The 'Silver Fox' – Harry Glassy, who later went to Crewe – won the over-50s Mr Wales title one year. He worked on the coal stage in a shirt and daps. Ponty was a cold place in the winter.

Examination cards were on the wall of the Examining Fitter's office, on the east side of the shed, and we'd sign them off when jobs were completed. There were the X Exams, 3-5 and 7-9 week exams. One day 'Scratchy' put a tin of beans on the cooker in the Examining Fitter's office. It exploded and impregnated the X Examination cards on the east wall of the shed with beans!

Shed work

I worked on '72xx' levelling pipes, which were prone to leak. It was a two-day job. Four-inch rubber pipes with two ends were supplied by Swindon, and these would be fitted in the round shed, or outside on the No 7 and No 8 roads. The back end of these engines would flex when going around points, and one engine had a cracked frame.

Aberbeeg didn't have an air compressor to rivet over firebox stays – they had to rivet them over by hand – so once 'Prairie' No 4593 was swopped with No 5516 so it could be repaired at Ponty.

One weekend a pannier ran through a stop block at Branches Fork, and broke the back axle. The engine came back to Ponty with the rear axle supported on a trolley. It was stored on the Lift Road, with the side rods and other parts stored outside in a wagon. The leading and driving axles were OK, but the rear axle had sheared at the back of the wheel. I was involved in lifting it on the Lift Road, and replacing the trolley with packing under the rear buffer beam. The rear set of coupling rods had buckled, but the front pair were OK. A check was made on the horns on the rear axle, and there was a concern that the crank pins on the remaining four wheels could be out of square.

Gerry Smith, the foreman from Ebbw Junction, had a crankpin alignment apparatus, and brought it to Ponty. It was a tri-square with a vee bottom. It would line itself on the crankpin and had radial feelers.

You could adjust each feeler, and check the measurements at four points to ensure that the crank pin was square to the wheel.

Some BR 9Fs came new to Ponty, and were there for six months until reallocated elsewhere. I changed the brake blocks on them. They would run through the shed, or on to the Tap Road, and be turned on the triangle, via the West box, Loop Junction and the Station South Junction.

I once changed the tender brake blocks on 'Britannia' *Polar Star*. This engine had to be re-railed after it came off the track at Milton, near Didcot. It was on its side in a field. They welded two rails to its wheels and strapped it. They then attached rails bent into a 'U' shape, and rolled the loco upright using sleepers. The latter were then removed and a track built, and the loco was removed to Swindon. An apprentice at Swindon made a suggestion for building a re-railing apparatus and was given £5. Swindon then spent thousands buying a German-built re-railer modified from the Swindon idea! However, it wouldn't work on diesels, as the engine was unsupported and the mountings would break.

The worst jobs were working in smokeboxes, bedding in steam pipes.

One engine had a leaking smokebox lance cock. The lip on the top was cracked off, and Driver John Drayton was getting his hands wet. He said, 'If we drilled a hole by there, instead of those drips it would go straight through there.'

I remember adjusting the brakes for Driver Arthur Garrett, who was on a job going through Ledbury Tunnel. 'I ain't going to be stuck in there,' he said.

'43xx' No 5322 wouldn't steam, and when viewed from the front the chimney wasn't vertical; it was as if

the smokebox wasn't aligned correctly. After it had been running, if you went in to the smokebox one side was scoured clean by the exhaust, with all the ashes piled up on the opposite side.

A shed fire alarm test is recalled. Lou Davis was in charge of the fire brigade team. It was decided to assume that the shed stores, of all places, were on fire (there was a 40,300-gallon tank[6] above it). In the north-west corner, where the motor drove the machines, was a manhole in the floor to a stop valve. The water pipes went all around the shed, for boiler washing. The idea was to get maximum pressure on one line. There was a piece of paper, designating certain people to shut and open certain water valves. Hoses were run out, but when the order was given there was no pressure, only a spider crawling out of the end of the hose! Charlie Acker knew the location of water valves around the shed.

'68xx' No 6840 *Hazeley Grange*, fresh from Swindon, newly painted, was put on the Stores road, facing south for Newport, as a spare engine for a Royal Train. Someone decided to embellish it further, and used cleaning oil from the shed, then pink fluid from a barrel, which was applied using spray bottles to wash the cleaning oil off it afterwards. The pink spray took the paint off, leaving the engine pink on one side; it was turned to face north to hide the error, and was never used on the Royal Train!

Arthur Garrett of Pontypool Road (right) with diesel tutor Harry Waring (left) and H. Newman.

Superheater elements are recalled being removed. These were banged and bumped, but to get them out they had to be pulled off the front of the header. They could be tight to get out. A chain block was put around the superheater element block and the lamp bracket of a 3,500-gallon tender. The engine was then chocked, the handbrake applied and the chain block handle pulled. Malcolm Hewlett, working with a lad called Ben, was pulling a superheater out and connected the chain block to the handrail at the back of a low tender, one of the 3,500-gallon type. He pulled the chain block handle, only to pull the handrail out of the back of the tender!

Johnny Cross was as mad as a hatter, and would jump from tender to tender with bags of water; he was like a gazelle.

For a while Mr Watt was the shed master, and would scoff at the methods used at Ponty, saying we were behind the times, and this would upset Les Norkett. For instance, Mr Watts would expect an engine that had had its axle box remetalled to be put out on the main line immediately, whereas Ponty would put a tank engine with axle box repairs out into the Birkenhead Sidings to run it in a bit before being returned to traffic.

Accidents

A man once fell through the roof of the round shed. He was from Abergavenny, a member of the signal gang. Another man from Abergavenny lost a finger when the ring on his finger caught in a truck outside. Ossy Williams also lost a finger when working on a brake adjusting screw. There was a dovetail key in the keyway, and he was grinding the dovetail to make it square when the grinder took his finger off.

Turntable repair

I fell in the turntable pit one day, after returning from the Mason's pub the worse for wear! The turntable was repaired every five or seven years. The men repairing arrived with empty wagons – a wagon of sand, a box van with cement, an open wagon with chippings, and another empty one (for rubbish from the turntable). They used the handcrane and jacked up the turntable; the main bearing was changed as well as the segment castings around the wall of the pit. These castings had sockets for securing the locking pins when the table was rotated and set for an exit road, and the sockets would wear; when lowered, the locking pin at the coal stage end of the table didn't align with one of the sockets, so the locking pin edge was modified to make if fit.

When repairing the turntable, one night they broke into an underground spring, and there was a panic, but Charlie Acker knew about it – he was an old hand, with lots of knowledge.

Ebbw Junction, 1961

When I was at Ponty I had six months at Ebbw Junction working on diesel shunters before returning. Gerry Smith, the Ebbw Junction loco foreman said to me, 'Go back to Les Norkett –you can apply for Ebbw from your home depot.' I was 21 and wanted to get married. Les had found this out, and when I got back to Ponty he said, 'Oi, come here. Number one, you're not going to Ebbw. Number two, if you get married, you must be a fool.' I got married aged 21 in 1961.

Gerry Smith said to me, 'You'll probably come down here one day as a fitter, and will have to do it.' He was referring to using the German-built Detrack re-railing apparatus. He said, 'Go out with Allan Jones,' who was an apprentice. We re-railed the loco, and stopped with the re-railing gang if nothing was going on. The engine concerned, No 2848, was lifted behind the factory, where the diesel depot was later built. There was a group of sidings used for storage, all but one of which were later lifted. Chargehands Malcolm Collins and Gerry Stephens came and checked on progress. The loco was lifted using an attachment to the safety valve, and we left the equipment attached to the loco. No 2848 was selected for rerailing exercises as the result of an accident at the

Glebelands, where it had run through the end of the up loop at the Maindee triangle.

St Philip's Marsh shed in Bristol had equipment for lifting an 'ROD', using chain attachments. The loco was attached to a cradle and you would start to jack it up jacking against feet on semi-circular rings. You would then jack against the next foot on the ring.

One day a 9F left the tracks coming off the docks, having been routed on to the wrong line. Pill shed had been there with their little breakdown gang, but the 9F had spread the track. The loco had got to the other side of the railway bridge, and the job was now Ebbw's.

Allan Jones said to me, 'We've got to re-rail a 9F.' When we got there, the drawgear had been cut between the engine and tender, and the fire thrown out. The re-railing gear was put in the horizontal plane, the engine was picked up, and the gear was slid through. The loco was slid sideways on temporary track to the next track over. The traversing jack was hydraulically operated, using opposing jacks. Swindon had added their own bits to it.

3. Loco Fitter Bob Garrett

Eric White came over from Caerphilly Works to be a relief coppersmith. Harry Bounds was the carpenter and had a workshop under the arches of the coal stage. You might be having your hair cut in there and Les Norkett would walk in! Harry used to call it the taper, and singe your hair.

Ernie Stevens did the ATC batteries. He was a boxing trainer. He was afraid to do anything. He didn't like changing the unit in the cab, with the bell and the box, and had to have a fitter with him. Walter Toombes had photos of efficiency in the carpenter's shop. Rollei Price would apologise to Marian every other day – he'd be under the loco, and swearing.

I remember my father Arthur prepping three locos, and when I walked around the back of the tender Bert Hobbs said the jobs has been cancelled. It was the first time I heard my father swear.

I remember driver Phil Williams ('Full Load Phil'). I had already done the brake adjustments, but Phil would say, 'I'm going to Dowlais Top tonight and want the brakes adjusting'. I would go underneath and, as a joke, tap the brake rodding with a spanner – then Phil would be contented! As a fitter you knew what the job was, and the loco.

You went to the pub at lunchtime. One day, coming back after lunch, looking down from the viaduct towards the long shed, I saw Les Norkett, in his green sweater. I crept up the back of the long road of the long shed. I was working on a safety valve joint in the round shed, and got back up on the boiler. Les was waiting for me.

He said, 'Where have you been, then?'

I replied, 'Waiting for it to cool down a bit.'

'Well, come back in the morning 0150 it will be nice and cool then,' said Les.

Ex-GWR '53xx' No 5322 wouldn't steam. The idea was to move the chimney, and line the centre up with the blast pipe, but it wasn't successful. There is a photo of my father on the footplate at Abergavenny, with Lionel Brakespeare.

Chapter 4: Shed and yard

1. Driver Tom Davies

I worked at Pontypool Road from 1918 to 1964. I left school aged 13 to work as a dipper in the local tinplate works, then in a coal level and the newly sunk coal mine at Hafodrynys Colliery.

Cleaning

I started as a cleaner, six weeks after my 15th birthday, on 3 January 1918. I worked as a cleaner for a couple of weeks from 4.00am to 4.00pm; if you were a cleaner you worked a 12-hour day for 4 shillings a day,

A. Merry Crowd.

L. HICKS, THE HIGHWAY
PONTYPOOL RD, NR PONTYPOOL.

Tom Davies is seen here as a young man, fifth from the left (arrowed) standing on the boiler handrail of 'Saint' Class No 2918 *Saint Catherine*, photographed alongside the coal stage ramp.
Ken Davis, Tom Davis, J. S. Williams collection

Some 40 years later, in 1959, Driver Tom Davies and Fireman Terry Nicholls prepare 'Castle' Class 4-6-0 No 4098 *Kidwelly Castle* at the north end of the shed. *Ken Davis, Tom Davis, J. S. Williams collection*

ASLEF dispatch riders pose in Victoria Street, Griffithstown, in 1955. Sitting in the centre are, left to right, Tom Davies, Eddie Jones and Mr Baker (a former Branches Fork driver). Behind them, third from the left, is Bill Canning. Behind Mr Baker is Arthur Trumper, and to the right is Tommy Tamplin. Second from right is Albert Stopgate. The building on the right is Griffithstown Community Hall. *Ken Davis, J. S. Williams collection*

with an early finish of 2.00pm on a Saturday, i.e. 70 hours per week. Of this 70 hours, 10 were regarded as overtime, which was very often lost if your conduct was in question, or if there were not enough engines in to clean you were sent home with loss of pay. It was wartime when I started at Ponty, and partial blackout conditions were still in operation.

Call boy

I was transferred from a cleaner to a call boy, on the night shift from 4.00pm to 4.00am, knocking up drivers and firemen to make sure they were all right and certain to come on duty for the trains they had to work. This was undertaken as a precaution to ensure that the punctuality of the service was maintained. It was a much nicer job than having to go into the filth and oil to clean dirty engines, but to be a call boy, going out all hours of the night from 11pm to 6.00am certainly required a strong nerve, which one does not always have just after one's 15th birthday!

It was a trick of fate that landed me with this job. Around this time there was some sheep-stealing going on in the district allotted to me, and the lad who was callboy in that area did not relish meeting this gang of ruffians in the night, so he just packed the job in, and as I was the junior hand I had to take the job.

A few nights passed with little incident, until a little later in the week at about 2.00am I was going through the gate of Jarrold's field when I came face-to-face with four of these dreaded sheep-stealers. My heart sank to my boots, as the penalty for sheep-stealing a few years previously had been death by hanging. However, all they wanted to know from me was whether I had seen the policeman. I told them I had not, so was allowed to continue my 'knocking up'. However, they later found the Police Sergeant, whom they promptly beat up and left unconscious not very far from the gate where I had left them.

The partial blackout in operation during the 1914-18 war made it a little easier

At an unknown location 'Saint' Class 4-6-0 No 2945 *Hillingdon Court* is seen with members of a footplatemen's Improvement Class. *Terry Jones collection*

for crime of that kind to take place and I must say it brought out many undesirable characters who were not very pleasant to meet when out on your own at night.

Fireman

I was made a fireman in July 1923 and was sent to Senghennydd (where 400 miners had lost their lives in a mine explosion in 1913). I spent only a few months there, but it was quite an experience working on those small Rhymney engines, taking long trains of coal from the Aber and Rhymney valleys down to the docks at Cardiff, Penarth, Cadoxton and Barry, where at that time coal was being exported to most parts of the world. While there may have been a recession in other industries, the coal trade was really flourishing, with the many miles of dock sidings chock-a-block with trains of coal, sidings at the bottom of each valley full, and the coal hoists on the docks working night and day. All these are now replaced by oil storage tanks for the importation of oil. I was returned to Pontypool Road in September 1924.

During the Second World War 'USA' locos arrived at Ponty in 1943. They were massive locos, with their 7-ton coal and 5,000-gallon water capacity, but no 'cow-catcher'.

Improvement Classes

These were held in our Mechanics Institute every Sunday afternoon at 2.30. Our instructors were enginemen, either drivers or perhaps passenger firemen, who had made a study of the steam locomotive, and were capable of passing on their knowledge in lectures to the classes, senior and junior, to men wishing to become engine drivers.

In spite of the fact that one had to have a very

practical and theoretical knowledge of the locomotive, and Board of Trade rules governing transport, no provision was made by the railway companies to enable one to learn the trade, so it was left to the men themselves to form classes, and instructors gave their services in their own free time.

Our building, The Mechanics Institute, was built by a trust that had been set up in June 1872 with a first issue of 300 shares at £1 each, at an interest rate of 5% paid by the GWR, amounting to £20 per annum. The main source of income, which provided wages for a caretaker, was four billiard tables that provided a pleasing diversion for those who chose to play on them at a charge of 4d an hour, meaning 1d each if a four-hand game was being played. Cards were another amenity that was provided, with instant dismissal if the eagle eye of the caretaker saw any exchange of money in gambling. There was also a library to cater for the cultural needs of the more serious members of our fraternity. So the 'Stute' provided a practical support of that old proverb 'all work and no play makes Jack a dull boy'. In later years, when economics crept in, it was found that subscriptions and income from all sources were not sufficient to pay for wages and maintenance, so the Institute was given, as a free gift, to what is now the British Rail Staff

A train of empties for Blaenavon Furnace Sidings crosses Pontymoile Viaduct, as seen from School View, Pontymoile, in the early 1970s. *J. S. Williams*

Association, and has now become another club with the sale of intoxicants.

2. Fireman Henry Williams

Early days

My Dad, George Williams, was firing at Severn Tunnel when he met my mother. He later became a fireman at Pontypool Road. He worked the Admiralty Coal Trains during the First World War – trips from Admiralty Sidings to Chester. He worked to Chester one day, stayed overnight and came back the following day. No 2385 used to work these, together with '28xx' Class engines. They'd use anything on these trains as long as it would move! The engines had no vacuum brake, just a steam brake. Later on, Dad was made a driver for Aberdare. He had to go there and lodge, and when there was a vacancy at Pontypool he could come back. I used to live in No 9, School View in Pontymoile, opposite the Cwm Road, in the last but one house next

to the viaduct. I'm the seventh sibling and I married Bill Jancey's only daughter.

On a Saturday night the last passenger train to Blaenavon Low Level, the 'Rodney', would go up about 11.00pm and return as empty stock; it would rattle down through there and we often used to think it was coming through the house!

During the Second World War there were many stored engines on shed, it was awful. There was no room for engines – the shed was full. No 7 Road was full of engines and they even had engines in Coedygric Sidings, which had five roads. Roads Nos 1 and 2 were full of engines and cleaners were expected to keep them cleaned and fires lit. At the coal stage they built an overhead building so that fires could be dropped without being seen by enemy aircraft; it contained fire hydrants to extinguish the ashes. The ash shelter was built over No 1 road at the coal stage (the Tap Road), and No 2 road, which had the stop block, opposite the stores.

Engines would also be stored under the

Pontypool Road loco depot is seen here in 1930, as viewed from the Turnpike at Pontypool. The Lower Mills sheet steel works and Phoenix galvanising works dominate the foreground, adjacent to the West Junction. This plant was linked by rail to Pontypool town forge, but had a rail connection to the Middle Junction on the 1920 Ordnance Survey map. *E. Harvey, J. S. Williams collection*

viaduct by the timekeeper's office.

With my Mum and Dad and sisters, we'd walk from Pontymoile up to the Turnpike, down to the Jockey, across the Jockey Field, and underneath the railway at Pontypool Road North box. We then walked past the gas tanks on the down sidings at Pontypool Road station, which were used to fill gas tanks on passenger coaches, although this had been discontinued by the time I joined the railway. They were round tanks, like big cylinders. We went up the station approach, across the road, and down to where the cattle pens and the sidings were, where spare coaches were stored if one had a hot axle box. We then turned left, then right, alongside the cattle pens and across the bridge at the Afon Lwyd, then down and turned right, under the railway bridge, and along the Black Ash path back to the canal at Pontymoile and back home. There was a black tin shed where Travis Perkins is now, and Mr Bevan had a coal merchant's supply there, using an old Ford lorry. When Mr Bevan retired, in the war, timber was sent there by the Ministry of Supply, and stored in a big pile 30 feet high. The railway to W. J. Harris's scrapyard was hardly ever used after the war, as heavy timber was stored outside the yard, and after the war the track to the yard was lifted.

During the very bad winter of 1947 there was snow on the Blaenavon Top Line and a train became stuck at Blaenavon Furnace Sidings, near the Whistle pub. They had drained the boiler. There was only one engine at Pontypool Road that could be put on the snowplough – No 7424. It was auto-fitted for the Wye Valley and worked the Monmouth line. Three engines were used on the plough – the '74xx' and two '72xxs' – and my Dad was on the '72xx' in the middle. Permanent way people were there and told them push through. They had a couple of goes. My Dad went through and when they came back the levelling pipe between the tanks had come off completely, so they had to throw the fire out. His engine was uncoupled and pushed in a siding out of the way at Furnace Sidings, and the other

engines got on with it.

When I started at the shed after the war the two air raid shelters (at Hart's Yard and the New Sidings) were still there, as was the ash shelter at the side of the coal stage.

Cleaning

I started at Ponty in 1949, having left school aged 15. When you became 17 you could work nights, then start calling. The running shed foremen I remember are Joe Richards and Bert Selwood, and Arthur Haymer was the chargehand cleaner.

I started as an engine cleaner. I cleaned 'Bulldog' loco *Seagull*; it was in the shed, on the Lift Road under the big lift, for years, but I can't remember it running.

I remember cleaning No 6400, which was used for the 12.02pm Pontypool (Crane Street) auto-train. It shone like silver. I even cleaned the inside motion. The driver asked the chargehand cleaner, 'Who cleaned this engine? When I was oiling up, my shoulders were catching oil from the red-painted stretcher in front of the firebox.' There was no pleasing some drivers.

Four cleaners were sent to Pontypool Road station – two at the top end, two at the bottom – to assist the firemen of expresses for the north or south to pull coal forward. Two cleaners would get onto the tender to do this. You would work maybe 8.00am to 4.00pm or 7.00am to 3.00pm on this task, for trains going to Swansea or Torquay. Expresses would stop at Abergavenny (Mon Road), Hereford, Leominster, Ludlow, Craven Arms and Shrewsbury.

Call boy

I then went calling, in Griffithstown, and up to the top of Blaendare Road. I started at 10.00pm and hung around, and at 12.30am I would start calling. There was a phone box at Blaendare Road by where Pearson's electrical store is today. You had all of Griffithstown to cover. The worst one was the top of Pontymoile. You had the top of the Race, and one on Stafford Road – that was a hell of a walk. It was either 10 minutes early or 10 minutes late. I used to walk down into the Cwm, up over the field and down into Stafford Road. One night I walked up over the field, crossed the lane (from Pontymoile to Penyrheol), and was walking down the other side when all of a sudden there was a 'clip, clop, clip, clop' – a horse had followed me, all the way to near Stafford Road, as I had to call old Phil Williams at No 95 ('Full Load Phil').

On another occasion there wasn't much lighting about. The paper boys used to have their newspapers come up on the Western Welsh bus, and they were wrapped in paper. I had been up to the Park Estate Offices to call Tom Brown, and was walking down to go up to Hillside Drive. I was by the bus stop at Pontymoile where the roads from the Cwm and Blaendare joined near the Vale of Neath railway bridge at Lock Cottage by the side of the bridge. All of a sudden a piece of this paper came down out of the trees in front of me.

Lock Cottage was on the right-hand side of the road, after it came under the railway bridge and up around to Blaendare and the Cwm. Frank Hide lived there; he was signalman at Pontypool Road South, which was a two-man box.

Walter Tedstone lived by the Prince of Wales pub, and I called him as well. He was a driver at the time.

Shed work

Sand used to come from near Porthcawl in a seven-board wagon for the sand house furnaces. You could have a job emptying the sand wagon, then you

were allowed to go home. We used to get stuck in, empty it and go home!

Another job I undertook was cleaning the loco shed, using a shovel, broom and a wheelbarrow.

The turntable in the round shed was used to run engines through to the long shed and the back end (No 7 Road). When I was a cleaner the turntable was in a poor state of repair, and had broken its back. When turning a '28xx' or '38xx' inside the shed, it was a hell of a job to get it to balance. Instead of having the driver and fireman and shed turners to turn it, they'd ask us cleaners, as young boys, to turn the engine on the table. 'There's one on the table we can't shift – come and give us a hand.' There'd be three or four cleaners at each end of the table, helping to push it round.

Engines were positioned on shed during three shifts by the shed turners, seven days a week. A former main-line driver and a passed fireman would receive instructions from the running foreman, then the engines were positioned by looking for their numbers on the engine board for the next day's duty. '28xxs' and '72xxs' were stabled in the long shed, and small tank engines, such as '45xxs', '56xxs', '41xxs' and pannier tanks, in the round shed. No 7 Road, at the back of the shed, began at the back of the coal stage and extended down to the South Junction, north of Coedygric Road Viaduct; it would be used to stable '68xxs' and '49xxs'. For No 6400, the shed turners would look on the engine board and position it in the round shed on a road on its own ready for the 4.30am

A '45xx' tank engine is stored outside the wagon repair shed, south of Coedygric Road Viaduct, together with a '72xx'. *J. S. Williams collection*

Blaenavon auto-working the next day.

One day when I wasn't there – it wasn't my shift – someone came off the ash pit with not a lot of steam on, and couldn't stop the engine at the shed door, and it landed in the turntable pit. Crash!

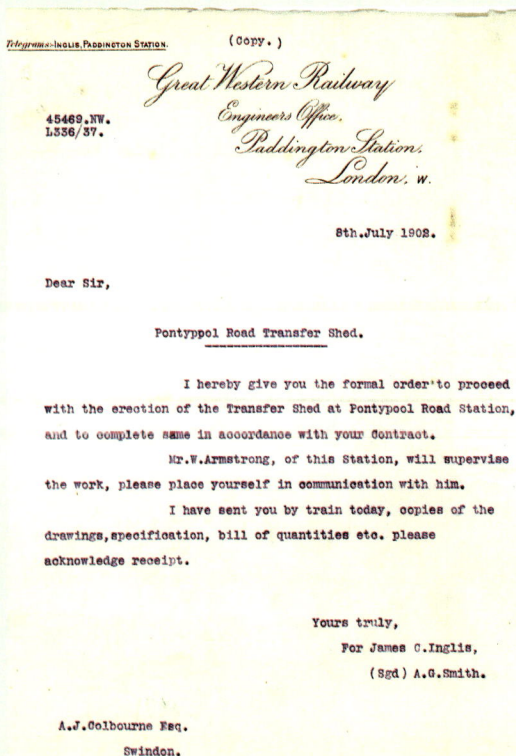

Another accident occurred when my brother in law was on the Abergavenny banker with No 349. He had a Cardiff driver with him and they had brought back some coaches that had been taken to Abergavenny to be cleaned before they went to Cardiff. My brother in law said to the Cardiff man, 'Go on, you don't want to come down the shed – I'll put him on the pit to drop the fire.' But going onto the pit he misjudged it and hit an engine on an adjacent road that was fouling his road. The buffers met and bent the buffer beam. He had to run after the driver before he went on his way. The engine was repaired at Caerphilly.

Yard infrastructure

The wagon repair shed was at Coedygric Road Viaduct. There was a railway alongside, used to store engines for repair or waiting to go to Caerphilly or Swindon (the Dead End Siding). I have taken a '72xx' to Caerphilly Works for repair; we went via Cardiff, or you could go via the Vale and get off at Ystrad Mynach and go down to Caerphilly.

Left: The goods transfer shed at Pontypool Road was authorised to be constructed on 8 July 1902, as per this memorandum issued by the GWR at Paddington. *Phil Williams collection*

Right: Looking south from the viaduct on 3 June 1964, the Carriage & Wagon Department sidings are seen on the right, south of the wagon repair shed. On the immediate left are the New Sidings, with their shunting spur in the background, and the connection from the sidings dropping down on the left to join the low-level goods line to Panteg Junction. On the right is the Old Yard, with the Eastern Valley branch dropping down to Panteg & Coedygric Junction in the distance. The double track in the foreground is the Up and Down Goods line between the East Junction and Panteg & Coedygric Junction. *M. Hale, Great Western Trust*

Coedygric Sidings are seen looking south during 1966. The New Sidings are on the left. Behind the cabin in the centre are the Up and Down Main (Goods Relief) lines, and reception sidings for the wagon repair shed. In the distance on the right is the Old Yard, adjacent to the wall. *Robert Hall*

Panteg & Coedygric Junction looking north on 8 August 1961. *M. Hale, Great Western Trust*

Ex-GWR '5205' Class 2-8-0 No 5208 is seen at Coedygric Junction with a train of washed small coal from Hafodrynys New Mine on 25 September 1964. *Kidderminster Railway Museum*

A pair of Class 25 diesel-electric locomotives pass Panteg & Coedygric Junction signal box circa 1977. *J. S. Williams*

Another coal train from Hafodrynys New Mine approaches Coedygric Junction, this time hauled by Type 4 diesel-electric loco No 1914 on Thursday 3 September 1970. The remains of the Old Yard dominate the foreground. *J. S. Williams*

'Western' Class diesel-hydraulic locomotive No 1053 *Western Patriarch* is seen at the same place with coal from Hafodrynys New Mine on 25 April 1972. *J. S. Williams*

Viewed from the Old Yard, another 'Western', No 1009 *Western Invader*, leaves the New Sidings after storing empty coal wagons on Thursday 3 September 1970. *J. S. Williams*

On Saturday 2 December 1978 the 'Welsh Wonder' rail enthusiasts' passenger train heads north through Panteg & Coedygric Junction, heading for Blaenavon Furnace Sidings and hauled by Class 20 diesel-electric locomotives Nos 20122 and 20022. *J. S. Williams*

A ground frame controlled points from Coedygric Sidings into New Sidings, where the Class 25 diesel-electric locomotive is standing in August 1971.
J. S. Williams

The New Sidings shunting spur is seen on the left, with the New Sidings connection to the low-level goods line seen in the previous photo.
J. S. Williams

Shunting activity in the New Sidings, as viewed from Coedygric Road Viaduct in the early 1970s.
J. S. Williams

The 'coal field' had been the old coal stock in the war, but was lifted in the 1950s, and the coal used for firing engines. However, it was hopeless – it had been frozen, had got wet and disintegrated. We were expected to fire with that.

The Loop Sidings were a series of very short roads; a long train, perhaps to Shrewsbury or Birmingham, would be split into three parts and stored in three adjacent roads at the Loop Sidings. The running line between the Loop Sidings and Station South was a single line, running alongside the coal field (opposite the Birkenhead Sidings), with sidings on either side, and was known as the Up Loop. It was under the jurisdiction of the marshalling yard – it was nothing to do with signalmen. At the end of this road, towards Station South Junction, there was a catch point and a signal. There you used the phone on the signal post to ring Station South signal box and say, for example, 'This is the two o'clock Dudley and we're off up to Dudley,' and you were let out by the Station South signalman.

If you were at South Junction and went straight on, towards West Junction, you'd initially land up in the Loop at the Loop Junction, where you used the Up Goods line, known as the Loop. There was a stop board there because the train would be shunting back and forth, and you weren't allowed passed that stop board until you were invited by the head shunter. You'd wait there until you were called. The Loop header shunter was paid extra money for turning the point to turn the engine.

The Loop shunters' cabin was situated at the bottom of the Skew Field, at the Loop Junction. In the days of the coal field, there was a klaxon on a post near Hart's Yard, operated by a button on a post by the Loop shunters' cabin. The shunter would be at the Loop Junction, giving signals '1, 2, 3' to 'stop', '4' to 'ease up', '1' to 'go from me', '2' to 'go to me'. We used to be down there on a train of maybe 40 or 50 wagons from Newport or wherever, and would be out of the sight of the shunters, as we were at the northern end towards Hart's Yard, listening out for the klaxon.

Traffic from the valleys (via Cwm Glyn)

Ex-GWR '57xx' Class 0-6-0PT No 3685 is on the bi-directional line known as the Up Loop at the back of Pontypool Road shed on an unknown date. 'WD' 2-8-0 No 90706 is seen stored at the south end of the Engineer's Yard, with the Birkenhead Sidings on the left. The engine is approximately opposite the shed water tank. *Kidderminster Railway Museum*

to go up north was pulled into the Loop and pushed into the Down Loop, next to the single Up Loop running line between the Loop Junction and Station South. The Northern Sidings Pilot would then come over and pick it up for the Northern Sidings, or it might be pushed into the Birkenhead Sidings for dispatch north.

The gasworks had a lot of coal going in. It produced tar for a firm in Bristol, and had its own diesel.

All but two of the New Sidings had stop blocks. The Reception road for Coedygric Sidings was in the middle of those sidings, as they had no stop blocks.

Right: From left to right, Harold Davies (shunter), Vic Evans (engine driver) and Tom Morgan (shunter).

Ex-GWR '8750' Class 0-6-0PT No 9644 is seen at the Loop on 21 September 1964. *Rail-On Line*

Platelayer Arthur Tibbs is seen in the Birkenhead Sidings in the 1960s, with a 'Hall' Class engine in the background waiting to work a train. The wagon examiner's office and greaser's office are on the extreme right-hand side. Arthur was present when the single-span bridge at Varteg Road, Blaenavon, leading to Cemetery Sidings and Vipond's Top Pits at the Varteg, was removed in the 1960s. *Arthur Tibbs, J. S. Williams collection*

Ex-GWR '69xx' Class 4-6-0 No 6914 and BR 9F No 92242 stand at the back of the coal stage in the Birkenhead Sidings on an unrecorded date. *R. K. Blencowe collection*

The Northern Pilot is almost opposite Hart's Yard in the Up Loop with a train to be pulled out to Station South and propelled back into its own sidings. There are flat wagons in Hart's Yard. *Kidderminster Railway Museum*

The Northern Pilot, No 9730, is seen in the Northern Sidings at the back of the East Junction signal box on 24 May 1960. *F. A. Blencowe, R. K. Blencowe collection*

On 24 May 1960 one of the yard pilots, ex-GWR '77xx' Class 0-6-0PT No 7740 with a wagon of scrap, stands on the spur between the Northern Sidings and Station South Junction. As the date of this photo is identical to that of No 9730 in the Northern Sidings, it is surmised that this engine may either be another engine acting as the Northern Pilot later the same day, or is the Old Yard Pilot collecting scrap for Panteg Steelworks. The source of the scrap is unknown, as the spur to W. J. Harris & Sons scrapyard was disused. *R. K. Blencowe collection*

The GWR designed an 0-6-0 tender engine for hauling trains between Pontypool Road and Birkenhead, and they were nicknamed the 'Birkenhead Goods' engines. No 927 is seen south of Station South signal box. The presence of buffers in front of the engine may indicate that it is performing banking duties to Cwm Glyn. *J. S. Williams collection, via the late Dave Fry*

The coal stage

The centre chute was used when I was at Ponty; it had an electric lift that raised coal to a tipping height of 14 feet compared to 11ft 6in for the north and south chutes, which were not in use. 970 tons of coal a week was used, and fire droppers dropped enough ash and clinker to fill 20 wagons of ash a week[6]. Two wagons would be lowered into the coal stage, and two coalmen were employed, each wagon being emptied by one coal man. Four tubs were used to empty two wagons, two tubs per wagon. The wagon door would be opened using a coal pick to knock the catches out, and it was supposed to rest on two tubs, one each end. If the door rested on the tubs, to ease shovelling a steel sheet was pushed into the wagon, under the coal, and that made shovelling easier, as the floor of the wagon was rough to shovel off and made the task hard work. Sometimes the door missed the tubs, and hung vertically, and coal fell onto the coal stage floor, which was made of steel plate, with a smooth surface. The coalman would fill one tub, and partly fill the other; the full one would be pushed towards the electric hoist.

The lift was flush with the coal stage floor; you pushed the tub onto the lift and pressed a button to raise it to the required height. The tub was then pushed forward against a vertical plate; this was counterbalanced, so when the tub hit the plate it rotated and you pushed the tub along this plate, which had rails on its upper surface, until the wheels hit the curled up ends of the rails. You then lifted the handle at the back end of the tub and, like a wheelbarrow, it pivoted on the front pair of wheels and coal would drop through the open door. One person could upend the tub to drop coal. When empty, the tub was lowered and pulled back onto the floor of the lift, and the plate automatically rotated to its

Ex-GWR '77xx' Class 0-6-0PT No 7724 is seen alongside Pontypool Road Station South Signal Box during shunting operations on 18 August 1962. *M. Dart, Transport Treasury*

vertical position. You lowered the lift, filled another tub and repeated the process.

I worked on the coal stage as my first firing job; I worked with Tom Howells, who was stone deaf, wore glasses and chewed twist. I would put the tub under the lift for him. There were marks on the wall of the coal stage an engine should be stopped for coal to be tipped; I would always get off the engine to avoid any coal being dropped on me!

When the coal was tipped, the tub was pulled back. Sometimes coal would drop onto the cab roof, and had to be swept off. To get onto the roof, you stepped off the counterbalanced plate, but then the plate would automatically rotate back to the vertical position, leaving you stranded on the roof. I used a brush to pull it back down, after sweeping coal off a cab roof – there was no health and safety in those days!

The coal stage fireman's job was to move an engine under the coal stage, coal it up, and leave it by the shed doors. I did this turn just after I started firing. As a fireman on the

Above: GWR '28xx' Class No 2824 awaits its turn on the ash road in September 1936; the coal stage ramp is in the foreground. *Kidderminster Railway Museum*

Left: Ex-GWR '57xx' Class 0-6-0PT No 4600 stands at the base of the coal stage ramp, date unknown. *Kidderminster Railway Museum*

Below: GWR 'Bulldog' Class 4-4-0 No 3456 *Albany* is seen at the back of the coal stage some time before 1912. There were two sidings at this location. *J. S. Williams collection, via the late Dave Fry*

Engines are being stored at the back of the coal stage on an unrecorded date. *Phil Williams collection*

coal stage, it was your job to make sure that there were no lumps of coal likely to drop off between there and the shed doors – after that it was nothing to do with you. You had a brush and used it to brush the cab off. At that time 'ovoids', a patent fuel, were being used, and one day these were being tipped into the bunker of a '45xx' tank engine until it was completely full, and there was a fair heap on top of the cab. I stood on top of the cab brushing them off, and one got under my foot and tumble, tumble, I went over the side and landed on a heap of ovoids on the ground, spreading them under me.

They got a first-aider called Gordon Morris (who repaired clocks and was nicknamed 'Tick-Tock'), and he walked me up to Panteg Hospital – I wasn't put on a stretcher. I saw the doctor and there were no bruises then, but the next day I had bruises and I didn't work for two days!

Wagons were pushed up to the coal stage – No 1429 used to do that. I used that

engine on the two-coach colliers' train to Hafodrynys, and when coming back to shed it was known as 'Snackey's Pilot', i.e. it was the shed pilot. It was used in the 'ash hole' for wagon loading on the fire pit, supplying coal for the coal stage and for shunting the sand wagon at the back of the sand furnace.

The carpenter's shop was on the end of the coal stage – you walked in and he'd sharpen your saw for five bob. I remember fireplaces in the coalman's cabin, and the toolman's place for shovels.

Firing on the Pilots

The pilots were the Old Yard, South and Northern Pilots, which faced north, and the Loop, Coedygric and New Sidings Pilots, which faced south. The Panteg Pilot faced north, and the Coedygric Pilot had no shunting truck, as it was a transfer pilot. The only banker pilots were the Northern Pilot and the Loop Pilot.

Ex-GWR '8750' Class 0-6-0PT No 9644 heads towards the South Sidings signal box on 21 September 1964. *Rail-On Line*

An ex-GWR '72xx' 2-8-2T arrives at South Sidings signal box from Cardiff or Severn Tunnel via Panteg Junction. The three-arm signal in the right background controls traffic from the West Junction, and in front of it is a freight train in the Loop Sidings. Two shunters are seen on the ground. There are two stop signals opposite the signal box; the taller of the two, on the left, is from the shed to go down the cutting to Panteg Junction. The single signal on the right is to go to Coedygric Junction, via the west side of the wagon repair shed. The lift for the beer for the canteen is seen on the left, adjacent to the viaduct steps. *J. S. Williams*

This similar view is also looking north towards the shed. In front of the office (for guards and yard staff, and women cleaners in the war) on the right is Wilson's Leg with wagons stored on it; in front of this is the dead-end siding. Outside the signal box are the merging Up and Down High and Low Level goods lines. North of the signal box this pair of lines splits into four roads, to the left to form the Up and Down Loop towards the Loop Junction, and straight on to form the up and down lines that proceed past the Loop Sidings and Hart's Yard towards Station South Junction. At the bottom end of the triangle (adjacent to the Skew Fields) was a stop board where down trains would stop before proceeding into the yard from the West Junction. The diesel shunter is standing in No 1 South Siding. *J. S. Williams*

I started firing engines when I was 16. My first firing turn was on the Coedygric Pilot, with a driver from Cardiff who walked strangely, so we called him 'Jitterbug'. The first day I was with him I stood by his side and had to tell him what the shunter required by watching his hand signals – reverse, stop, forward, ease up. The engine was maybe a '57xx'. After a while you get the drop of it – watch the clock, watch the boiler, if you wanted more coal put some on and shut the door.

Some of the old drivers were taken off the main line – green-carded – and put on these pilot jobs, and they were fussy. If you got out the pep pipe to clean the footplate, they'd say, 'Don't go putting too much water about, I've got rheumatics,' that sort of thing. I had an old driver from New Inn called Charlie Hobson. He was all right, and some got on with him OK. He had a fad about the gauge frame – you had to take it apart to clean it. He used to roll his own cigarettes, and the silver paper from the packet had to go up the back of the gauge frame.

The Coedygric Pilot was a transfer pilot in a way, for trains coming from the north, which arrived at Coedygric Sidings and the New Sidings alongside. Any wagons

for the valleys were put on the South Road and shunted into the South Sidings. You would then pick up what was to go on down to Cardiff and the West of England. The South Road ran from Coedygric box towards the South Sidings, and was at the back of the shed beyond No 7 Road, at the bottom end of the Birkenhead Sidings. (The Loop Sidings were up against the Skew Field, towards the West Box.) The engine faced towards Panteg Works.

The Coedygric Pilot also received traffic from the north from such places as Hereford. This went to the Old Yard, via Coedygric box. If the Coedygric Pilot had traffic for Panteg Works, he would say to the signalman, 'Old Yard and below.' He might then drop a couple of wagons to the Old Yard via Coedygric box, and have one wagon next to the engine behind the down platform at Griffithstown station (down by the goods shed), leaving it there to cross over and come back up. The Coedygric Pilot never had a shunting truck, whereas the Old Yard Pilot did, for traffic from Pilkington's works.

The Coedygric Pilot was known as the 'transfer pilot' – it would go to the back of Panteg & Coedygric box for the Old Yard, and onto the south road for the South Pilot.

Coming up from Panteg works, water would be taken at the Old Yard water column, as did engines working trains from Severn Tunnel Junction; auto-trains for Blaenavon would take water at Panteg station when working to Blaenavon Low Level.

The Old Yard pilot used the line from Coedygric signal box to the Old Yard for transfer work. There was a weighing scale there, underneath the bank for the Eastern Valley line, to weigh railway wagons; it was located in a recess in the wall. The Pilot would also pop down to Pilkington's glassworks, perhaps with a load of sand,

Above: North of Coedygric Road Viaduct, a passenger train heads south on the main line, with the Northern Sidings in the background; the engine is an ex-GWR 'Hall' Class.
J. S. Williams collection

Right: A freight train approaches the East Junction on the Up Main line.
J. S. Williams collection

Below: Viewed from the Northern Sidings, an ex-GWR '41xx' Class 2-6-2T heads south with a passenger train on the main line. The New Sidings are seen in the background.
J. S. Williams collection

returning with wagons of ash, weighing them and charging Pilkington's. It also received traffic from Panteg Works coming up through the cutting at Coedygric box up to the South Junction, and pushed traffic back in.

Looking north between Panteg & Coedygric Junction signal box and the footbridge at Panteg & Griffithstown station was the site of the old Coedygric engine shed. In 1949 all that remained was a galvanised shed, owned by the Gwent Wagon Company, which repaired railway wagons. They cut headstocks for coal wagons, using 10-inch by 6-inch pieces of timber, with all joints cut by hand. They also made solebars, as well as other parts. They had a blacksmith's forge there for making bits and pieces.

The Panteg Pilot would go out in the morning, to go down to Weston's Biscuits and the Cold Storage premises in Llantarnam and shunt them out, then come back to Lower Pontnewydd on the main line and shunt, and Panteg Works on the way back. It would go up to the Old Yard and drop a few wagons off there, and drop a few off at the Loop Siding. It would then run around and pick up a van and the remaining train to work to Panteg Junction, waiting underneath Coedygric box where the 'tunnels' were; south of the tunnels was a signal to avoid blocking the New Sidings connection, and we would stop there. The shunting spur for the New Sidings was over the top, on the right, on the bank. You had to brake the wagons coming down, and pick up the brakes just outside Panteg Works, after you passed Panteg Junction.

Sometimes you would be required to push a train into Panteg Works, after leaving the South Junction. You disconnected the van, and proceeded to the dead end by the tip then push back into the works. This was via the connection between the 'tunnels' and the New Siding slope. You would then stand aside and wait for the works engine to put wagons ready for you to take to the Old Yard and South Junction.

The New Sidings running line was used for traffic to Panteg Junction or to Coedygric. I only ever saw traffic go to Panteg Junction. The train to Severn Tunnel and Exeter used this route, with a Ponty engine. One night we had eight cattle trucks on the train to Severn Tunnel – it comprised all sorts of wagons, and the engine would be a '56xx' or '42xx'.

Cardiff trains from the New Sidings went over the 'tunnels' (the bridge over the line by the New Siding shunting spur), down to Cwmbran and the Old Mon line to Newport. The train to Cardiff from the New Sidings and Coedygric Sidings would go to Cwmbran and to Newport via the old Monmouthshire line and service all the places along the way, then out via Alexandra Junction at Newport to Cardiff.

The old Monmouthshire Line extended from the back of the old Cwmbran station to Newport. A goods train for the north came

A goods train enters the New Sidings reception road.
J. S. Williams collection

Left: Looking towards the shed, the Loop Junction is on the left. *J. S. Williams collection*

Below: An ex-GWR 0-6-2T returns to the shed on the upper Up Goods Relief line, via the East Junction, after dropping off a train in the New/Coedygric Sidings. *J. S. Williams collection*

Right: Looking north from Panteg Steelworks on 19 May 1964, the low-level goods lines from Panteg Junction are on the left, passing under the railway bridge that took the high-level goods line from the East Junction to Panteg & Coedygric Junction, whose signal box is seen on the left. The New Sidings connection is on the right, with its shunting spur in the foreground. Between the bridge and the shunting spur was one of two air raid shelters. The points on the left were the entrance to Panteg Steelworks. *M. Hale, Great Western Trust*

The truncated remains of the low-level goods line to Panteg Junction are seen here; the junction itself has been removed. The cottages north of Panteg Junction signal box are on the left, behind the car transporter train; access to the cottages and signal box was via the wooden path crossing the main line. *J. S. Williams*

A footplate ride from the New Sidings to collect a train of coils from Panteg Steelworks, with Severn Tunnel Junction Driver Dennis Collett (right) and secondman Mostyn Richards in July 1971. When this train was propelled back to the New Sidings, the locomotive began to slip, causing grass beneath the diesel to catch fire! After Panteg Junction was closed in the 1960s, rail access to Panteg Steelworks was via the New Sidings. *J. S. Williams*

up from Cardiff on this route, and went into the Northern Sidings, which had seven roads. If the train was pulled into the Northern Sidings, the brake van was uncoupled and left at the end of the sidings so that a train could be formed on it to work later from the sidings. The Cardiff engine was uncoupled, and reversed back to Station South to proceed down the Old Mon Line to the New Sidings.

Alternatively, the train might propel back into the Northern Sidings, where it would be met by the head shunter, who had changed the points in front to maybe the No 4 or No 2 road. He uncoupled the brake van, on the move, which then entered one of those roads under its own momentum and was put on the side out of the way. It was protected by the under-shunter, and the guard remained in it. The points were then changed and the whole train was propelled back, brakes put on and the train engine uncoupled. The Pilot picked up the van and put it on the other end of the engine, so that when run out it was on the Pontypool Road end, and right for Cardiff. The train engine went to the New Sidings reception road, took water and stood by the cabins.

The Cardiff train was then assembled in the New Sidings, using the New Sidings Pilot. A train from the north, and Ebbw Vale, would be formed for him. The Cardiff engine would be in the road by the water column, by the shunters' cabin, examiner's cabin and inspector's office, and the footplate crew had their food. If the Northern Pilot was available, that engine took the van from the Northern Sidings to the New Sidings, instead of the train (Cardiff) engine. There was a loop by the shunters' cabin

Fireman Eric Telfor stands next to ex-GWR '57xx' Class 0-6-0PT No 3708 in the Northern Sidings on 4 March 1965, adjacent to the shunters' cabin. *Rail-On Line*

by the water column, so that a train could be formed by the pilot engine, which would run around into the adjacent siding.

The Cardiff engine then backed onto the train, and the New Siding Pilot pushed the brake van on the back. The Cardiff engine worked back to Newport using the Old Mon line, passing Coedygric box, Panteg station and Cwmbran station, then off to Cardiff, after servicing all the factories. One was the British Brattice Company, a rubber firm,

Yard foreman George Jones (left) and head shunter Rollei Thomas stand by the Northern Sidings shunters' cabin in the early 1950s. *Dick Bassett, J. S. Williams collection*

located in Maindee by the Odeon cinema. It made conveyor belts and this train delivered stock there on the way back to Cardiff. When the train arrived in Cardiff it was dropped off at Long Dyke, the engine, a '56xx', uncoupled and taken to shed.

The 9.10am Manchester used a 'Baby Scot', which couldn't go on the turntable at Ponty, so it was turned on the triangle. It went up to the West Junction, dropped down to the Loop, and proceeded to Station South on the bi-directional line. To save time it would take water at the same water column as the Control Banker, at the water column by Hart's Yard.

3. Fireman Colin Polsom

I started at Pontypool Road on 9 September 1959 as a cleaner, and finished in 1964 as a fireman, the week the Vale of Neath closed. My regular mate on the engine was initially Bill June in the Branch Link, Evo Evans, then Les Evans, in the Control Link. I never ran out of steam, but came near! The job was as dirty as you wanted it to be. I learned a good philosophy from the code of conduct and morals from a lot of people at Pontypool Road that lasted me the rest of my life. The hardest thing of all was bad mates, but I was very lucky and didn't have many. When I started there were still old GWR men who taught you codes of conduct, such as appearance, cleanliness, etc. I went by passenger train to Aberdare on the Wednesday before I started my new job on 15 June 1964 at British Nylon Spinners at Mamhilad. I had just got engaged to Sandra.

Cleaning

On my first day I cleaned two engines in the round shed. In the morning I cleaned *Heatherden Hall*, then *Highnam Grange* in the afternoon.

We cleaned the engine for the 1.42pm Cardiff, and I was desperate to learn at every opportunity. I would get on the footplate, and especially liked people such as Gwyn Hewlett, an older fireman who took us

youngsters under his wing. Glan Price from Glyn Neath was another lovely bloke, as was Harry Oswald. One day we were getting one of the 'Star' series of 'Britannias' ready, and I thought, 'How does Harry sit in that seat?' You could go on the engine and build a fire for the fireman, and listen. The 1.42pm was invariably a 'Castle' or a 'Britannia', and the work was done on the Tap Road, although it should have been on the Cabin Road. You got the lamps ready and helped them out.

Drivers

One day I was on an engine waiting for it to be coaled at the coal stage and looked across to see Driver Mel Smith on the Old Yard Pilot. He was tidying up with the pep pipe, and went to lean on the door, but it was open and he fell off the engine!

Horace Smith also drove the Old Yard Pilot; he was from Worcester, lived at Blaendare and was a cracking man. He knew how interested I was in the job, so whenever I went to work with him he would ask me questions about the engine. Where does the steam go when it leaves the regulator valve? Where would the eccentric be when the big end is in the back? I used to like it. I was young, but while my mates would go for a pint or play snooker, I was working.

One Friday or Saturday afternoon shift I wasn't feeling pleased with myself, as my mates were enjoying themselves; we'd broken the back of the shunting and were having our tea. Horace began to ask me a question and I told him I wasn't in the mood – I was feeling sorry for myself. He said to me, 'What's up over that bank?' I said, 'Panteg Hospital.' Horace said, 'I'm telling you any one of those people in there would swop places with you today.' So I stopped feeling sorry and carried that philosophy in my life to this day.

I was spoiled – I hadn't been cleaning long, and was of a generation of firemen who were promised driving jobs within ten years, yet there were drivers like Harry Howells, Harry Waring and Bas Jenkins who had been firing for nearly 20 years and had to go to

Aberbeeg to get a job as a driver, then come back to Ponty. I was up for this, and wanted to learn as much as I could, and here was this man Horace, who was giving me his time, to help me do it. I had a lot of turns with Horace, and was very grateful to him.

I once had Driver Jack Drayton on the Old Yard Pilot. He stood leaning against the regulator handle and told me he had wasted his life, as he was in the *Guinness Book of Records* for having made more than 24,000 staff suggestions. He was telling me all these facts and figures. This was one of the Pilot Link jobs.

On the 'morning prep' you booked on at 3.00am to get five engines ready. I would pushbike from Pontnewynydd. It was hard graft. You had to locate the engines. The most important two were those for the 5.10am Crewe and 4.50am Chester passenger trains (times are from memory), worked by 'Halls'. You were allowed an hour to get a tender engine ready. Because they were going on these jobs, they'd come off the coal stage well coaled up and tidy, with a bit of clean fire. If they had to be turned, the tenders had to be filled to balance the turntable.

First you found the engine, usually at the bottom end of the long shed so it wouldn't get blocked in. You went to the lamp room at the coal stage and got two lamps, making sure they were trimmed and full of paraffin,

a bucket of tools (hand brush, spanners, oil can), a shovel and a coal pick. These were carried from the lamp room to the engine. The coal stage was at the top end of the shed and the engine would be by the bottom end, so if you had to do that five times it wasn't much fun. The engines would be a 'Hall' or a 'Grange', or a foreign engine such as a BR Standard or a 'Black Five'. The engines would then go to Pontypool Road station for passenger work or fast goods, or pick up a train in the South Sidings.

If you went in to work and the baffle plate was down in the smokebox, you might find that the boilersmiths on the night shift had gone home a little bit early. What did you do? Tell the foreman? No, you did it yourself. If the sanders didn't work on shed you'd get a fitter to sort it, but on the road you did it yourself.

It was taboo to let the tank or tender overflow – you made sure it didn't. I was on a tank once (it may have been a '56xx' or a '41xx' for the Vale passengers) and my mate turned his head away, with the water valve full open; I kicked the bag, which buckled up and drowned him.

Morning prep was a hard task. You might get on an engine in the long shed that had not long been lit up. The shed was dark and murky, and the smoke would be just falling off the stack and there would be very little water in the boiler. You had to cuddle that fire up with care to get enough heat, but at the same time you needed enough steam to top the water up – it was a balancing act. You did a bit to the fire, checked the sand boxes, then went back to the fire. You wouldn't have been prepping it long before the crew arrived; the idea was that the fire was prepared ready for the crew to fine-tune it ready to take the engine off shed on time. If it was in good order, the boiler would be at three-quarters of a glass. You never had an engine blowing off or making black smoke from the chimney. If you went through a

Diesel driver tutor Harry Waring at Newport (Godfrey Road) on 19 June 1963.

station with black smoke or blowing off, there would be a report waiting for you by the time you got back on shed, to explain why.

On one occasion I was prepping a Chester or Crewe loco with good coal. I was topping up the boiler with the injector and, looking across, saw John Pike with 'Full Load Phil', his mate. John was prepping the engine. You always checked around the engine before you put the injector on, as any leaking joints sprayed hot water. Phil was oiling the eccentrics. John looked out both sides, couldn't see Phil, and put the injector on. The clack joint on the safety valve was leaking, and a dribble of hot water ran around the boiler barrel straight down Phil's neck. It could have happened to anyone. Phil threw the oil feeder out from the engine just as the running foreman Ted Tanner was walking down the long shed with his hands

Fireman Charlie Reynolds (right) and Driver Rollei Jones (a young driver who died young) stand alongside a '41xx' 2-6-2 tank engine. Rollei was the son of senior fitter Rollei Jones.
J. S. Williams collection

in his blue smock. He pirouetted on one leg in the opposite direction. The air was blue!

4. Fireman Charlie Reynolds

I began my career on the railway at Pontypool Road on 12 February 1951 as a cleaner. I later became a fireman, progressing to a steam driver, then a second man and driver on the diesels. My claim to fame is being the fireman on the last tender engine to cross Crumlin Viaduct, and being the second man on the last train of coal from Big Pit, on a Sunday in October 1979; it was taken to Severn Tunnel Junction, with the NCB diesel attached to the rear of the train. I booked on at 5.00am and finished at 7.00 pm.

In 1968 I was the fireman on Great Western steam loco *King George V*, taking it from Newport to Hereford in light steam, towed by a Type 3 'D68xx' diesel loco, after overhaul in Newport, for use at Bulmer's cider factory in Hereford. During that journey, it was put in the up loop at Abergavenny early in the morning. I blew the whistle, and was told not to do that! In October 1974 I was one of two firemen to fire *Flying Scotsman* from Newport to Shrewsbury; I accessed the footplate via the tender corridor. I have also driven *Duchess of Hamilton*, owned by the National Railway Museum. I finished on the railway in 1999. The last steam engine I drove was 'King' Class loco No 6024 from Gloucester to Newport in 1996.

Family history

My father was born in West Bromwich, and my grandfather got a job in Pontnewynydd Forge in 1907, and lived in Forge Hammer Row, by the Forge Hammer pub; they were forge houses. Not long after getting the job, grandfather was killed in the works in 1910. He was a moulder; wagons of moulding sand were dropped to a certain point and he would unload it for use in the steel moulds. There was a pillar at the side of the track, and my grandfather was pinned between it and the wagons. This happened at 11 o'clock in the morning, and when the Inspector came men had been there beforehand to slew the track over to hide the evidence. One person in the works complained to the Inspector, saying this was incorrect, and he was sacked – he couldn't get a job this side of Swansea.

Father continued working, but had to pass the site where his father had been killed every day. It upset him badly. In 1911 Partridge Jones and John Paton Ltd, which owned the works, sent him to Llanerch Colliery (which the company also owned) to work underground. During the First World War he joined the Royal Artillery Regiment, and was sent to France to fight. He was wounded twice – in the arm and in the face. He then returned to work at Llanerch Colliery. In 1938, while drying his face with a towel, he felt a sharp pain – a metal splinter had worked out from under the skin, a piece of shrapnel from the First World War.

He wouldn't use the baths at Blaenserchan after working a shift underground, as they were about half a mile further up the valley. Instead he cycled home and bathed there. He was afraid of catching a cold on the return home if he bathed at Blaenserchan, due to the change in temperature from being hot then cool outside. When Llanerch shut, he was transferred to Blaenserchan and was one of the first miners to retire at 65 years of age, in 1964. At 60 he had asked for lighter duties until retirement. He passed away, aged 90, in 1989.

As a youngster I rode the beer lorry at Pentrepiod to go to the Robin Hood pub during school holidays. The lorry reversed up and drove down; it went up to Sayce's Farm, where it could turn. The pub had a bracket in the wall to lower beer barrels by rope onto a four-wheeled cart, or pull them up the slope and empties down to the river bridge where the lorry was situated.

The works hooter at Pontnewynydd would blow at 6.00am and I would walk the mountains as a child, but my parents always told me to look where I was walking.

I lived in Waunddu with my parents and brother, and was in the junior school at Cwmffrydoer when both runaways from Blaenavon High Level station took place. The first was during the day, and it ran into the loop at Cwmffrwdoer at about 11.00am The engine was driven by Bill Dauncy and the fireman was Jack Lawrence.

A few weeks later at about 9.00pm the second runaway occurred. I heard the whistle blowing. In the dark it looked like the engine and first four wagons were on fire, with flames coming from their brake blocks. I shouted, 'Dad, Dad, another runaway!' I ran upstairs to the bedroom, which looked across to Gwenallt.

Dad replied, 'Don't be so bloody soft there's no engines up here this hour of the night.'

'You're too late, Dad – it's out the other side,' I replied.

Below Gwenallt loop, beyond the stop block, there was a bridge over a culvert. The loco ran through the block and jumped the culvert – it gave the impression of a hen sitting on a nest, with the spoil pushed around it.

The driver was Edgar Charles of Griffithstown, with fireman Ted Ashman of Pentrepiod, and guard Jack Timms. Jack later recalled that as soon as the driver whistled to leave Blaenavon High Level, after having the brakes pinned down, he knew that the train had insufficient brakes. He rolled up into a ball in his van and didn't expect to get over Garndiffaith Viaduct. Near the cinder tips at Pentwyn the teenage fireman jumped off and ran home in the dark. He told his father what had happened, had a bath and went to bed. About 3.00am railway officials knocked on the door saying there had been a runaway and they couldn't find the fireman. Ted's father said, 'He's in bed.' Edgar Charles stayed with the engine and put his foot against the boiler. On impact he broke his hip. The fire irons are said to have shot from the top of the tank and through the rear cab windows.

Great Western men had only done

passenger work to Brynmawr until 1941, then started running past Talywain to Furnace Sidings for the first time as a wartime measure. The men weren't used to working these trains from Blaenavon, as they had been worked by the LMS until May 1941.

Pontypool Road shed

There was one foreman per shift, either Joe Richards from Griffithstown or Arthur Lewis. Mr Belson was the chief clerk. There were six shift foremen, two on each turn; a few drivers would also do this.

About 500 men were employed there. Each yard employed six men per turn, inspectors, and wagon repairers.

You could access the shed in three different ways. The first was from the road viaduct at Coedygric, down the steps and past the Traffic Office at the side of the wagon repair shed. Another way was via the wooden footpath across the main line and the two goods relief lines, at the top side of the East Box. Access to this area was via the Black Ash path, which originated at the canal basin, then down the side of the triangle from the West box to a walkway under the main line at the side of the Afon Lwyd; this path turned left to the station, or right to the road viaduct at Coedygric.

Using the Black Ash path to the station, you walked from the shed past the stores and over the railway crossing by the East box to the Northern sidings. You passed the cabins, then about 40 yards later crossed over the railway to a gate in an opening in the fence, down to the tunnel under the railway line (the Black Ash path to the West box), past there to the old station yard, up the hill by the station master's house on the road to the main road, then down the other side to the station. This was the official walking route. In the wet you stopped on the track. This route was timed to be 16 minutes – every walk was timed. Old drivers and guards had heavy bags to carry on this route.

I used the Black Ash path to get to the shed, leaving it by the West signal box and walking down the track by the bottom end of the shed.

The other route was via the Black Ash path, under the railway, then turn right to the gasworks and the Northern Sidings. There was a gate to the Northern Sidings, and access as described above.

The wagon repair shed at Coedygric Road

Pontypool Road shed as viewed from the East Junction signal box on 24 May 1960.
F. A. Blencowe, R. K. Blencowe collection

Another view of the sheds, this time from the south end of the Loop Sidings.
R. H. Marrows

'Castle' Class 4 6 0 No 5073 *Blenheim* pilots No 5025 *Chirk Castle* past Pontypool Road loco sheds at the East Junction, with a northern passenger working on 16 August 1954. *Reproduced with kind permission of the Railway Correspondence & Travel Society*

Another 'Castle', No 5095 *Barbury Castle*, heads north while engines await their turn on the ash pit in the background. *Kidderminster Railway Museum*

The former GWR brick-built Pontypool Road West Junction Signal Box is seen derelict and vandalised on 18 April 1965. *Kidderminster Railway Museum*

Viaduct was used for a long time for wagon and brake van repairs. Access to the yard and loco shed from the south end was by walking down the steps from the viaduct, past the offices on the right-hand side to the end of the building, then past the steps to the loft, the wagon repair shed entrance, kitchen, boiler house for heating the canteen, and toilets. The wagon repair shed had two roads, with a cripple siding for wagons between it and the Goods Relief line. This was accessed from the Panteg end, and wagons would be shunted in from the shed end. You could go in both ends as a repair shed for wagon repairs.

The Traffic Office was located at the side of the wagon repair shed. Going down the steps from the viaduct, on the side there was a square steel framing – this was an old lift for taking goods from the wagon repair shed up to delivery lorries on the road.

Part of the wagon repair shed was turned into a canteen. At the bottom of the steps was an office used as a guards' cabin, then

An ex-GWR 0-6-0PT passes south through Station South Junction with a freight train, as viewed from the Black Ash path.
J. S. Williams collection

An unidentified ex-LMS 'Royal Scot' Class 4-6-0 approaches the West Junction signal box. The Black Ash path is to the left of the signal at the base of the embankment .
J. S. Williams collection

An unidentified ex-LMS 'Royal Scot' Class 4-6-0 is seen on the triangle adjacent to the West Junction signal box.
J. S. Williams collection

there were the offices at the end nearest the shed where the bosses were: yard master, yard chief clerk and yard office staff. The guards' room had lockers all the way around it. You walked around the corner and up the stairs to get to a store. If you walked around the building and along by the side, you went into the canteen. It was closed in 1964, and moved to the 'Oily Rag' railway club in Griffithstown. The canteen staff and the drinks licence went with it. Written above the doorway was 'Pontypool Road and Griffithstown Temperance Society'. The former canteen was then turned into a mess room for footplate staff. Drivers and firemen also had a cabin by the stores at the top end of the loco shed, which contained a wash hand basin at one end and benches with wooden backs around the walls.

Preserved No 3440 *City of Truro* came to Pontypool Road once. It was turned on the triangle, and stopped in Birkenhead Sidings, behind the loco shed, where I had a look at it and got up onto it. It was waiting to go to the station, from where it was working an excursion train.

The coal stage building

There were four rooms underneath the building. The first, nearest the shed, was a cabin for the driver and fireman who worked on the stage. The next room was the lamp room, near the coal tipper on the second floor; this was a long room. Lamps off the engine were filled here, wicks checked and lenses cleaned. It had a big fireplace and was always hot – coal was picked up off the floor outside, or dropped down by the

Ex-GWR 'City' Class 4-4-0 No 3440 *City of Truro* is seen at Crewe Steelworks Sidings after bringing an enthusiasts' special to a Crewe Works open day via Pontypool Road in the late 1950s.
J. S. Williams

coalman. At either end there were doors, one each end of the building, to go to the coal platform. The third room was where the ATC batteries were kept and charged to stop them going flat. The last room, at the station end of the building, contained lockers, and was for the coalman, fire-droppers and the ashpan man.

The second floor was all steel, and carried a single track. Operating the coal stage was very intensive manual work. On each shift two men worked on coal, two men on fire-dropping and one man worked on ashpans. Wagons of coal were pushed up the steel coal stage base to the top, and braked. Up to ten wagons of coal could be stored on the coal stage at the start of the day. One wagon would be inside the coal stage building for unloading. Two steel tubs, or drams, were used; one end had a swinging door that could be locked. Two tubs were put against the wagon, and the wagon's side door opened onto them. Coal was shovelled off the door into the tubs, then any overflow on the coal stage floor. The tubs were then pushed onto the tipper, raised clear of the roof of the engine or tender, and the coal tipped in. A '72xx' tank engines took five tubs, a '42xx' tank engine three, and tender engines would have eight.

The coal stage was shunted every day, two or three times in the morning. A lot of coal was needed to coal up the engines. Empty wagons were braked down one at a

time from the building, using both brakes, and put in a siding. If the track was blocked at the bottom of the coal stage you couldn't get an engine on shed. The empties were shunted as one train into the siding; if any loaded wagons were still on the train, these were put onto the loaded train ready to go back up. The wagon on the engine was stopped where the coal stage men wanted it.

There were three roads outside the coal stage: the Through Road, the Tap Road next to the coal stage, and the Cabin Road next to the cabins by the stores. At the end of the coal stage was a tap for clean water.

Around the shed

Water columns were located at the New Sidings and at the Old Yard, there were three on the shed, and one at Birkenhead Sidings behind the shed. At the station at Pontypool Road there was one on each of the two bay platforms, one at the north end of the up line, and one at the south end of the down line. There was one on the Up Goods, and one on the down goods. There were no water columns at the Northern Sidings, which were the newest sidings.

The shed stores had a water tank on top of its roof for feeding the water columns, and was supplied with water from the canal near Griffithstown swimming baths. The tank was cleaned out on a weekend every few years

Ex-GWR 2-6-2T No 5103 takes water at the Birkenhead loop by the water column, circa 1960. Hart's Yard is on the left. *Kidderminster Railway Museum*

– when an engine blew off, it would stink. Water for the station was taken from the canal by Panteg Cemetery.

I recall the sand houses, one behind the coal stage, and one at the south end of the shed, in front of the timekeeper's office. The latter was a steel-sheeted building and had a steel opening in one side that you could pull down to throw sand through from a wagon alongside. If you were spare, you were sent to shovel sand through these openings into the back of the sand house. The sand in the wagons was always soaking wet. Inside the sand house there was a big hopper with a fire grate below to feed the coal in, and a central chimney above passing up through the centre of the hopper. The sand ran down and below the hopper, past the chimney, and would be glowing red. If you carried a bucket of sand it would be warm against your legs, and you would need a piece of waste as protection. Most engines had four sand boxes; the back sanders were used for reverse running.

Removing smokebox ash was the last thing to be undertaken before the loco moved on to the shed. There was a road alongside to position wagons onto which the ashes could be loaded.

The booking-on office was in the round part of the shed; you booked on and the running foreman told you your engine.

I spent three months cleaning, and two weeks were spent on nights, calling. The first engine I cleaned was No 6849 *Walton Grange*. On a day turn this engine would be cleaned on the Tap Road by the coal stage ready for the 1.42pm Cardiff train from Pontypool Road. It was cleaned every day. On the afternoon shift you cleaned other engines. I didn't do much cleaning as I was firing quite a lot as a cleaner.

I was on nights, calling mainly, but as I was 16 years old I had a few firing turns, and was made a fireman in May. I worked days, afternoons and two weeks of nights.

At night there was good lighting in most of the yards. There were big floodlights against the viaduct on both sides, shining onto the yard, and there were a lot of lamp posts around the yard. Where the men had to work was always well lit.

At the shed, lights shone towards the sidings. At the Northern Sidings lights shone at the Black Ash path.

The West box had a light outside for the steps to the box only; this area wasn't well lit at night. You walked up the track on the sleepers. The West box could be accessed from the Black Ash path by a set of steps; the path was lit.

Pontypool Road sidings

There were eight yard pilots: Loop, South, Old Yard, New Sidings, Coedygric, Northern, one on the station, and one on the shed (to move coal around, and into the gasworks via the concrete bridge; the gasworks' diesel would push these into the works).

Little Mill Sidings were situated at Little Mill Yard, opposite the signal box, and were used to form and re-form trains for the Vale of Neath, Bristol and Cardiff. Two early-morning freight trains for Bristol and Cardiff went here to shunt. Vale of Neath freight trains were banked from here to Cwm Glyn near Hafodrynys. The morning Little Mill freight to Swansea also started from here to go via the Vale of Neath.

The carriage sidings at Pontypool Road station were used to store carriages for the Eastern Valley workings, and the auto-coaches.

Trains entered the glassworks sidings via the line at the back of the Station South box. They would go into the station on the Up Goods, to the bottom by the

carriage sidings, then push back in by the Station South box. Trains of sand went in for making the glass, and wagons of glass were taken out by the Northern Pilot and dropped onto the back road alongside the Up Goods. Stopping there, they would then be pushed back out by the Station South box and through the crossovers to the Northern Sidings. Sometimes the train of glass would be stored elsewhere – on the Down Goods to the Birkenhead Sidings and another set of sidings called Hart's Yard, which was used for coal storage for a long time; there was still coal there in 1951. Management stored coal against a big freeze; it was a wasteful method, as not all the coal was picked up.

Before Hart's Yard, the original coal storage location was the 'coal field' before Pilkington's glassworks was built, using the Admiralty sidings. When Pilkington's was built, Hart's Yard was used instead. The Northern Sidings were also used for coal storage during the war and into the 1950s; they were the best sidings in the yard, with long roads and a nice shunting spur. The Bristol to Manchester vacuum would go into the Northern Sidings, and you went to Llantarnam with the Northern Pilot to

Ex-GWR '56xx' Class 0-6-2T No 6661 leaves Station South Junction with a Vale of Neath train heading for West Junction on the triangle, with Pilkington's glassworks in the background. In the foreground are the points leading to Hart's Yard (left) and the engineer's yard on the extreme right is the Up Loop. Date unknown. *Kidderminster Railway Museum*

Ex-GWR 2-8-0 No 2894 is on the Up Goods line approaching Pontypool Road Station South Junction. The ash pit steam crane is seen on the right. *R. K. Blencowe collection*

give it a push up. No 385 is remembered on this job, but was no good. At the Station South box, you pulled the train back into the Northern Sidings, otherwise it had to propel back. You pulled back to the shunters' cabin, where you were uncoupled to go into another road alongside, which was empty. The train was then propelled back into an empty siding.

A few coal wagons for the coal stage were kept at the back of the shed, but as a rule they were kept in Hart's Yard, at the bottom end of the Birkenhead Sidings if Hart's Yard was full, or sometimes in the Northern Sidings by the gasworks – you had to go down to the station by the Station South box and push them back up. Shed coal was normally kept in the sidings adjacent to the two running roads next to the Skew Field side of the shed (the Birkenhead Sidings). You pulled them out, put them on shed and put the empties back in the Birkenhead Sidings.

The old Northern Sidings contained seven long roads, all having easy access, and two shorter ones next to the main line, at

the bottom end. Trains could be backed into the Northern Sidings from anywhere, one such being 261, the Bristol vacuum, with chocolate, a train that was run at night. Trains from Cardiff or from the Vale of Neath that had wagons for Pontypool Road, or wagons with gasworks coal, used these sidings. The Saltley train (for Birmingham) started from here, with a crew change at Worcester or Shrewsbury. A lot coal was stored in these sidings, and Severn Tunnel yards were also full of Welsh coal.

The gasworks was accessed from a spur in the Northern Sidings; you ran across an overbridge at Black Ash path to put coal in. The gasworks had a little diesel to shunt internally. Coal would be shunted into the gasworks once or twice a week.

Hart's Yard was used for stockpiling coal – the old Admiralty naval siding had been used in years gone by. Coal was unloaded and stockpiled between the tracks, and covered up. The old Northern Sidings were also used to stockpile coal until the gasworks opened. The Northern Pilot would put coal in there for the gasworks.

Ex-GWR 0-6-0PT No 8781 is seen in the gasworks siding, with the Northern Sidings in the foreground and the gasometer behind it on 11 August 1962. M. Dart, Transport Treasury

The Loop Sidings were situated by the back of the South box by the viaduct. These were dead-end sidings.

Trains from the Vale of Neath were shunted off by the South Pilot, and wagons transferred to Coedygric to work trains from there. Two trains started from the Coedygric Sidings or New Sidings for the Vale of Neath; this was for the coke ovens working off the Vale of Neath, above Pontypridd station. One train was at night, the other in the morning.

New Sidings and Coedygric Sidings were side by side, under the arches of the viaduct. If you were on a train from the north, at night a banker pulled you out of the New Sidings to Station South; you braked as you went onto the Up Relief outside the Station South box, inside an indicator signal. The end of the train was opposite the station, where the banker uncoupled. At this location, you could go past the shed to the Loop, Birkenhead or South Sidings, or to the Vale of Neath. The guard told you

to be ready to go, then the banker gave a couple of 'crows' on the whistle. You replied with 'crows', the couplings clanged, and the banking engine pushed the train gently for the West Junction and the Vale of Neath.

Main-line trains from the north to the New Sidings entered by the North Box at the far end of the station, and came right through to the East signal box, which turned them down to the New Sidings reception road.

A single track ran from the New Sidings past the shunters' cabin, then dropped down to the New Sidings signal and out to Panteg Junction. There was a ground frame on the left in the New Sidings. In front of this box you switched down to go onto the shunting spur. If this wasn't done, you were pulled back to the Station South box and went down through the cutting by the East box.

Severn Tunnel trains came up in the morning, via Panteg Junction and the 'tunnels', and finished up in the New Sidings to go back via the single-track slope onto the Down Goods Line back to Panteg Junction. If you worked a train to Cardiff from New Sidings, it was sent down the Eastern Valley line, and the old Monmouthshire line to Newport, and onto the main line to Cardiff.

At the top of the Old Yard by the cutting was a water column and a signal. On the left-hand side was the spur for the Old Yard siding, between the cutting and the wall for the Eastern Valley. At the top of the cutting you went under the viaduct, past the South box and on up to the Loop. You stopped by the hand point on the Loop until the shunter or foreman told you where you were going. You either went up around the west to the Vale, or on towards Station South at the bottom end of Hart's Yard (which was a single track used for reversible working – you could go up or down it).

In the Old Yard there was a cottage by the viaduct that had been built for the men who constructed the viaduct, and the garden was alongside the track going up the side of the cutting leading down towards Panteg Junction. On right-hand side, walking towards Coedygric Junction, the first building

Viewed from Coedygric Road Viaduct, a diesel-electric DMU forming the 4.40pm Blaenavon (Low Level) to Newport (High Street) passenger service passes on the Eastern Valley line on 26 March 1959. *D. K. Jones collection*

was the ambulance hut, then there was a water tank that supplied the water columns for the yard.

I recall traffic for Panteg Steelworks, putting wagons in and pulling them out. Wagons were dropped in and pulled out just between the 'tunnels' and the bottom slope of the New Sidings. Ingots and steel slabs came out, and coal for the works went in. Coal came from anywhere, although Oakdale coal went to London for steam locos, and Midlands coal was fast-burning with a lot of smoke and heat.

The Old Yard Pilot, ex-GWR '96xx' Class 0-6-0PT No 9650, is seen on 25 September 1964 by the cottage adjacent to Coedygric Viaduct. The cottage was split into two parts; that near the viaduct, at the front of the engine, was used as the Old Yard cabin, and the half near the pigeon cots was used as a house. *Kidderminster Railway Museum*

Panteg Junction was used by the 'tripper' going down to take wagons into or out of Panteg works, and also for main-line trains going into Pontypool Road yard, where transfer pilots would move wagons to other parts of the yard. It was busy with trains from

Ex-LMS 2-6-2T No 40145 is stored in the Dead End Siding south of Coedygric Road Viaduct in 1958.
Driver P. H. Williams, J. S. Williams collection

the yard from the South box by the viaduct, and engineering trains to Panteg.

The Skew Bridge loop (Down Goods Loop on the Panteg & Coedygric Junction map) was regularly used to avoid passenger trains, or was used to push freight trains back into the yard. Freight trains needed a long time to get clear, as a number of passenger trains used the yard and went down the Eastern Valley – four a day – as well as other freight trains using the yard. They would normally push freight trains back into Coedygric Yard, but sometimes into the Old Yard. You then collected the brake van and went to the transfer sidings at Panteg by Panteg & Griffithstown station, dropping the van onto the back of a train, then went back up with a train of empties. The signal for this loop was opposite Griffithstown swimming baths on the down line.

Panteg Hospital had a siding and two or three wagons of coal were dropped off a train of empties going to Pontnewynydd Yard at night; the full wagons were coupled behind the engine for this. After Pontnewynydd Yard, the train would return to East Usk Sidings, leaving there at 11.30pm and going back to Pontypool Road.

Pontypool Road rostered links

You started cleaning, and were then made a junior fireman assisting on the shed with the shed driver or coal stage driver. Then, if a vacancy arose in a link, you covered that link. You went from the pilot link to the bankers, the banking link to the bottom branch. It was their way of teaching you the job. Pilot work was good.

There were 14 links worked by the footplate crews at Pontypool Road. Some of these are as follows:

The Pilot Link was the first link. There were 24 turns on this link. Each link had its own driver. My first mate was Rollei Jones, and he was with me for 18 months. I then worked with Ted Preece, 'old Presto'. With Rollei the job came first, and everything had to be done right. He was a disciplinarian, firm but fair. All Ted Preece was interested in was saving time. I finished on 9 March 1953 to go into the Army in April. When I came out I went into other links. I had three weeks of route learning as a refresher from being in the Army.

Rollei was very severe but taught me a lot of things. They didn't like the engine blowing off in the yard when they were working. Rollei challenged me: 'If you keep the engine quiet today I will fetch you a bottle of beer in tomorrow'. I kept the fire quiet – Rollei wanted the engine quiet for the rest of the week. He was over the moon. A couple of shovels of coal to build the fire up, then open the firehole doors to keep it cool. On passenger jobs and heavier jobs you had to be alert. There was a lot of work on the pilots in the yard.

ICI was shunted by me, twice, using the Little Mill Pilot. You got the empties out and put coal in.

Pilot work had regular drivers on the South, Old Yard, and New Sidings Pilots. The other Pilots were worked out of the Pilot Link. The South Pilot was standing drivers, but when a driver became 60 he could apply for work of lesser importance. By doing that it meant he was asking to go onto the Pilots, and he would be on them for the rest of his working life, until he was 65. Certain drivers didn't like the main line and were like a cat on hot bricks when you worked with them.

i. The Northern Pilot was always live drivers (those who worked everything), as the engine was required to bank from Llantarnam on the afternoon train – the 261 Bristol to Manchester freight. It would put off and put on at Pontypool Road, in the Northern Sidings. Only the 261 was banked from Llantarnam, using the Northern Pilot.

There were 12 or 24 turns in a link. You had one day off a fortnight. You had Monday off one week, then Tuesday two weeks later. This was subsequently changed so you had one day off a week.

ii. The Banking links had 12 turns. The Control Banker would work Little Mill to Pontypool Road, or to Nantyderry to pull a dead train in, or bank to Cwm Glyn. Bankers covered work at Abergavenny and at Crumlin. Banking from Llantarnam Junction was covered by the Northern Pilot. Banking from Panteg Junction up to the South Junction was undertaken by the Old Yard or South Pilot.

iii. There were three Branch links, all with 12 turns per link. The links were broken down into the Bottom, Middle and Top branches.

The Bottom branch link typically covered Pontnewynydd Yard (if spare), Glascoed goods (morning and evening), Abergavenny banking, spare turns, the Cwmbran Pilot and Llantarnam biscuit works. This link also covered Hafodrynys and Cwmbran, and shunting the coal yard at Pontnewydd, or Cwmbran and station coal yards.

The Middle branch link covered the Monmouth goods, Ebbw Vale via Crumlin, East Usk and Uskmouth jobs.

The Top branch link had 12 turns, and covered three day turns, five nights, four afternoons and a week of rest day cover. Typical work involved working the coke ovens at Pontypridd, down to Cardiff with the night goods, to Ebbw Vale, and down to Uskmouth.

iv. The Relief link had 24 turns. This link involved working the bottom main-line goods and the middle and top main-line goods links. Working in the Relief link you didn't know what job you had. Within it was the tow turn, when you booked on at a certain time. There were eight of these, covering around the clock. You covered everything at the depot, and you went everywhere.

v. The Bottom Goods link to Hereford, Cardiff, Severn Tunnel, Aberdare.

vi. The Middle Goods Link to Bristol, Margam, Aberdare to Glyn Neath.

vii. The Local Goods link, where you went working trains a bit further away.

5. Wagon Examiner Andrew Atkins

I started my career as a wagon oiler. I progressed to wagon examiner and moved to Pontypool Road, where I worked in all the yards. My mother died aged 47 in 1966 and I was offered a relief job, as an examiner and shunter. I have worked at all the collieries in Gwent, as well as Newport Alexandra Dock and Newport Mon Bank. I started at Oakdale Colliery in 1967 until 1989, and was then transferred to Ebbw Vale for 12 years, then to Llanwern Steelworks until 2007, when I retired.

I started on the railway in July 1961 at Hafodrynys New Mine. My first job was to oil empty British Rail 16-ton railway wagons at the tippler. There were four shunters at the New Mine – two at the top end and two at the bottom end. Three trains of empties would arrive in the morning, from Hereford, Droitwich and the Hereford Pool, which was a train of 50 empties. The empties were put in different sidings at the top of the screens for different sizes of coal – peas, beans and small coal. Markham Colliery sent a lorry filled with small coal that wasn't washed.

The weigher put the wagon labels on and the examiner examined the wagon. At the tippler, to move the wagon forward once they'd tipped it they dropped a loaded wagon against it. Tom Hewlett would say to me, 'Come on, sonner, I've made the tea.'

The Swansea vans came through about midday, for Manchester Docks. We had a cabin at Hafodrynys close to the track; we'd see them come through and get out of the cabin in case they derailed!

I had worked at Hafodrynys for a fortnight; I was then off for a fortnight for the miners' holidays. I was transferred to Pontypool Road during the annual miners' holiday of 1961 and was sent to work in the wagon repair shed. Everything was repaired, including the wheels. Crippled wagons were sent for repair – there were so many that some were sent to Thomas Ward of Cardiff to be repaired. Any type of wagon was repaired. Every afternoon, after the staff had finished for the day, the repair shop was shunted. If you didn't have to go underneath, the wagon was repaired outside, while anything requiring lifting was repaired inside the building. You could often have a hot box

on a train for Quaker's Yard. My first job in there was to fit a hammer head to its handle. I then assisted on wagon repairs.

I worked in all the yards at Ponty. I worked nights on 12-hour shifts, and pushbiked to Ponty Yard via the Black Ash path.

The Loop cabin was between the wall at the Skew Fields and the South Sidings signal box, at the top end of the Loop Sidings. We used to break up our coal outside, and I was in the cabin one night when a pair of feet come by. It was a tramp. I said, 'Mate, why don't you whistle or do something? Don't turn up unannounced.' We had a bench locker, and could sit there; there was a mirror so we could see who was outside. A couple of nights later a lot of police arrived, walking towards our cabin. They were looking for Harry Roberts, from Blackpool, who had killed two policemen.

I was on Ponty station one night when a pigeon train arrived, and Charlie Reynolds, who was then a fireman, was relieving it. I asked, 'How far are you taking this?'

'It's nothing to do with you,' he replied. I turned my shoulder and left.

I once examined wagons in the siding at Guest Keen & Nettlefolds, Cwmbran, which had labels saying 'Panama Canal via London'.

When my mother passed away in 1966 my boss said to me, 'Whatever you do, don't rush back. Before you come back, come and see me.'

I was off a fortnight, and he said, 'I've got a job for you.' I was put on relief work at Ponty. I started at Ponty station, as an examiner, examining passenger trains, and freights from West Wales that had relief at Ponty. I would ring the signalman and examine the train, which would be on the Up Goods line by the North box. When examined, I would ring the signalman and say, 'OK, go, relief is on.' I don't think a train left on my shift without being examined.

When Ponty shut in 1967 I was offered three jobs; the first was Llanwern, and the second was Oakdale Colliery. I went to Llanwern first and didn't like the work.

I asked my boss if I could go to Oakdale Colliery instead. I started there in 1967 and worked there for 22 years until it closed in 1989. Coal was sent to three places in Margam, including Margam Yard and Margam Hump, as well as to Llanwern Steelworks. Oakdale had one train of empties in the morning, which went to Markham Colliery to pick up coal for washing at Oakdale, as Markham had no washery. The driver of the Markham train left the engine at Oakdale, and officially caught a bus back to Ebbw Junction. However, a second Oakdale train arrived in the morning, and the driver of the Markham rode back with the driver of that train. The bus stop at Oakdale was by the Rock pub, which involved walking down a steep hill. However, getting a bus to Newport was difficult.

We travelled to Markham Colliery on the train, in the guard's van. The guard said, 'Sit down, Andy.' It was a rough ride! Instead of going up quietly, the driver opened right up! You could hear the empty wagons bumping each other. Halfway between Oakdale and Markham was Llanover Colliery, which belonged to Abertillery Water Board. There was one of our wagons in their siding, and I took the red clip off it.

I remember Driver Ted Preece, a former Ponty driver based at Ebbw. If Pontypool Rugby Club were playing home you had to look out. We had a derailment at Oakdale, on our property. Ted came up with breakdown vans and said, 'How long are they going to be?'

I said, 'I don't know, Ted – why is that?'

'Ponty are playing home,' replied Ted.

I said, 'Have a word with Control.'

I was in the cabin when he rang. He said, 'Yeah, they're chock-a-block up here with coal wagons – you give me permission to leave the breakdown, and I'll give them some space up here.'

And he did, and went home! Ted got away with it. 'Zapper' Ted we used to call him, and his son is the spitting image.

In later years Gloucester men would work a train of coal from Oakdale for Scunthorpe Steelworks.

Chapter 5: Vale of Neath

1. Driver Tom Davies

Admiralty coal trains 1914-18

As it was wartime, the railways were actually taken over by the Government's Board of Trade, but this did not alter very much the practices that were in operation on the old GWR. Footplate staff were continually being changed in their turn of duty, owing to the fluctuation in the volume of traffic.

At one period in the war, one train of coal left the Admiralty Sidings at Pontypool Road every hour around the clock for Chester and Liverpool where the Royal Navy's ships were being bunkered, and similar trains of empties were being run in the opposite direction to South Wales. (see the Introduction). In addition to this traffic, all passenger and freight services were maintained.

The backbone of this extra freight work was the '28xx' Class 2-8-0, 50 of which were stationed at Pontypool Road; their power seemed unlimited and their free-steaming qualities enabled them to perform their jobs even when the clinker from a dirty fire was falling out of the firehole doors. These engines would haul trains

PRIVATE, AND NOT FOR PUBLICATION.　　　No. 11

BRITISH RAILWAYS
WESTERN REGION

SERVICE TIME TABLES
PONTYPOOL ROAD
AND
NEATH JUNCTION;
MERTHYR AND PONTSTICILL JUNCTION, HIRWAUN AND QUAKER'S YARD (H.L.)

SEPTEMBER 26th, 1949 until further notice.

IMPORTANT NOTICE.

The Time specified in the Time Tables is the Departure from the Station when the times of arrival and departure are not stated, and in such cases the Trains should ARRIVE in sufficient time to enable the work to be done in order to leave the Station at the time appointed. The advertised departure times in a number of instances are slightly earlier than the Service Book times and the former must be used in all quotations to the public. The trains must also leave at the ADVERTISED time whenever practicable.

Out-of-date copies of this Service Book should be returned to distributing Office for disposal as waste paper when a new Book is received.

6918

The Vale of Neath route as operating in the 1949 timetable. *Phil Williams* of 45 10-ton coal wagons. [Author's note: 32 of these engines were stationed at Pontypool Road during the First World War, based on shed allocation records researched by the well-known author John Hodge.]

Vale of Neath, winter 1963

I had to take the snowplough, which was attached to an 0-6-0 tank engine, and proceed to clear snow from the line between Pontypool Road and Aberdare. We made pretty good progress, with just a little more regulator required when encountering a few drifts, until we came to the western end of Crumlin Viaduct, when it became necessary to put the fireman down to examine the points; there were no signals working, and while there was a green flag from the signal box, the driver had to satisfy himself that the points over which he was to travel were closed properly, so the fireman would do so before proceeding. On this occasion we had a Locomotive Inspector aboard, who volunteered to drop off and examine the points, which he did, but he didn't realise that the track over the viaduct was laid on wooden baulks about 18 inches above the deck of the bridge, and when he stepped off the bottom step of the engine he sank down into the snow. This produced a scream of sheer terror, as he thought he was falling through the bridge deck!

After his remark, 'All's well that ends well,' we proceeded on to Nelson & Llancaiach, where we stopped for water at the end of the platform, all still covered in snow. The station master came from his office and rushed down to the water column where I was standing. He said, 'Driver, I know I should not be asking you to do this, but it is an emergency. There are no road communications of any kind between here and Mountain Ash [a small mining village about 6 miles away], and there is a midwife here that has been called out to an urgent case. There is absolutely no way for her to get to Mountain Ash, and I wondered if you would take the risk, and take her with you on the snowplough?'

Well, after a little consideration I agreed, for really the footplate was sacrosanct to all without special passes and, fully aware of the risk to my job that I was taking, I went to the lady and assured her in no uncertain manner that it would be a very rough ride for her to take. Undismayed, she climbed aboard and away we went. It was not too bad for the first couple of miles, just clearing snowdrifts of 3 or 4 feet, until we came to the entrance of the single-line tunnel, which was our goal. The snow had accumulated pretty badly, for the tunnel went through the bottom of a mountain, and when I put on a bit of steam to have a run at it, it just piled up to half block the tunnel mouth; there was such a bang when I struck it that I thought I had either become derailed, or perhaps brought some of the tunnel stonework down. Anyway, we got through intact, and our passenger, although a little bit frightened, assured me that she was all right.

With no more trouble she disembarked at Mountain Ash station with her little brown bag and, after profusely thanking me, said, 'Won't this make dramatic reading in tomorrow's *Western Mail*, when my brother, who is a reporter for that paper, gives me his report?'

I said, 'Oh, dear lady, if this is reported I shall get the sack, so you had better keep quiet until some day when you may write it in your memoirs.'

We proceeded on to Aberdare, where a steam lance was brought from the loco shed to blow away the packed snow that had accumulated in the engine's motion. These steam lances were a replacement for the rods that were used to clean out boiler tubes; they were connected to a steam valve at the front of the smokebox and, while they did an excellent job in blowing the tubes clean when in the shed, they were absolutely invaluable when used for clearing snow from points and the rods that ran alongside the track from the signal boxes, and of course anywhere else they may be needed.

One of the worst features of these snow-clearing trips was the tremendous carnage that took place – sheep used to gather in the numerous railway cuttings and get buried in the snow. There was no way of knowing what was beneath the snow when using the plough, and it was only when the thaw took place that the true picture was revealed, with hundreds of carcases that remained to be loaded into a special train chartered for that purpose. One cannot say it was a very desirable job to be performed by the platelayers, loading up mangled sheep, but as it was a task that had to be done, it was accepted as part of their work.

2. Railway enthusiast Terry Jones

My father, Austin Jones, was a former West Mon Grammar School pupil, and undertook an engineering apprenticeship at the Big Arch, Abersychan, under Partridge Jones and John Paton Ltd, in the loco shed in the early 1920s. For the period between 1925 and 1941 he was the Colliery Engineer at Quarry Level, and from 1931 this duty included Blaendare Level. When at Blaendare he purchased TVR No 789, which he named *Blaendare*, and GWR 0-6-0 No 808.

In the 1930s until 1941 I lived on Crumlin Road, in a bungalow near the bottom of the Race, at Pontypool. In 1939 my father accepted a position to work at Lower Varteg Colliery/Vipond's Top Pits, becoming the Colliery Engineer there in 1941. My mother didn't want to move back north of Pontypool. I was sent to live with my grandparents on the Varteg, until accommodation at Salisbury Terrace, Varteg, was obtained for my parents. My father initially went to Lower Varteg, but was not then in charge as Mechanical Engineer – that came later, in 1941.

I am a lifelong railway enthusiast, and the following are my memories of railways in the Eastern Valley in the 1930s and 1940s.

Coal trains

'Aberdare' tender engines are recalled working trains of coal down the Vale of Neath line towards Pontypool Clarence Street station – sometimes they used 'ROD' ('30xx') tender engines. I remember asking my father why the 'RODs' didn't make a ticking noise like an 'Aberdares' when coming down; the answer was that the 'ROD' wasn't fitted with a vacuum brake, only a steam brake. A vacuum-braked engine would make a 'tick, tick, tick' noise from the vacuum pump. I watched these trains as a youngster. 'RODs' were not popular – you couldn't stand steady when firing.

'56xxs' are also recalled on these trains, but not '43xxs' or '28xxs' – but I was very young at the time.

Cwm Glyn banker

Empties going up the Vale of Neath working towards Hafodrynys were hauled by an 'Aberdare' ('26xx'), pushed

Looking west, the Cwm Glyn banker, ex-GWR 0-6-0PT No 9644, banks a train towards Cwm Glyn on 14 December 1963.
R. H. Marrows

up the bank by the Cwm Glyn banker. The banking engine at this time was 'Dean Goods' No 2385, the only one of its class at Pontypool Road. The wagons were private-owner wagons with the colliery owners' names written on them.

The banking engine ran back down the bank at a fair speed. My father worked at Quarry Level and Blaendare Level at the time, and once said that the fastest wheels he ever saw on an engine was on one of the '20xxs', which had been used as the Cwm Glyn banker, when running back down to Pontypool Road yard from just above the Mynydd Maen Colliery. My father told of the pay differential in the 1930s between drivers and signalmen: drivers earned £4 10s, and signalmen about £2 15s, while firemen would get, say, £3. The drivers had an easy job on this turn; up at Cwm Glyn, once they lost

An unidentified ex-GWR '42xx' Class 2-8-0T approaches the railway bridge opposite the Mason's pub on Station Road, Griffithstown, with an Eastern Valley working for Talywain or Blaenavon Furnace Sidings. *J. S. Williams collection*

the bit of gradient they shut off, 'blew for the board', the signal came off and they were sent into the loop. They stood there for 20 minutes, the driver sitting on the seat with his feet on the reversing lever, waiting for a train.

Some of the '20xxs' and '57xxs' are

Below and top right: The last train of blended coal from Hafodrynys New Mine washery passes Station Road and the Mason's pub, Griffithstown, on Sunday 1 April 1979. *J. S. Williams*

recalled, as well as '27xxs', on this banking turn. I used to stand on the bank by my father's bungalow and watch the banking engine push the wagons past the bottom of the Race. I observed that only maybe 15 wagons in a train of, say, 45 wagons had the couplings compressed – the rest remained taut.

While 'RODs' and '66xxs' were used on goods trains, I recall pannier tanks with three coaches providing the passenger service to Neath, before and after the war; '56xx' tank locos performed this duty before the '41xxs' arrived at Ponty. My father was in Trosnant Sidings one day and watched a passenger train run past towards Clarence Street station and brake, but it ran past the station and had to push back into the platform – it was going too fast.

'20xx' tank engines on hire to Lower Varteg are recalled running quite fast down the Eastern Valley line over the railway bridge by the Mason's pub on Station Road, Griffithstown, and down to Coedygric Junction to run back through the yard onto Pontypool Road engine shed.

I moved house to live on the Varteg at Salisbury Terrace in the 1940s when my father accepted his new position at Lower Varteg Colliery from Mr Bythway. When walking from the bus stop and across the footbridge at Clarence Street station from the Pontymoile side at about 8.40am, I remember a brand-new '41xx' tank engine working the Vale of Neath passenger service from Pontypool Road to Neath. This was one of two of the class just allocated to Pontypool Road; it was No 4135 or No 4137. These two engines replaced the panniers and '56xxs' on the passenger trains. I stopped on the footbridge to watch one of these engines run through the cutting and into the station.

Matthew Redwood, a West Mon pupil, had heard that a new steam locomotive, No 1000 *County of Middlesex*, would be going through Pontypool Road one Sunday afternoon in 1945 at about 2.00pm. I went home, scrambled my dinner, and got on my pushbike from Varteg to get to see this engine come from the station and down through the cutting at Coedygric Road Viaduct.

One day 'Bulldog' No 3453 *Seagull* was seen stored at Pontypool Road by the road viaduct at Coedygric, in a siding against the bank of the Eastern Valley line (in the Old Yard).

3. Fireman Derek Saunders

Vale of Neath passenger trains were the 8.40am and 2.28pm to Neath; for a time I worked to Swansea with this train after running around the train at Neath. The 7.45am passenger to Aberdare was worked with a '63xx' tender loco. There were two passenger turns to Neath worked by Ponty men, Neath men working the remainder. The 8.40am was worked by loco Nos 4138 and 4135 (No 4131 was also at Ponty). '41xx' Class tank locos were also used on the Blaenavon trains, and a Sunday excursion to Porthcawl. The 2.28pm used a tender engine, a '63xx' maybe.

To arrive at the South Bay at Pontypool Road from the Vale of Neath, the train crossed over onto the Up Main line in front of the Station South signal box. If you worked a light engine off shed to go to the station, you stopped outside Station South box on the Up Goods Relief line and waited for the 'dummy' (ground signal), then reversed onto the Down Goods Relief. You then moved forward and crossed over onto the Up Main line to proceed to the station.

Coaches for the Vale were stored in the up or down carriage sidings in front of Butt's Siding at the station. When you arrived at Ponty station with an engine fresh off shed, sometimes the shunter would have put the carriages in the South Bay ready for you, using the Station Pilot. Otherwise you picked them up in the carriage sidings, and the shunter had to couple up; if you picked up the coaches in the bay (put there by the pilot), the fireman had to couple up. It all depended on the shunter. When you arrived back at Ponty station at the end of the shift, the Station Pilot would pull the carriages off you, and you would then take the engine back to shed.

After the 1955 strike I fired with a driver

Ex-GWR 0-6-2T No 6628 takes the 10.55am to Neath through Pontypool Road Station South Junction on 3 June 1963. This working used a Neath loco crew. Pilkington's glassworks is seen in the background, built on the site of the First World War Admiralty Coal Sidings.
M. Hale, Great Western Trust

who had worked through the dispute. We had a light engine off shed to go to the Northern Sidings. We stopped on the Up Goods line outside the Station South signal box and had to reverse back across the main line, for which you needed the 'dummy' to be cleared. I wouldn't tell him the 'dummy' was off, so he got another fireman to go with him – he didn't know where the signal was. I said to the foreman, 'The driver's always right, is he? You haven't heard my side of it.'

Ystrad Mynach had its own passenger train, and the coaches were put off at Ystrad Mynach yard.

The Nelson auto-train was the 6.42am; one or two coaches were used with a '58xx' or '14xx' tank loco (Nos 5818 or 1422). We would also use a '64xx' pannier on this job. The footplate crew worked one trip to Nelson and back, then went on the ash pit at the shed, using another engine to shunt wagons of ash off the ash road. The 6.42am was prepared on shed around 5.40am. I remember pulling out of the Station South Junction, up round to the West, and we almost came to a stand before reaching the West box. Dai James was firing and forgot he had the injector on.

Ponty also worked the pick-up goods and Neath trains on the Vale. On the pick-ups you shunted everywhere. You had an hour at Hengoed for shunting. Nelson and Quaker's Yard were also shunted.

I worked to Swansea via the Vale once with Dai James ('Bubbles') to Landore Low Level. We were accompanied by a pilotman from Neath. It was a passenger train, possibly a football special.

TVR No 385 left the shed on one occasion to work a goods train to Aberdare. The engine had a steam brake only and no vacuum, so could only be used on freight work. By the time the train reached Crumlin the steam pipe to the steam brake had failed, and the train ran away, crossing Crumlin Viaduct at around 30mph. It may have come to a halt by Penar. The driver should have noticed something on shed. This incident occurred during the war or just after, and is based on 'hearsay' from footplate staff at Ponty shed.

'28xxs' were used on the Vale of Neath for Llanelli or Neath jobs. Passing over Crumlin Viaduct with a '28xx', you could feel the structure shake. No 2840 is recalled working on the Vale line. If you had a freight

Crumlin Viaduct as viewed from its eastern end. *Phil Williams collection*

train to work over the Vale and were on
the Down Goods line at Ponty station, you
would stop opposite the South Bay and
take water if it was required.

'66xxs' Nos 6634, 6636, 6667 were used
on the Blaenavon passenger and Vale of
Neath passenger trains, while '45xx' tank
locos were used on the 6.10am Abertillery;
Nos 4533 and 4597 are recalled.

The so-called 'Third Line' went into
the back of the platform at Clarence
Street and extended as far as the West
box at Pontypool Road yard. I can never
remember this being used, but in my time it
was used for wagon storage.

There was a three-legged footbridge at
Maesderwen, crossing the line between the
canal bridge and Pontymoile to connect
Maesderwen with Fountain Road. It had
two legs on the Maesderwen side, and one
on the Fountain Road side.

Engine No 4229 was mostly used on the
Blaendare Pilot, and driver Jack Merryfield

Crumlin Viaduct (Showing Height)

Left: A westbound freight crosses Crumlin
Viaduct some time before 1929 when the
railway across it was reduced from two lines to
one. *Phil Williams collection*

Below: On 31 October 1962 an unidentified ex-
GWR '28xx' Class 2-8-0 heads east across the
viaduct. *Kidderminster Railway Museum*

The Vale of Neath railway bridge at Pontymoile Canal Junction is removed in 1967. *Robert Hall*

used to work it. It worked to Hafodrynys, to do the shunting and return with coal. Blaendare Junction, at Hafodrynys, didn't exist during my time on the footplate; the only signal boxes in use were at Cwm Glyn and Cefn Crib, near Hafodrynys.

I remember one of the '42xxs' working in the siding at Hafodrynys Deep Mine. One day I saw a wire hanging down from a post, so I thought I'd wrap it round the post when we went past. It was live – it nearly wrapped me around the post, and was swinging back and forth!

Ex-GWR '73xx' Class 2-6-0 No 7320 heads the 7.40am Neath-Pontypool Road train past the closed signal box at Cwm Glyn on 4 June 1963. *M. Hale, Great Western Trust*

Ex-GWR '56xx' Class 0-6-2T No 5647 heads west past Mynydd Maen, west of the Lower Race, in August 1963. *Both ProRail*

Glyn Tunnel was straight at the Hafodrynys end, but had a curve to the right at the Crumlin end.

I only remember Hafodrynys washery at the New Mine working. I can't recall the washery at Mynydd Maen Colliery working, at the bottom of the Race near Pontypool.

For the bank at Cwm Glyn, eastbound trains came to a halt at the stop boards and the guard and shunter would pin down the brakes. Half a dozen brakes were pinned down at the first stop board and you pulled away; the guard rode on the engine and the shunter put more brakes down at the second board, where the gradient was steeper.

On one occasion, with a train from Aberdare or maybe Penar, I remember the guard saying to me, 'Have a look out and see if the shunter is all right.'

I said, 'Who the hell are you? There's my boss, look, George Turley.' He was my driver. I said, 'You do your job – you go down and walk with the shunter.' We called the guard 'Doctor Hemmins' – his name was Bert Hemmins and he had medical remedies for everything.

4. Fireman Graham Merryfield

I worked the 8.48am passenger train to Neath, normally with No 6115. This engine was also used as the Crumlin banker, as well as

Station Pilot turns at Ponty. Sometimes the 8.48am used a pannier tank.

You had a '56xx' on the Dowlais tanks, but I also worked it using a pannier tank. I worked this turn with Arthur Edwards. At the shed I filled the firebox full and levelled off the bunker, then went back to the coal stage to have the coal stacked up to the roof. You left the shed about 11.00am and picked up the train in the Loop Sidings, consisting of vans and empty ammonia tank wagons. The train worked to Dowlais and returned with full ammonia wagons. You got relief at Ponty station, where another Ponty crew worked the train to Hereford, returning light engine to Ponty.

Upon leaving the Loop Siding at Ponty, you travelled over the Vale of Neath to Maesycwmmer Junction and up to Dowlais, where you had a banker at the top. You then returned with full wagons. At Crumlin High Level you stopped for a banker to assist. This engine dropped down from Crumlin Junction, ran across the viaduct, dropped down to Penar, crossed over and came up behind you at Crumlin High Level station; it then banked you up to Hafodrynys, at Cefn Crib. Arthur would not always want a banker at Crumlin, working this train unassisted to Cefn Crib. By the time you got to Ponty the bunker was empty and there wasn't enough coal to get to Hereford; I worked this train on to Hereford with all the rubbish and dust left in the bunker.

The Dowlais tanks cross Crumlin Viaduct, for Pontypool Road and beyond, on 9 August 1961.
Paul Chancellor collection (Colour-Rail)

Crumlin Junction, with the Vale of Neath line passing over the viaduct, and the 'muck hole' line to Llanilleth on the right. Ex-GWR 0-6-0PT No 4668 sets off across Crumlin Viaduct on 4 June 1963. *M. Hale, Great Western Trust*

An undated view of Crumlin Viaduct in the days of double track, before 1928, as seen from Crumlin High Level station. *Phil Williams collection*

In a similar view, a Pontypool to Neath train crosses the Ebbw Valley section of Crumlin Viaduct on 27 April 1960. In the background the Crumlin banker assists a train from Ebbw Vale towards Crumlin Junction and up to Cefn Crib. *R. K. Blencowe collection*

Left: A Pontypool to Neath train enters Crumlin High Level station on 27 April 1960 hauled by ex-GWR '97xx' Class 0-6-0PT No 9712. *E. T. Gill, R K Blencowe collection*

Below: Ex-GWR '37xx' 0-6-0PT No 3717 is seen at the High Level station with an eastbound passenger train on 8 June 1964. *Paul Chancellor collection (Colour-Rail)*

Ex-GWR 0-6-2T No 5642 enters Crumlin High Level station, date unrecorded. *Phil Williams collection*

On 3 September 1958 a train for Pontypool Road crosses the Kendon Valley end of Crumlin Viaduct after leaving Crumlin High Level station, hauled by an unidentified ex-GWR '41xx' 2-6-2T. *Kidderminster Railway Museum*

On 18 June 1960 the 5.35pm Swansea-Pontypool Road train crosses the viaduct and approaches Crumlin Junction in the distance. An unidentified ex-GWR '56xx' Class 0-6-2T hauls the train. *Kidderminster Railway Museum*

Above: An unidentified ex-GWR 0-6-0PT crosses the Kendon Valley section of the viaduct with an eastbound freight on an unknown date. *Phil Williams collection*

I worked on the Crumlin banker with a pannier or No 6115, which was normally on this turn, or No 5164. There was also a night Crumlin banker, which normally used a pannier. The banker ran down to Penar, crossed over and went up behind the train at Crumlin High Level, banking it to Cefn Crib at Hafodrynys. The 9 o'clock Penar was a heavy train, pulled by a pannier tank, and stopped at Crumlin High Level for the banker to Cefn Crib. If there was nothing to do on the Crumlin banker, I walked across the viaduct and leaned over the railings.

I also worked the night banking turn at Cwm Glyn, starting at 10.00pm and finishing at 6.00am. You banked anything that came along, such as a tanker train coming in for Swansea, or a goods train. Sometimes you banked one or two trains during the shift, or maybe nothing at all.

No 4639 was used as the Cwm Glyn banker, but tonight it would be the Crumlin banker, driven by Arthur Edwards. He came off shed at 10.00pm and pulled down past the South box, by the signal. When the

board came off we went past the West box and Arthur gave the engine full regulator and pulled the lever back. We went through Hafodrynys like nothing on earth – I was looking across waiting for the regulator to be closed. There wasn't much fire left. I looked across the footplate again going towards the Glyn Tunnel at Hafodrynys, but Arthur didn't shut the regulator until we were going down into the tunnel. Then he slammed the brakes on, and we entered the tunnel, still moving fast. At the end of the tunnel was a bend, and I thought we were sure to jump the rails there. As were entered this bend it was like the loco had glanced off a wall. I was frightened to death. We got to Crumlin Junction, down by the signal box, and back over the points and up to the signal box, where Arthur stopped and jumped off to go into the signal box. I drove the engine into the siding. We had done the trip from Pontypool in less than 5 minutes.

There were two trains to Ebbw Vale using one diesel, which would take more than a '72xx'. Also the steam-hauled train would

The eastern portal of the tunnel at Hafodrynys is seen on 6 June 1963. *R. H. Marrows*

An eastbound freight approaches the western end of Hafodrynys Tunnel. Unusually it is not assisted by the Crumlin banker. *W. Potter, Phil Williams collection*

An eastbound coal train approaches the western end of the tunnel, assisted by the Crumlin banker. It may be a train of coal from Oakdale Colliery. *W. Potter, Phil Williams collection*

Left: Ex-GWR '66xx' Class 0-6-2T No 6605 of Aberdare shed heads the 4.49pm train to Pontypool Road at Hafodrynys Platform, west of Hafodrynys Tunnel, on 8 June 1957. *M. Hale, Great Western Trust*

Below: Looking west at Hafodrynys Platform from a Neath-bound train on 10 April 1964. *F. A. Blencowe, R. K. Blencowe collection*

Ex-GWR '46xx' Class 0-6-0PT No 4639 calls at Hafodrynys station with an eastbound passenger train to Pontypool Road on Friday 12 June 1964, the day before closure. *D. K. Jones collection*

require a banker from Llanilleth to Crumlin Junction, coming back with a loaded train from Ebbw Vale.

One day there was a runaway on the Ebbw Vale train from Cwm Glyn. This was the 6.10am off Ponty shed. Diesels were kept around the back of the coal stage. I worked an empty train from the Loop Siding at Ponty to Ebbw Vale steelworks with driver Arthur Edwards and a Ponty 'D68xx' Type 3 diesel loco (later Class 37). We were to come back with steel coils. We didn't need a banker at Crumlin, as the diesel could take the train unassisted to Cefn Crib.

The train was heavy, and coming back down to Cwm Glyn we should have stopped at the stop board to have brakes pinned down. The train had some vacuum-fitted wagons, and Arthur thought we had enough brakes. We went past the stop board and the train was getting faster and faster. Arthur put the vacuum and air brakes on, but to no effect. We went through Clarence Street at a fast speed, blowing the horn, then around the corner to the West signal box. The signalman at Trosnant Junction had alerted his colleague at the West box, who set us

for the sand drag on the triangle, up a rise between the running line and the Black Ash path. In we went and stopped about a foot or so from the end – there was gravel and sand everywhere. It stopped us, mind. Ideally we could have run through to the station.

The 2.13pm 'muck hole' to Llanilleth pulled us out with a '72xx' driven by Ted Hounslow. We didn't get on the diesel again – someone else took it back to the shed. Arthur had a severe reprimand, and the guard was on the sick after this incident.

Arthur Edwards's recollections of the incident

I started at Ponty in 1941, and was lodging in Coedygric Road. It was the first time I saw snow in my life, as I was born in Briton Ferry and we never had snow there. I am now in my 90th year [2014].

We were relieving men on a diesel. The driver was called Fletcher, from New Inn, originally from Newport, and was nicknamed 'Spitter Fletcher', as he had a habit of spitting. We went out to relieve a train from

Cardiff, with a guard from Abergavenny. We went to the Loop cabin to relieve the train, which was more than an hour late. The guard said, 'It was just my luck – I wanted to get away today.'

When I got aboard, I said, 'Where have you been?'

The driver replied, 'We had trouble with the brake, but it's all right now.'

Therefore we didn't have the brake checked. We went engine and van from the Loop Siding to Ebbw Vale and I forgot all about what he said about the brake – we were just engine and van, see. We got to Ebbw Vale, picked a few wagons up, not many, and dropped back down to Llanilleth, where we picked up 18, with six vacuum-braked wagons. We went across to the signalman to have a word with him and asked, 'Can we have the road now all the way to Pontypool?'

'Yes,' he said, 'you are all right,' and away we went.

Up from the 'muck hole' we changed staffs at Crumlin Junction and headed down towards Cwm Glyn. I eased the brake a bit, trying to hold the train, but we didn't stop despite having six vacuum-braked wagons and vacuum on the diesel. Around by the builder's yard (at the Clarence, just before Clarence Street station), I thought, 'There's nothing happening.'

Graham was sitting on the side, with his legs hanging out of the cab – I can see him now. 'Graham,' I said, 'we are not going to stop at the West,' and we hadn't even got to Clarence Street station. I said, 'If you want to get off, now's your chance.'

This image flashed through my head – if he's got us set for the main line and a train comes up, we'll smash into the side of it. I'd forgotten about the sand drag. Suddenly we came to a dead stop. We were in the sand drag. But there was a passenger due on the Vale. The signalman at the West box said, 'You're all right, we've got a "72xx" coming out and we'll pull you out of the sand drag.' The '72xx' came out of nowhere, and pulled us out, like a cork out of a bottle.

On the Monday morning I thought, 'Oh my god,' as Inspector Ron Perry was waiting in the lobby. 'Come here, Mr Edwards, I hear you've had a bit of an accident.'

I said, 'Yes, it's not me you want, it's Fletcher – he's done the dirty on us really.'

'Anyway,' said the Inspector, 'it's all been hushed up. There's no Registered Caution. That diesel should have a vacuum tender coupled to it for extra braking.'

Of course, to go in a sand drag you are marked for life – everyone knows about it.

Another diesel job was a train to Margam (Port Talbot Steelworks). Two diesels were used on this job, working a train of red oxide wagons from Hafodrynys to Port Talbot, returning with empties. Two bright-green 'D68xxs' were used, and when getting near Port Talbot on the bank the fire bell would ring.

1929 accident at West Junction

Another much earlier accident is worth recalling at this point. On 6 July 1929 the 7.40am rail auto-car from Nelson to Pontypool Road left Pontypool Clarence Street station against danger signals and, after proceeding about 600 yards, struck the rear vehicle of a special goods train that was standing at the West Junction home signal, preparatory to entering the goods yard.

The rail auto-car consisted of engine No 753, an 0-6-0 tank, pulling one eight-wheel bogie trailer coach, No 152. The goods train consisted of 49 wagons, of which the rear four were a brake van, two loaded coal wagons and one LMS wagon containing pig iron. Ahead of these were two 30-ton Great Western 'Macaw' wagons, and these, together with all those ahead of them, were not damaged. The train was drawn by engine No 2803; a banking engine had been detached from in front of the engine a minute or two before the accident. The total length of the goods train, excluding the banking engine, was around 1,080 feet.

The weather was fine and the rails dry. The goods train left Clarence Street at 8.10am and came to a stand at the West Junction up home signal at 8.14am. The

Pontypool Road West Junction as seen on 6 June 1963. The tracks to the left led to Pontypool Station South, while those to the right lead to the Loop. The line on the extreme right is the 'Third Road', from the Loop Sidings.
R. H. Marrows

An early view showing the west end of Pontypool (Clarence Street) station, with the signal box in its original location. The Eastern Valley line to Pontypool (Crane Street) is in the background, together with the siding to Clarence Street goods shed, accessed from the Vale of Neath line.
Mark Vrettos collection

banking engine, which had been working down from Cwm Glyn attached to the front of the train, was detached and ran ahead. The road was then set for the goods train to enter the yard and the signal pulled off accordingly. Driver Lewis made an attempt to start, but was unable to do so due owing to the number of wagon brakes that had been applied for the gradient. Neither driver nor fireman of the goods train noticed the collision nor felt any impact, but the driver, looking back preparatory to a second attempt to start, saw that something had happened to the rear vehicles of his train, and told the guard, who went back to investigate.

The goods train had been waiting at the home signal, where there was a stop notice for all goods trains, for about 5 or 6 minutes prior to the collision. Of this time about 3 minutes had been occupied getting the banking engine clear and the remainder in releasing the brakes. This delay was not in any way greater than usual.

The rail auto-car had arrived at Clarence Street station at 8.19am, about 1 minute late; it had been checked at the home signal in accordance with Rule 40. The signalman at Clarence Street had not received the 'Train out of Section' signal for the goods train from West Junction, or had pulled the starting signal for the rail auto-car. As soon as the station work had been completed Guard Powell got into the central entrance door of the trailer coach and rang the bell to proceed; the bell rang in the engine cab.

Driver Higgins did not look at the starting signal and pulled away. Fireman Hough was looking back along the train and thereafter turned on the injector. Guard Powell occupied himself with writing his journal. Signalman Bartlett was make entries in his train register while the auto-car was in the platform – then, looking out, he noticed it passing around the bend. He could do nothing except send the prescribed emergency signal to the signalman at West Junction box, and inform him by telephone what had happened. While doing the latter he heard the noise of the collision. Responsibility was apportioned to Driver

Higgins of the rail auto-car. [Author's note: Driver Phil Williams, known as 'Full Load Phil', recalled seeing this accident many years ago. Someone was taking photographs from the Maesderwen footbridge, but was told to stop by a Great Western official.]

5. Fireman Gwyn Hewlett

Reg Dimry was a good mate. I worked the goods over the Vale of Neath with him when I was in the passenger link. We used to go to Margam over the Vale, with a mixed train of English coal for Margam yard. English coal and Welsh coal were missed at Port Talbot for use in the steelworks. We came back with a train of box vans picked up at Neath, with a '68xx' or a '49xx'. We had relief at Ponty and the train went all the way to Shrewsbury.

Ex-LMS 8F 2-8-0 No 48525 approaches the eastern end of Pontypool (Clarence Street) on 14 December 1963. *R. H. Marrows*

A westbound passenger train crosses the Crumlin Viaduct in 1930.
E. Harvey, J. S. Williams collection

The train of coal coming south might also be routed via the main line, and not travel on the Vale. In later years we lost this job to Hereford men, who worked double-home with it to Llanelli.

The 2.40pm to Neath used a '41xx', which you worked with three or four coaches. There you hooked off, went on shed, trimmed the bunker and turned the engine. It would work back as the 5.59pm Neath to Ponty, arriving at Ponty at 8.00pm

I had ex-LMS 8F 2-8-0s on the Vale, on coal trains to Margam. These were a nice engine, and would pull the same load as a '28xx'. You picked up the train at Little Mill and travelled via the Vale of Neath to Margam. You might pull off in the yard at Neath, or go to Llanelli and the engine would come off there. You had any engine on freight work.

Another job was to pick up an engine at Neath shed in the late evening, travel tender-first to the yard to pick up the train, possibly for Coleham, Shrewsbury, then work back on to the main line and get relief at Ponty.

I once crossed Crumlin Viaduct with a '53xx' coming back in a thunderstorm without a banker. You could feel the viaduct swaying. The worst bit of the line was up to Cwm Glyn – the rest was easy. 'Kings' were always banned from Crumlin Viaduct, but I fired 8Fs and a BR '75xxx' over it.

You went in the loop at Cwm Glyn if there was a passenger train about. The brakesman had a cabin by the side of the signal box, and he would come out and brake your train, together with the guard.

6. Fireman John Pring

Gwyn Hewlett and I started at more or less the same time as cleaner boys at Pontypool Road, in 1947. I am sure that a lot of his memories will match many of mine, but my memory of the 14 years I had there is very good, particularly when it comes to individual characters.

Gwyn and I were called up for National Service and met up again in the Royal Artillery at Kinmel Park training as Signal and Wireless Operators.

Ex-GWR 2-6-2T No 4126 crosses the first span of Crumlin Viaduct with a westbound passenger train in 1963. *ProRail*

Bankers

The Control banker was a three-turn shift, and the engine could be utilised to go to assist trains almost anywhere in the Pontypool Road vicinity. The engine used on this job was mostly a '72xx', No 7206 being the most regular one; this class was built in 1934 based on the '42xx', but with an extended bunker giving a bigger coal supply. They were very strong and fine engines to work on, and a great favourite with most Western men.

This banker would stand in a small siding near the bottom of the West Junction, very close to the main Station South Signal Box, with very easy access to the main line. Most of its work was from Llantarnam Junction to Pontypool Road and from Little Mill Junction through to Cefn Crib for heavy freights heading for Swansea and West Wales. This could be a very busy job with many special fast freights on the main line from Llantarnam, and many coming up from the West of England with fresh vegetables and fruit.

VIEW towards TRINANT, CRUMLIN.   7581.

Above: Crumlin Navigation Colliery can be seen in the distance of this view across Crumlin Junction and the eastern end of Crumlin Viaduct. A banked train of coal is present at Crumlin Junction. *R. H. Marrows*

Llanhilleth Colliery.   No.166

Left: Llanilleth Colliery, looking north, a location known to railwaymen as the 'muck hole'. *Phil Williams collection*

GWR '1076' 'Buffalo' Class 0-6-0T No 1078 is
seen at what is believed to be Llanilleth Colliery
Middle Junction in the Ebbw Valley, acting as
the Crumlin banker. Date unknown.
Phil Williams collection

The Abergavenny banker was a jointly
shared role for Pontypool Road depot and
the Midland Region shed in Abergavenny.
The engines used on the Ponty turns were
usually the ex-Taff engines Nos 349 and
385, not one of the favourites as they were
poor steamers and not very good as banking
engines.

The Crumlin banker was loco No
2385 ('Crumlin Castle' as it was dubbed at
the Pontypool Road depot by drivers and
firemen, particularly those working in the
Banking Link). This Dean 0-6-0 was first
introduced in 1887, and was considered as
one of Dean's most successful mixed-traffic
engines. It was worked almost exclusively on
the three-turn Crumlin banker turns, based
at Crumlin Junction; being a small tender
engine it was able to carry adequate coal and
water required for the very busy schedule of
banking performed.

Banking tasks were assisting heavy freight
and coal trains from Penar Junction to Cefn
Crib over the Crumlin Viaduct, as well
as the line from Llanilleth, known as the
'muck hole', to Cefn Crib through Crumlin
Junction. Both inclines were quite steep;
that from Llanilleth was single line around a
climbing bend, and in wintry conditions we
used a lot of sand to prevent slipping on the
greasy rails. I am sure that any footplateman
who worked this job can relate some very

unpleasant working conditions, particularly
during the winter – running tender-first
down to Penar over the viaduct through
rain, snow and howling gales could be pretty
uncomfortable. Only having a rather small
cab, even with a canvas storm-sheet attached
did not provide very much protection, and
on such nights you could have your heavy
railway raincoat on for the whole shift. We
sought the haven of Penar Junction signal
box and the hospitality of the signalman to
make a can of tea and thaw out.

No 2385 kept its Great Western green
livery right through to the end of its days
and was always cleaned when on shed. It was
used on the odd excursion to Weston-super-
Mare, routed from Severn Tunnel via the
Gloucester line and over the old bridge over
the Severn at Sharpness. I was fortunate to
work one of these trips down to Weston and
back, and the old girl handled the job well.

7. Aberbeeg Fireman Ron Prettyjons

I started at Aberbeeg as a cleaner, and left
for two years in the Army.

When firing on iron ore workings we used
a tank engine from behind the signal box
at Aberbeeg. There would be six or seven
trains a day. They were loaded at Newport
Docks, and one scoop would fill one wagon.
One day I was banking an iron ore train from
Aberbeeg when all of a sudden the bottom
came out of an iron ore wagon – there was a
massive bang, and the ore came out of   the
bottom.

They had nine 9Fs at Newport and,
when initially used, there was a problem
with the design of the regulator. An incident
is recalled at Aberbeeg when the leading
engine was taking water. When it moved
off the regulator stuck open and there were
sparks everywhere – and the engine cut itself
into the rails. They altered the design of the
regulator after that incident.

I sometimes wanted to finish early, and
so would my driver, Mr Hill. I would say to
the signalman at Aberbeeg that the driver

was 'driver ill ready to go to shed'. We would shovel the coal off on to the track to make sure we had none before going back to the shed.

I used to shunt Llanilleth with coal trains. I worked to Cwmtillery with a '42xx', and pulled them down with a brake on every wagon. We would steam them down. I worked Six Bells, the South Celynon Washery, North Celynon and Marine Colliery at Cwm, Ebbw Vale, where coal was washed. *Menelaus* shunted the colliery. Ebbw Vale was the furthest north, where a lot of shunting was done, and Brynmawr was the limit – it was a perishingly cold place. Crumlin Navigation Colliery, as well as Cwmcarn and Risca Collieries, are also recalled. I never worked the Penar branch. Coming down through Cwm early in the morning I would put small coal on the fire, and dirty the washing in nearby houses!

When based at Severn Tunnel I worked a train from there to Didcot, getting off at Swindon. The fireman of a train coming back from Paddington, the 5.55pm working, was taken ill and I was asked to go on it and bring it back to Cardiff. The engine was a 'Britannia', and as I left Swindon I filled the firebox right up, then at Badminton I filled it right up again, which nearly took me to Cardiff. From Badminton it was mostly downhill. Approaching the Severn Tunnel was interesting; you fired going through the tunnel, and picked up water at Magor; there was a light at this location at night.

I also worked the Monmouth Troy branch up to Tintern when based at Severn Tunnel. Tommy Rees came from Aberdare to work at Severn Tunnel when I left to work in Llanwern.

For the Royal Ordnance Factory at Glascoed we would take people from Brynmawr and Ebbw Vale in separate trains using Aberbeeg engines, joining them up at Aberbeeg. The same procedure was used for Barry Island trains. Returning passengers had

Situated immediately north of Crumlin Viaduct was Crumlin Navigation Colliery, in the Ebbw Valley. The ventilating fan steam engine is preserved, and is now in storage at Nantgarw, as part of the former Industrial and Maritime Museum collection from Cardiff Bay. *Phil Williams collection*

MARINE COLLIERY, NEAR EBBW VALE.   W.4644.

Marine Colliery, at Cwm in the Ebbw Valley. *Phil Williams collection*

red cordite on their hair from the munitions. The train would use two tank engines, a pannier and a '56xx'. There was one train in the morning and one at night – one to Brynmawr, the other to Ebbw Vale. Typically it was an eight-coach train split into two trains of four coaches. This was the only time I worked Ponty for a job.

I worked over Crumlin Viaduct from Llanilleth, to take engines to Aberdare for repair. It would sway as you went over it, and the wind was felt.

8. Fireman Henry Williams

The 'Third Road' extended from the end of the Loop Siding at Pontypool Road, past the West Junction, through Pontymoile, up the back of Clarence Street station, and back in under the railway bridge at Clarence Street, stopping there. It was used for wagon storage.

When Hafodrynys Washery opened I was on the banker at Crumlin Junction when they brought the washery cylinder through on a 'Crocodile' wagon; it had to go through the tunnel at Hafodrynys.

At Trosnant Junction there were two sidings where they would repair wagons for the Gwent Wagon Works at the Lower Race.

I never got to work the Nelson auto-train. A '14xx' would take a coach from Pontypool Road to Nelson, only in the morning, but not in the afternoon. It was a school train.

I once took a special train of three cattle wagons to Maesycwmmer. Cattle trucks were sent to Pontypool Road station and put onto the back of a train going to Maesycwmmer, where they were taken off and the pilot there would take it the local slaughterhouse.

Above: Signals for Maesycwmmer East Junction are seen on the east side of the A472 roadbridge, with the signal box in the distance, on 27 July 1963. *Trackbed.Com*

Banking from Penar to Cefn Crib and Pontypool Road to Cwm Glyn

Eastbound trains would be banked from Penar up to Cefn Crib box, where the front engine shut off and the banker dropped away as the train rolled over the top towards Hafodrynys. No brakes were pinned down, so you would control the train with the engine hand brake, off and on as required, to suit the road, and the train was brought to a stop at Cwm Glyn signal box.

On arrival the guard, who was in his van, put down brakes, aided by the brakesman at Cwm Glyn. As they approached the engine they put down drakes on each side of the wagon. The engine would be blowing off with a full head of steam in case you had to drag the train from Cwm Glyn; no matter what brakes were put down, it would be blowing off at Cwm Glyn box. You then either continued towards the West Junction at Pontypool Road if the line ahead was clear, stopping at the next stop board below Cwm Glyn, or were put in the loop at Cwm Glyn to allow a passenger train to pass. In bad weather there would be poor braking from wagons that had been under the screens, as the brake levers would be iced up. At the second stop board, below Cwm Glyn, more brakes were put down. At the West box the guard would get out of his van to pick up the brakes before proceeding forwards to the Loop Junction. When he got to the driver he would say that they were either all up, or he had left so many down. You would stop at the Loop Junction stop board, and whoever was about would pick up the remaining the brakes.

You mostly cut off banking at Cwm Glyn, easing off at the platelayers' cabin there. Sometimes, if the train engine in front was struggling, it would be banked to Cefn Crib; however, it wouldn't be pushed too hard as there was a downhill bank from Cefn Crib

Ex-GWR '57xx' Class 0-6-0T No 5741 approaches Maesycwmmer Junction on 23 February 1956 with an eastbound freight. *D. K. Jones collection* to Crumlin Junction, and the train had no brakes pinned down going down the bank to Crumlin. There was a sand drag at Crumlin Junction, which was always weed-free.

I remember No 2385, the Crumlin banker, as 'Crumlin Castle', and once went on it tender-first to Hengoed in fine weather from Crumlin Junction. The engine had been in the sidings at Crumlin Junction, opposite the signal box, and we reversed back down over the viaduct and through High Level to Hengoed. We had to bank a train from Aberdare. You had a little cab, and tried to put a storm-sheet up. It was all right when you got it going. This was a one-off, banking from Hengoed, as there was engineering work at Hall's Road, so we couldn't bank from Penar.

We had to travel from Crumlin Junction and run past Hall's Road to get to Penar. Penar was one of the few places on the Western Region where a banker was hooked onto the train; it wasn't allowed to run loose until it got to the other side of the Crumlin Viaduct, then it was uncoupled and propelled the train to Cefn Crib. The reason for this was that if the train engine failed on the viaduct you couldn't get an engine there to hook it off. If the banker failed on the viaduct, the train engine would have to pull the banker off it. You never stopped a train on the viaduct.

When it was scrapped, No 2385 was replaced by a tank engine. As a trial, a BR '80xxx' tank was tried out, based at Crumlin Junction, but was considered unsuccessful and the trial was not continued.

In between banking turns the engine was kept in one of two sidings opposite Crumlin Junction signal box. We'd be waiting there and the signalman would shout 'Banker!' I then walked over to the box and picked up the electric token, always taking care to read it. One said 'Llanilleth', the other 'Crumlin High Level', and you could pick up the wrong one! There was a tablet machine, and you put the token on a ring. If banking, the banker had the token. (If double-heading on the main line, the inside engine had the token.)

Double-headed engines were used for the Aberbeeg-Glascoed ROF passenger train. The pair left Aberbeeg shed to pick up the return carriages from Glascoed; they were known as the twins, and were a priority working.

When banking from Penar the guard would look at his watch before leaving, then we started pushing from there. When we got to the viaduct the double-headed engines used for the Glascoed train had left Aberbeeg shed. Our train was too long for the refuge siding at Crumlin Junction, so if we were late, impeding the movement of the twins from Aberbeeg, we had to be split at Crumlin Junction, the train being put in the two sidings opposite the signal box – the guard would tell us before leaving Penar The train engine had the first half of the train, and the banker would push his part of the train into the sidings to let the two engines go by. There was nowhere else to put us except at Cwm Glyn.

I next went into the Banking Link with a driver from Banbury called Alf Batley, who looked just like a gypsy. He had black eyes and shoulder-length hair. We used to be parked at the entrance to Hart's Yard, at the 'perch', on the side of the triangle leading to the West Junction. There was a signal and a catch point here. We had a '72xx', and the levelling pipes between the side tanks and bunker would always leak; they were a casting, and this would shear. I was forever putting water into the tank. I once drew up a design for a flexible pipe to cure this problem; I gave it to Les Norkett, but it never went any further.

The Control banker banked up to Cwm Glyn, Little Mill and Llantarnam, the engine being controlled by Newport Control. When banking a train from Little Mill to Cwm Glyn you filled the tanks before you started using the water column in the Birkenhead Sidings, by the exit signal. But by the time you had banked the train to Cwm Glyn you would need to fill up with water again, straight away, and go back into Hart's Yard for the next banking task.

One day my father was driving the Little

Mill and Llanelli train, and Alf and I were banking him with a '72xx', starting at Little Mill, where the sidings were very long and all dead-ended. We came up onto the goods line at Pontypool Road station, and had to stop because a passenger train was going over the Vale. We'd pushed him from Little Mill, and Alf said, 'Put the handbrake on,' which I did, and put the chain on the brake handle. We now sat there waiting when all of a sudden my father, on the front end, blew the whistle – toot, toot! Alf said, 'He hasn't dropped off to sleep up there yet, then?'

I took the chain off to get ready on the handbrake, but it wouldn't move. Alf had blown the brake up and destroyed the vacuum, so eventually I got a coal pick and gave the handbrake handle a whack. My Dad was on the move by then, so of course we couldn't get up behind him, because there were too many curves, and we would get buffer-locked. So we had to wait until we got nearly at Clarence Street station, by which time father had gone from Station South all the way up to Clarence Street. He was blowing the whistle – 'Where are you?'

Anyway, Alf said, 'I'll shift him when we get to the Clarence.' It was OK for him to say that, but I had to fire the damn thing. We eventually got up behind him and blew the whistle, and were pushing the whole train and my Dad. The regulator was up in the roof! Alf decided when we got up to Cwm Glyn, that was enough.

Another day on the banker at Little Mill, I was cleaning out the fire after taking over at 4.00pm. I put the bar in to clean the fire and it caught between the firebars! I got the pick and tried to hit it out. Alf said, 'We'll sit on it.' So that's what we did, and brought half the brick arch down! I had to throw all that out then, and had to explain it on shed.

Blaendare Pilot

This pilot brought two trips of coal a day from Hafodrynys Colliery (Deep Mine), and picked up empties from the South Junction. One day in about 1953 I was working with Jack Merryfield as my driver and we had a runaway. Jack had half a stomach. We had taken the empties up and put them in the top end of Hafodrynys Colliery, then picked up the coal and van and were on our way down with a '56xx'. We stopped for brakes at Cwm Glyn; we had an Irish guard by the name of Paddy Ryan. We left there and came down OK, stopping at the West Junction for a train coming up. Paddy came down and said, 'Ten.'

I said to Jack, 'I don't know – Paddy's here and he's given me the number ten.'

Jack replied, 'All right, he's probably picked up ten brakes for us to get away.' He opened the regulator, shut it, and we were away!

'Oh hell!' he said. 'He's taken them all up and only left ten brakes down.' So of course, we couldn't stop. Jack put the engine in reverse but to no effect. So on went the brake whistle. We were approaching the Loop Junction and they were shunting across the road. The driver of the Pilot that day was a man called Ron Voyle (later a Locomotive Inspector and a well-known person on BR preserved steam runs in the 1980s). He could see what was happening, slammed on his brake and tried to snap his train. But it didn't happen. So to ease our train he got some wooden trucks and put them in the way. We ran into the side of them, but I had jumped off before that!

Harry Rawlins, who was a loco shed fitter, recalls being taken out to see this accident by fitter Rollei Jones. The '56xx' had hit the train and gone over it, and had begun to tilt sideways – there was coal everywhere. It stopped everything for a day – they couldn't use the Loop. Trains using the Vale were pushed out to Coedygric, with a guard's van on the south end, then dragged across the Monmouthshire line and past the side of the shed (from Panteg station to Pontypool Road).

Balanced workings by the Blaendare Pilot involved taking the empties up to Hafodrynys Deep Mine and bringing full ones down to the West Junction, then bearing off to the right to the Loop Siding, leaving them there. This engine would do two trips in a day. It was then put on shed, and you would sign off duty. The next driver and fireman would come along at about 4.30-5.00pm, service the same engine and take a train down to the Liswerry branch in Newport, to Stewarts & Lloyds, and come back to Ponty about 2.30am, into the Northern Sidings.

Wagons from Hafodrynys, in the Loop Siding, were then marshalled all over the place. Some were pushed into the Birkenhead Sidings, opposite the 'coal field'. The Northern Pilot then came from over by the gasworks, backed up in there, picked them up, went out towards Pontypool Road station, then backed them into the Northern Sidings.

I recall a train of coke hoppers for the Patent Fuel Abercwmboi Phurnacite Plant coming all the way from Bromsgrove, and entering the Coedygric Sidings reception road, up through the middle. It was hauled by a '28xx', '38xx', '68xx', '49xx' or even an ex-LMS 'Black Five', and comprised 40 or 50 empty coke wagons. The engine uncoupled, went to the ash pit to drop the fire, then ran through to the long shed.

The next thing you saw was the Cwm Glyn banker proceeding to the East Junction and onto the old Monmouthshire line to pull the wagons out the way they had come in, up to the station. A pannier tank or '56xx' then came off shed and got on at Station South, blowing its head off, the rear engine was uncoupled prior to banking, and off they went. The '72xx' would be on the back and shove the lot to Cwm Glyn. The train then proceeded to Abercwmboi; it later returned to the Midlands with patent fuel ('ovoids').

'Popeye'

'Popeye' had been sent to Pontypool Road from Tredegar as a punishment. I was on the 12 midday Ebbw Vale train with a '72xx'. We booked on at 11.10am, giving us 45 minutes to get the engine ready and at 12 o'clock bring it off shed. Well, OK, you could just about do it. 'Popeye' would get there about 11 o'clock, having already been in

the pub at the end of Station Road. He was always tanked up from the previous night. I did what I had to do. Then he said, 'Come on, we'll go for water now.' There was water at the south end of the shed.

I put the bag in, he opened the water valve and disappeared. I thought, 'Where is he?' He was in the canteen, with his tea can, to fill it with beer. The South Pilot pulled our train out, and we backed on, then up past the West and on our way. When we came to Crumlin Junction we got our staff (the token) and brakes were put down to get us down to Llanilleth. At the bottom was a signal and a catch point, and boarding to keep people off the railway. This line was known as the 'muck hole.' Beyond the boarding was a pub, the Royal Oak. 'Popeye' got off, climbed over the fence and was in the pub filling up his tea can. Between Pontypool Road and here he had emptied his tea jack and filled it up again. To stop the signalman giving us the road to go on, 'Popeye' put a brick in the catch point to stop the signalman from closing it. On this particular day, as he went to lift the brick out the signalman pulled the point and nearly had his hand.

When we got on the move, we passed the signal box at Llanilleth and the signalman said, 'What the hell's wrong with that point up there?' 'Popeye' come across to my side and said, 'The kids have been there messing about and thrown a lot of rubbish in there. You nearly had my hand off cleaning it out.'

We then proceeded to Aberbeeg, where we had to drop some wagons off. So we pulled up and stopped, the guard came up and hooked them off, and up to the platform we went. I was looking now ready to go and back them in, but 'Popeye' wasn't there – he was over on the other platform to fill up his can again. So I had to drop the wagons off and pull up for water.

The guard said, 'I don't know why they employ him,' and I replied, 'Neither do I.'

'Popeye' came back and up to Ebbw Vale we went, right through the yard, and the shunter uncoupled the engine. We went down back to the bottom end of the yard, now travelling bunker-first. 'Popeye' was gone again. We were on the road where we were needed, and I put the bag in for water. We were then directed onto our train. 'Popeye' appeared, bouncing off the wagons, sozzled. This one day I had had enough of it, so I stood in the gap between the tank and bunker when 'Popeye' tried to get up.

'Come on, out the way,' he said.

I said, 'I beg your pardon, you don't talk to me like that.'

'I'm the boss,' said 'Popeye'.

'Well,' I said, 'you're not bossing this boy – I'm quite prepared to take you on.'

'Popeye' started swearing, and the yard foreman came along. 'Hey,' he said, 'we can't have this – we'll all have the sack.'

I said, 'You only have to sack one person and that's him. If you get shot of him you'd have peace.'

'Popeye' climbed on board and went for me, but I knocked his arms away. I said, 'Don't try that again – I'll kick you straight between the legs. You can do what you like, but you are not driving this train. I want to get home in one piece.'

So I had a word with the foreman. We had about 14 wagons with tent tops and high bars, all covered. I said to the foreman, 'Can you get these wagons all fitted up?'

I drove and fired that train all the way home. I'd had enough. When I put the engine on the pit, I went down to the office and got hold of Joe Richards. I said, 'I want to see the boss in the morning, Jack Russell. I am not firing to that man no more.'

Joe said, 'You can't do that – he'll have the sack.'

I said, 'Good job.'

The next day I went to see Jack Russell, and told him all about it. He said, 'This is a serious accusation you are making.'

'Yes,' I said, 'it's serious. I'm still alive. You knew full well what he was like going through the sand drag at the West with No 4600 and nearly coming out the other side. The man's a menace.'

I had to go with 'Popeye' the following week on the two-coach colliers' train, the 5.30am from Pontypool Road to Hafodrynys.

I wasn't speaking to him. All I was saying was, 'Right-o, right away, right back, drop back, stop, green light,' whatever. 'Popeye' started getting a bit worried. 'Oh,' he said, 'we can't go on like this.'

I said, 'It's you who can't go on like this, it ain't me – I haven't done anything. You're a menace.'

They had him in the office, and I was moved across to work with Alf Batley; another fireman took my place to work with 'Popeye'.

A couple of weeks later I was in the relief cabin (by the stores with the shed water tank on top), and there were firemen waiting for jobs. Someone opened his mouth and said, 'Be careful what you say – we've got one who is prepared to report you.'

So I said to him, 'Seeing you are so clever, and know everything about everybody, why don't you have a fortnight with him? I'll go with your mate and you can have him.'

Alf Batley came in. He said, 'What's going on here Henry?'

I said, 'Clever ones here know it all, they can do this,' then someone said, 'Henry couldn't keep a barber in hot water,' to which Alf replied, 'Never mind keeping a barber in hot water, I'll take him anywhere, and there are some of you here I wouldn't give the time of day.' There was a hell of an atmosphere in there and I was sent to Coventry.

On a previous trip with 'Popeye' we'd been to Ebbw Vale and come back, and had a banker from Llanilleth (we always had a banker from the 'muck hole'). We got to Cefn Crib and started to put the brake on, but were signalled to be turned into the loop to await a passing train.

'Don't worry about the handbrake, I'll manage,' he said, and we landed up in the bank at the end of the loop! The engine was a '72xx'. There was no buffer stop at Cwm Glyn loop, just the bank at the end of the track.

I worked with 'Full Load Phil' once on the Aberdare. We were picking up a dolomite container at Crumlin Junction that had come from Ebbw Vale, for use at

Taffs Well. I remember Phil once writing a report about the late running of his train, in which he stated, 'I am using an engine built in 1934, and coal which has been sat on the ground since the Second World War, which disintegrates when put in the firebox and doesn't burn, causing poor steaming, and you expect me to keep time!'

I once took a '56xx' through the flooded platform at Mountain Ash (Cardiff Road). You shut the dampers and stood on the seat in the cab. The tide of water created when passing through the platform flooded the waiting room!

The last engine I fired on the Vale of Neath route was a '28xx', coming back from Neath with a train of steel for up country. It was the last train of the night on a Saturday evening and we took the engine back to the shed. We had a banker at Penar – the guard decided that, based on the weight of the train, before we left Neath. I married driver Bill Jancey's only daughter in 1958 and left

the railway in 1959 to work at the British Nylon Spinners factory at Mamhilad.

9. Fireman Terry Warwood

The Stormstown was a 12-hour job, and I was after money. You booked on at 6.00pm, prepped your engine, a '56xx', and picked up the train. It was an 'H' code train, and the guard was a rules and regulations man; he said, 'H headcode fireman, H headcode,' to which I replied, 'What's that?' The guard would then get the lamps and do it for me. We had this guard every day on this turn.

You worked over the Vale to Hengoed, where you did some shunting, then went on to the Rhymney line to Caerphilly, where you did some more shunting, then to Pontypridd and up through the station, branching off to Abercynon and Quaker's Yard. We hooked off, went up for water, then back to the sidings and made a cup of tea.

Ex-GWR '66xx' Class 0-6-2T No 6634 was often used as the Crumlin banker, and is now preserved. Here the loco approaches the Lower Race with an eastbound train of empties on 6 August 1958. Note that Trosnant Sidings on the right have been removed. *Paul Chancellor collection (Colour-Rail)*

Then it was back on the train, and off again.

10. Fireman Colin Polsom

When firing '72xxs' to Ebbw Vale, if you kept the back corners filled the fire would feed itself. Coming back up from Llanilleth to Crumlin Junction was bunker-first, when you were exaggerating the shape of the firebox. I was coming back with the Ebbw Vale, with the fire sloping up against the front of the firebox, and things weren't going right! It was sorted out by the time we went over the top at Hafodrynys; it was then a nice fire for the fire-droppers to sort out back on shed.

The Oakdale was a 9-to-5 job. I worked with Jack Lewis as a fireman. We picked up empties from the Loop Sidings, and took the train to Oakdale. We then came back to Penar and had a banker, No 6634. It was the worst engine we had at Ponty. You would have a good train of coal.

Drivers

One week my mate was on another job, and Bert Hale was the spare driver and was booked on the Crumlin Banker. I was apprehensive. I was a young fireman who wanted to go home, and Bert would stay there all day if he could. We went over 'on the cushions', probably mid-afternoon. When we got up on the footplate the first thing he said to me was, 'See that water there, look? That's how I want it kept, three-quarters of a glass.' He had no sense of humour whatsoever. We had a gap in interests between an older driver and a younger fireman. In between

A Pontypool Road to Neath train approaches Crumlin Junction hauled by ex-GWR '66xx' Class 0-6-2T No 6690 on 10 April 1964. *F. A. Blencowe, R. K. Blencowe collection*

The train passes Crumlin Junction signal box, where the token is collected from signalman Jenkin Lewis for the single line across the viaduct.
F. A. Blencowe, R. K. Blencowe

banking it was difficult to make conversation.

It was quite an experience to go across Crumlin Viaduct as the fireman of a passenger train. I had to put my arm out to get the staff from Jenkin Lewis, the Crumlin Junction signalman, at a speed exceeding 8mph. I used to know Jenkin quite well.

If Ted Kilby didn't have a flare lamp or oil can in his hand he thought he was naked! He loved the job. One day I was coming back from Aberdare with the Swansea vans and a '38xx', and was coming up through to Quaker's Yard. There was a single-bore tunnel at Cefn Glas, and you could guarantee that from the time you went in there to the time you came out you couldn't see a light, it was that intense with smoke and steam. When we came out of the tunnel I looked and my mate wasn't there. I was frightened to death. But he had detected something, and was on the running plate outside the cab putting oil in. We had '38xxs' and 'Halls' on the Swansea vans.

One time I was on the Saturday Glyn Neath passenger out of the bay at Ponty station with Driver Arthur Edwards. This was a Control Link job. We used to go to Aberdare, back to Quaker's Yard, then back to Hengoed. We were regulars on this job. At Hengoed a lady was talking to the guard, wishing to meet the Cardiff connection at Quaker's Yard. Arthur was lively on the throttle and sure enough we were there on time, then

A train approaches the Ebbw Valley section of Crumlin Viaduct on the same day. *F. A. Blencowe, R. K. Blencowe*

On a return journey, on 13 June 1964, Jenkin Lewis picks up the staff for the Crumlin High Level Station-Crumlin Junction section of track. The next stop is at Hafodrynys, before the west portal of Hafodrynys Tunnel. This was the last day of the Vale of Neath line. *R. H. Marrows*

off we went to Aberdare. Arthur said to me, 'What's the running time now, from Aberdare to Hengoed?' I said, 'I don't know.' We came back from there like hell in the night. At Middle Duffryn, Mountain Ash, the road was bouncing us all over the place! A wonderful experience.

Dowlais and Stormstown

We had a '56xx'/'66xx' from Pontypool Road to the ICI Dowlais

Viewed at Quaker's Yard High Level on 18 May 1957, ex-GWR 4-4-0 No 3440 *City of Truro* and '43xx' 2-6-0 No 4358 take water while working the 'Daffodil Express' eastbound on the Vale of Neath line. *R. H. Marrows collection*

Quaker's Yard Viaduct is seen in March 1958, with an ex-GWR '53xx' Class 2-6-0 hauling a westbound freight. *D. K. Jones collection*

Chemical Works, with only eight tanks. We used to work to Bargoed, and have a Rhymney banker. Depending what mood they were in, or what time of day it was, they'd be lucky to knock the smoke off the stack! We'd go up there through Cross Faen, up towards Foch Chriw, and you'd look back and the banker would be useless – but some of them would give you a good shove. We came down over there one day, out of Foch Chriw, dropping down, and there was an entrance to Ogilvie Colliery across the railway line. A man used to come out of his little hut and wave – it's OK to go. We had a load on behind and we couldn't have stopped within 2 miles. Coming to Cross Fan signal box, the Home and Distant signals

Top right: Ex-GWR '56xx' Class 0-6-2T No 6605 approaches Quaker's Yard High Level on 9 November 1961. *D. K. Jones collection*

Right: Ex-GWR 0-6-2T No 5647 enters Quaker's Yard High Level with an eastbound passenger train in 1963 while an ex-GWR 'Grange' 4-6-0 waits on the left.
Paul Chancellor collection (Colour-Rail)

Below: The same engine takes water at Quaker's Yard High Level while working an eastbound passenger train, also in 1963. *Rail-Online*

were right on the steps of the box. I went in there once to carry out Rule 55, to let him know we were stopped at the red signal, and the signalman looked like Dick Turpin. He had a couple of pit props, and I sawed some up and had some blocks to take home for my parents' coal fire. It was a hard old slog if you

had to go to Hereford with the train on the way back. It was a 12-hour shift of hard graft.

The Stormstown job was another 12-hour shift, at 8pm. We went down through Ystrad Mynach with Evo Evans, and the engine would go on its own to Aber Junction. You had a single track, past the crematorium, to

Ex-GWR '41xx' Class 2-6-2T No 4101 leaves Hengoed Low Level with the 10.44am Rhymney-Cardiff train on 23 February 1957. An eastbound freight is seen at Hengoed High Level in the distance.
D. K. Jones collection

Ex-GWR '28xx' Class 2-8-0 No 2870 passes Hengoed High Level coal sidings with a westbound freight on 28 February 1957.
D. K. Jones collection

Ex-GWR '56xx' Class 0-6-2T No 5628 hauls a Neath-Pontypool Road passenger train at Hengoed High Level station in 1962. *D. K. Jones collection*

Nos 6655 and 5634 bank a coal train from Ogilvie Colliery at Darran & Deri, aided by train engine No 5605, in January 1964. *ProRail*

The same train is seen at Ogilvie. *Prorail*

Pontypool Road Driver John Drayton is seen at the disused Penar Halt while taking water with ex-GWR '45xx' Class 2-6-2T No 4593 in April 1958. This was the return working of the Pontypool Road to Porth (Rhondda Valley) train, 10.00am Porth to Pontypool freight carrying a mixed cargo of coal and coke. *J. Drayton*

Pontypridd. There were coke ovens at Porth, where you had to wait for someone to come up. You put a bucket on the signal and had a nap, waiting for the bucket to drop off the signal when it cleared. We took empties there, and coke back.

Last freight over Crumlin Viaduct

This was the 5.5pm to Hengoed, and Don Green from Abergavenny was the driver; he was a moody man, and I didn't know how to take him. Eris Smollick was the guard. Going towards Penar Junction from Crumlin Junction, in the distance you could see the Distant signal for Pontllanfraith. If you caught it by there, you'd tell the driver, but Don was moody so I wouldn't tell him. He was knocking the stack off the engine! We got to Hengoed, and to the Hengoed Hotel partying!

The last train was always the Swansea vans, and we always went before it. This particular day Eris was balancing on two hands in the hotel, and when we came out we watch the Swansea vans go through

with a '38xx'. We followed on behind after making up our train. I had to bring the fire around leaving Hengoed, and I remember going through Pontllanfraith and looking in the firebox, thinking 'I haven't got this fire right for Penar. But,' I thought, 'not a problem, we'll stop at Penar, and by the time the banker arrives I'll have the fire ready.' However, Don asked me to go to the signal box at Penar to get a can of tea; Don wouldn't go himself as he had fallen out with most of the signalmen.

I said, 'Don, I need to get the engine right.' Don said he would do it, so I went to the signal box. When I come back Don was moaning, and I had to put the fire right, then down around the corner comes No 6634, the last engine I wanted to see as a banker. I'm led to believe that this was the last goods train to go east over Crumlin Viaduct.

11. Fireman Charlie Reynolds

The Vale of Neath line was an up-and-down track. From Pontypool Road it was uphill to Hafodrynys, from where

Ex-GWR 0-6-2T No 5659 is seen at Pontllanfraith Low Level in 1964. *ProRail*

Crumlin Junction looking west on 6 June 1963. The Crumlin banker, No 6634, is seen in the siding opposite Crumlin Junction signal box, awaiting its next turn of duty. *R. H. Marrows*

you would drop downhill to Pontllanfraith. You would drop down again to Hengoed, and climb around the rocks to Nelson & Llancaiach, where it was level, then it was again downhill to Mountain Ash. There was a long pull from Mountain Ash to Aberdare, a bit of level then a 3-mile climb to Hirwaun. This was followed by a long drop down to Glyn Neath, with a flat run along the side of the river into Neath. Above Clarence Street station was the steepest part on the way to Aberdare, and a banker was available at Aberdare to bank to Hirwaun.

A 'Grange' was the biggest tender engine I worked over there, or an ex-LMS 8F, but I never worked a 'Hall'.

This is the view looking east through Crumlin Junction towards Hafodrynys Tunnel on the same day. The branch to Llanilleth is on the left, behind the water tower. *R. H. Marrows*

Great Western '53xxs', 'Granges', '28xxs', 'Austerity' 2-8-0s, 'ROD' 2-8-0s, panniers, '14xxs', '41xxs', '56xxs' and '66xxs' are recalled. A '66xx' or '41xx' was the biggest tank engine used over the route. '72xxs' were banned from Crumlin Viaduct, but those and '42xxs' were used on the route to Crumlin Junction to go down the bank to Llanilleth to get to Ebbw Vale.

Freight trains for the Vale, with goods wagons such as box vans, were collected from Little Mill yard, which was also used as coal storage sidings. Faster vacuum-fitted freights would leave Little Mill and go up the Vale.

Trains of empties for the collieries along the Vale of Neath were picked up at the Loop Sidings, or at Coedygric/New Sidings. You coupled onto your train in one of these three sets of sidings, and were pulled down to Pontypool Road station by

the banking engine, which uncoupled then banked the train around the triangle past the West Box and up to Cwm Glyn, where the banker dropped off the train.

Ex-GWR '56xx' Class 0-6-2T No 5633 passes Nelson & Llancaiach with an eastbound freight train in August 1963. The GWR/Rhymney Railway joint line to Dowlais (Cae Harris) is seen in the background. *D. K. Jones collection*

Yes, '72xxs' did cross Crumlin Viaduct! A train of vans is seen heading for Crumlin Junction on 12 May 1957, being hauled by an unidentified ex-GWR 2-8-2T. *Kidderminster Railway Museum*

Occasionally a train from the north for the Vale would be left at Coedygric/New Sidings. The banker would couple on the back and pull you to in front of the South box. There was a route indicator signal there to the West box, then to Clarence Street station and Hafodrynys.

There were two or three trains from the north going to the Vale. One job was to Pontypridd, dropping into Crumlin, then past Penar Junction, Pontllanfraith, through the tunnels and over Hengoed Viaduct. At the left-hand signal you went to Ystrad Mynach, Llanbradach,

Penrhos Junction and Pontypridd. This route was used on a Sunday to take Pontllanfraith Working Men's Club to Barry; you went to Caerphilly, through a tunnel to Taffs Well, over the bridge, through another tunnel and came out near Barry. You also came back this way. A '41xx' or '56xx' tank loco was used

A '56xx' 0-6-2T crosses Hengoed Viaduct, in the Rhymney Valley, with an eastbound freight on 23 February 1957.
D. K. Jones collection

on these workings. Coal to the coke oven sidings at Pontypridd was also worked over this route.

The Glascoed ROF train was two trains in one, from Ebbw Vale and Abertillery, coupled together at Aberbeeg, then up the 'muck hole' at Llanilleth.

A day's work

A trip to Neath was a day's work. There was a lot of traffic, and you might be in a loop for 20 minutes for a passenger train to pass. Freights travelled at 20mph and needed to stop for brakes to be pinned down or picked up.

You took water before going off shed, and went down to the station to pick up the train. You had water when you stopped at Nelson, and also at Aberdare. You had water at Neath before you left, and water at Aberdare again on the return trip. If you stopped anywhere by a water column, you took water. You would have water three times to Neath when working on a tank loco, but a 4,000-gallon tender engine with three to five coaches would get to Neath on one filling.

At the Station South box on the Relief line, you came to a big gantry signal. You could go up around the West to the Vale of Neath, to the back of the shed, or to the East box and the gantry signal there.

By the West box there was a stop signal to protect the junction, and a starting signal near the canal. Coming down from Clarence Street in the other direction, there were two signals on the down road, about 30 or 40 yards from the West box, against the Black Ash path. One signal would turn you down into the yard, towards the Loop Siding, the other would get you down into the station. A sand drag was located adjacent to the Black Ash path; it started by the West box and ended near the bottom end of the triangle.

The 'Third Road' extended from the West box towards the Loop Siding and Mynydd Maen Colliery and stopped by the fish ponds. The Third Road was later used to store crippled wagons between the West box

and past Clarence Street station, where there were four sidings.

The Control banker was kept on the 'perch'; this was a siding at Hart's Yard by the big coal stacks that could accommodate two or three engines, and had a signal at the end. To go off the shed with the banker you rang the signalman at the South box and travelled down there by the indicator signal on the left, by the sand drag; this was the indicator for the West Junction, Hart's Yard or straight on to the Loop Sidings, the Birkenhead Sidings or the shed. It was handy for everywhere – to go to the station or anywhere else.

The Control banker was normally a '72xx' and would set off from the 'perch' to go to Little Mill to bank a train for the Vale up to Cwm Glyn, or pull a train from the yard to bank it to Cwm Glyn.

On nights or late afternoons, the fireman on the banker used to get a fire-dropping shovel (left on the ground by the signal) and stand it against the signal. You could then have 10 minutes' sleep. When the signal was pulled off, the shovel would drop against the side of the engine and wake you.

'Brecon Wonder' (Colin Parry) once placed the shovel so that its blade was against the signal and the handle on the signal counterweight. The signal became jammed, and the signalman had to come from the South box. The shovel was subsequently taken away after a foreman from the shed was sent to see the driver.

The Little Mill Pilot banked trains up to Ponty if the Control banker had gone somewhere else. You might be unlucky and have to bank to Cwm Glyn. A lot of trains from Little Mill were for Aberdare, Neath and West Wales. The Little Mill and Llanelli train used to go over the Vale, and you had a '28xx' on this. You left Little Mill at 5.30am, banked by the big Control banker.

If a train was in trouble, say at Nantyderry or at Llantarnam, the Control banker would bank it to Pontypool Road. You needed a good fire at the back end of the firebox. If you had to go and work a train, you levelled the fire over the box and put more on to get it going. If you went to the loop at Llantarnam to assist a freight going north, you needed a bright fire, but could ease up on the fire getting back to Ponty. If you were on the 'perch' with too much fire and the engine was blowing off you would be shouted at by the driver!

You were never bored with the job. The fire-dropper might have left clinker, making the fire far from lively. Brickettes were shovel-sized blocks of compressed dust – it was all small coal. Ovoids were often used, but these would roll all over the place; they were 90% coal and 10% bonding. When breaking up brickettes on shed at the start of the shift, they broke to powder rather than pieces, and would block up the hatch on a tank engine. Coal would be broken up in the bunker on shed before leaving. Brickettes were easier to break up in a tender. Welsh coal was soft, and would burn well,

while North of England hard coal looked like shale, and would burn in seconds.

There were four signal boxes on the route to Hafodrynys. After the West box at Pontypool Road there was Trosnant box beyond Clarence Street station, and Cwm Glyn box at the fish ponds. Then you went under the road bridge and past the second pond. Blaendare box was situated on the right-hand embankment adjacent to where the Hafodrynys New Mine later had its sidings (by the concrete tower). Blaendare box controlled the full sidings from beneath the screens at Hafodrynys Deep Mine on the up side of the track. Beyond the colliers' platform by the level crossing was Cefn Crib box.

The 'Third Road' stopped before the ponds. It was used again when the New Mine opened in about 1957, and a junction installed to go out through Trosnant Sidings.

Ex-GWR '56xx' Class 0-6-2T No 5649 enters Pontypool (Clarence Street) with the 12.18pm Aberdare-Pontypool Road service. The so-called 'Third Line', which once served the Glyn Pits, Blaendare Trading Company, the Gwent Wagon Works and the Mynydd Maen Colliery, is seen on the left, with Trosnant Junction signal box on the elevated Eastern Valley line in the background. *M. Hale, Great Western Trust*

The original box at Cefn Crib was at the Hafodrynys end of the level crossing going into Hafodrynys Deep Mine. It controlled the sidings going into the screens at the mine, where empties were pushed. A new signal box was later opened to replace the old one, on the Pontypool side of the level crossing; it controlled the sidings to Hafodrynys Deep Mine and the empty sidings for the New Mine.

Left: An unidentified ex-GWR '72xx' Class 2-8-2T crosses the Vale of Neath line at Trosnant Junction on 13 February 1962.
L. Fullwood, Transport Treasury

Ex-GWR '56xx' Class 0-6-2T No 6687 passes the Lower Race, Pontypool, on 1 August 1959, with an eastbound passenger train for Pontypool Road. Again, the 'Third Road' is on the left, with the Mynydd Maen Colliery washery in the distance. *Paul Chancellor collection (Colour-Rail)*

Above: An eastbound freight, hauled by ex GWR '28xx' Class 2-8-0 No 2869, passes Mynydd Maen, near the Lower Race at Pontypool on 31 March 1956. The 'Third Road' is on the left, and a platelayer's cabin on the right.
C. N. Fields, Manchester Locomotive Society

Left: Hafodrynys New Mine is seen during construction circa 1956, with Blaendare Junction signal box in the middle distance. *J. S. Williams*

Below: Ex-GWR '56xx' Class 0-6-2T No 5645 stands at Hafodrynys New Mine as the Blaendare Pilot on 14 May 1959. *Trevor Owen, Colour-Rail*

East of Crumlin Valley Colliery, construction work is in progress for the two drifts for Hafodrynys New Mine, accessed by the tram bridge. Workings were constructed towards Cwmbran on the left and Tirpentwys on the right. *J. S. Williams collection*

Ex-GWR 0-6-0PT No 9600 passes Crumlin Valley Colliery platform and approaches Cefn Crib on 2 May 1964. My great-grandfather Thomas Williams resided in one part of the house on the right, adjacent to the mountain, when he was the Colliery Engineer at Crumlin Valley Colliery (Hafodrynys Colliery) and the Glyn Pits between 1912 and his death in 1925, aged 76. *Paul Chancellor collection (Colour-Rail)*

A new signal box was opened for the new sidings for Hafodrynys New Mine; it was a wooden box situated under the road at the bottom of the sidings, between Blaendare and Cefn Crib boxes.

The Hafodrynys Pilot brought empties up, and took loaded wagons for Severn Tunnel to Pontypool Road yard, to the Loop Sidings and those between the shed and the Loop Sidings.

A '42xx' tank loco, the Blaendare Pilot, was used in the morning with a train of empties to Hafodrynys Deep Mine. It could go to Hafodrynys by one of two ways, either up via Panteg Sidings (by Panteg & Griffithstown station) and in at Blaendare, or via the West box. The New Mine at Hafodrynys required '42xx' and '72xx' tank engines – '66xx' tank engines ccasionally, but they were too light and would slip easily. You

shunted between Cefn Crib and Blaendare signal boxes on this turn.

Trains were banked from Pontypool Road to Cwm Glyn only, on a gradient of 1 in 40, from Little Mill Junction or Pontypool Road. After Cwm Glyn box the track was level, but there was a slope to Hafodrynys where you could take twice the load, as it flattened out. Two to three hundred yards from Cwm Glyn signal box, by the Cwm Glyn side of the top fish pond, was a road overbridge – you pushed up to there and stopped. The fireman would change the lamps to run back through the crossover to the down line.

The whistle was blown twice (two 'crows') when you started to bank. At Cwm Glyn box the driver would ease down and let the train in front move away. You had to know everything about the road in order to avoid broken couplings.

Ex-GWR '72xx' Class 2-8-2T No 7241 brings washed small coal from Hafodynys New Mine through Pontypool Clarence Street on 13 February 1962. *L. Fullwood, Transport Treasury*

A view looking east from the roadbridge west of Cwm Glyn. *Mark Vrettos collection*

Ex-GWR '56xx' Class 0-6-2T No 5645 passes Cwm Glyn en route to Hafodrynys on 1 August 1959. *Trevor Owen, Colour-Rail*

On the same day ex-GWR '8750' Class 0-6-0PT No 9731 passes the first fish pond in the Glyn Valley, approaching Cwm Glyn from Hafodrynys. *Trevor Owen, Colour-Rail*

In August 1977 an unidentified Class 37 diesel-electric locomotive banks a train of small coal at Cwm Glyn, for washing at Hafodynys New Mine. The train was banked from Uskmouth in Newport. *J. S. Williams*

The train heads for Hafodrynys. The fish ponds on the left are now buried beneath washery waste from Hafodrynys New Mine. *J. S. Williams*

The signal box at Cwm Glyn was on the left, and there was a loop on the right-hand side, looking towards Hafodrynys, into which a down train would be pulled to allow a passenger train to pass. The road bridge was above the end of the loop. You either dropped back onto the down road, or took refuge in the loop under the side of the road embankment. The loop normally accommodated about 35 wagons, but a 40-wagon train required longer storage. In that case you pulled into the loop and out the bottom end on to the main line, then pushed back up the loop to a stop block under the bank. It wasn't often used this way.

It was here in the 1950s that a lorry ran down over the bank in the dark, and was spotted by a fireman on a banking engine after changing the lamps on the loco and about to run back down the line. The lorry driver was shouting for help in the dark, and luckily got it from the crew of the banking engine. The driver and fireman went to look – the lorry had landed the right side of

the stop block, and its driver could see rails through his windscreen.

By the signal box there was a spout where the signalman got his water. The top pond was above the road overbridge, above the end of the loop.

Working a train down through Cwm Glyn required having the brakes down or you would never be able to stop. At the bridge at Cwm Glyn you might be looped depending on traffic. There were two stop boards where you stopped to have the brakes pinned down. The first stop was right outside Cwm Glyn box, by the end of the loop. You pulled out of the loop with brakes down as far as the second stop by the garage, down at the bottom fish pond, normally with the guard and brakeman riding on the engine with you. There you stopped and adjusted the brakes, and had more put down; the driver would pull the train until it was difficult to pull. Thirty wagons required, say, 15 of them to be braked. You had to work hard coming down the hill as you had the brakes down; but

Above: The Cardiff Canton steam crane is seen at Coedygric, as viewed from Station Road, Griffithstown, on Tuesday 15 December 1971, the day after the coal train ran away from the second stop board below Cwm Glyn at Mynydd Maen. The driver, secondman and guard were all Ebbw men. *J. S. Williams*

if too many brakes were pinned down, the engine would be working hard and you would do a lot more firing! The ideal working was to pull hard, whether working up or down.

A few memoirs from diesel days are of interest at this location. On 14 December 1971 a coal train from Hafodrynys ran away from this second stop board. The driver and second man were a bit green. The train had stopped at Cwm Glyn, and was intending to stop at the second board, but the driver missed it. The guard had told the brakeman to go on back and ride on the engine, but the driver didn't blow the brake whistle. It was an all Ebbw crew. Julian Brachii, a driver for Arriva Trains Wales who began his railway career as a Traction Trainee at Ebbw Junction in April 1974, recalls the driver as being Stan Hancock, and the secondman was Ken Marshall. The shunter rode on the train, picked up the brakes at the second stop board, and walked back to the colliery. The author's mother heard the sound of the diesel blowing its horn at Stafford Road, Griffithstown, prior to the crash, and my father took the author and his brother to see the derailment after school on a Monday night. The author's father took photos of the accident the following day, but was limited to what he could photograph as BR bosses from Cardiff were in attendance. Some years ago my father met the guard of the train,

The scene of the accident, looking north. *J. S. Williams*

The accident as viewed from the New Siding shunting spur. *J. S. Williams*

who stepped out of the van to see a cloud of dust and hadn't felt the impact; he lived at Wattsville.

Julian recalls a second diesel runaway with the same driver, which didn't go through the catch points at Panteg & Coedygric Junction. He recalls that in the late 1970s two locos would come off Ebbw shed coupled in tandem, not in multiple, with two drivers and two secondmen. They worked a train of coal from Alexandra Dock Junction in Newport to Llantarnam loop. The front '37xxx' ran round to the back, then banked the train to Hafodrynys. This was when loaded coal trains went up there for blending with coal lifted there. The train was then taken to Aberthaw Power Station by Barry men in MGRs.

Both the old Deep Mine and new mines required you to put the empty wagons in at

Cefn Crib; they were then gravity fed back down into the sidings. Coal for the Vale from Hafodrynys would sometimes run over the Vale, requiring the Blaendare Pilot to put this ready. Eastbound freight trains working from Cefn Crib to Crumlin Junction didn't require brakes to be pinned down.

Oakdale Colliery coal went to Newport via the Western Valley, across Crumlin Viaduct to Hafodrynys. Hafodrynys New Mine's output went direct to Llanwern or

Runaway Type 3 diesel-electric locomotive No 6914 is seen in the New Sidings after the accident. *J. S. Williams*

Uskmouth.

There was a colliers' train to Hafodrynys, which went to a platform there. You then collected a train of coal and worked it back to Pontypool Road Yard, picking up the colliers later.

To take a coal from Hafodrynys Deep Mine you went through to Cefn Crib, over the top, then pushed the empties into the colliery sidings, leaving the van on the running road. Sometimes you put them off in two roads at the colliery. You then came back out to Cefn Crib box, and backed down to run around the van. Then you went to Blaendare box from Cefn Crib, ran back over the crossover into sidings on the mountain side, and took the loaded coal out from there.

The New Mine also had coal from Tirpentwys, which crossed over the road via the concrete bridge and into the screens for washing. It then passed over a weighbridge and was run one wagon at a time into one of several sidings. A '66xx' or '42xx' tank loco went into these sidings, but Margam trains in the morning had a tender engine, a '28xx', '38xx', 'Hall' or 'Grange', to Hafodrynys tender-first. A new signal box was built for these sidings between Cwm Glyn and Blaendare.

These trains would run down the Eastern Valley to Llantarnam and on to the main line, then through Newport station by five different ways – through Godfrey road, through the back platform road (No 1), No 2 road, the down main, or the down platform then through A or B tunnel. At end of the tunnel you might be on the relief or the main line at Ebbw Junction.

Other freight turns

A '66xx' tank engine was used on the Pontypridd coke ovens

Ex-GWR 2-8-0 No 3804 works a westbound freight at Trelewis in 1964. *ProRail*

turn at night, while the morning turn had a pannier or a '66xx' – it was a shorter train. There were always bankers available. The coke ovens were a mile above Pontypridd station. The train would stop there, put the wagons off, work back to Pontypridd, then travel across the long bridges by the cemetery and come out near Caerphilly. You could go to Taffs Well over the viaduct and Cadoxton and Barry, or down the big hill into Taffs Well and Cardiff Queen Street to Barry, or into Caerphilly station and Cardiff.

The Aberdare pick-up goods travelled from Pontypool Road and pick up and put off en route. It might go in at Hafodrynys Deep Mine and put something off there, via Cefn Crib old signal box. Maybe it would drop timber off or pick up, then drop down to Crumlin. It might put wagons off at Crumlin Junction to take down to Llanilleth or Aberbeeg. At Penar you always had a bit to-do coming back from Aberdare, but not when going. At Pontllanfraith there were sidings for coal hauliers, and you went in to drop some wagons off or to pick up empties. You stopped the coal merchants working when shunting the goods shed and the coal sidings.

Bird in Hand Junction was passed next, then on to Hengoed. Then you went around the rock to Nelson. You sometimes went into Deep Navigation Colliery at Trelewis,

Deep Navigation Colliery was to the right of this photo, and Taff Merthyr Colliery accessed by the points in the foreground. Ex-GWR '46xx' Class 0-6-0PT No 4612 hauls a Neath-Pontypool Road passenger train in August 1963. *ProRail*

Deep Navigation Colliery at Treharris was the deepest coal mine in the South Wales coalfield. The Vale of Neath Railway dominates the middle distance. *Phil Williams collection*

Treharris Collieries.

Former Barry Railway 0-6-0ST Class 'F' No 65 is seen as ex-GWR No 715, operating as the Deep Navigation Colliery shunting engine. *Phil Williams collection*

to move empties; this was the deepest colliery in South Wales. Then you travelled to Quaker's Yard, through the tunnel to Mountain Ash. There were about four collieries there together. Then you went past the Phurnacite plant at Abercwmboi, and up to Aberdare.

Aberbargoed trains used Maesycwmmer Junction to get to Aberbargoed. You were taken off the train and asked to bank a train on the other side of the valley if no other engine was available. This would be done if their own fireman was off sick or on holiday. You also worked to Fleur de Lis and Bargoed.

Crumlin banker

The Crumlin banker worked from Penar Junction to Cefn Crib box. Hafodrynys Tunnel, between the two, was curved near the Crumlin end. On the morning or afternoon Crumlin banker turn, you caught a train to Crumlin High Level and walked over the viaduct to the engine, which would be working the Llanilleth branch at the 'muck hole' If the engine was going to Penar they would fetch it to Crumlin High Level then take it through to Penar to begin work.

At other times you caught the colliers'

train from Pontypool Road to Hafodrynys Colliery. It stopped at Clarence Street and Hafodrynys colliers' platform, then you got on the banker at Cefn Crib signal box as the Crumlin banker crew would be relieved there, and they would then travel back to Pontypool Road on the colliers' train.

The banker was kept in a siding by the signal box at the Hafodrynys end of Crumlin Viaduct for use wherever wanted. It banked trains from Penar Junction that had come across the Vale of Neath or were bringing coal from Oakdale. You might go to Crumlin without being banked, but you would stop at the Hafodrynys end of the viaduct to be pushed through the tunnel and over Cwm Glyn. Alternatively the banker might travel to Penar and push you from there over the viaduct and up to Hafodrynys. You would also be banked from Llanilleth to Hafodrynys, up the 'muck hole', then the banker would drop back over the crossover to return to Crumlin.

The gradient at Penar was 1 in 50, but going over Crumlin Viaduct it was almost level. At the Hafodrynys end of the viaduct it was 1 in 40. At Penar Junction, there was the signal box, in the middle of the tracks, the double track to Oakdale and Markham,

Crumlin Viaduct is seen on 9 August 1961, with the Crumlin banker crossing it as ex-GWR '72xx' 2-8-2T No 7230 approaches Crumlin Junction with a train from Ebbw Vale via Llanilleth. *Paul Chancellor collection (Colour-Rail)*

An eastbound passenger train approaches Crumlin Junction on the same day. *Paul Chancellor collection (Colour-Rail)*

0-6-0PT No 3717, the Crumlin banker, is viewed from Crumlin Low Level station on 16 April 1963. It is running west light engine to Penar Junction, to bank an eastbound freight train. *R. H. Marrows*

It is seen again on the same day with 0-6-0PT No 3683, working an eastbound freight across the viaduct. *R. H. Marrows*

Looking east from Penar Junction on 22 August 1959, the Pontypool Road line swings away to the left, while the former Hall's Tramroad line passes through the 239-yard tunnel.
M. Hale, Great Western Trust

the line to Pontllanfraith, or Oakdale to Newport, and the line to Crumlin or the Vale of Neath. The banking engine was kept in a siding there.

The engine used was a pannier or a '56xx' or '66xx' tank, but not a '72xx', which were not allowed over the viaduct at Crumlin, but would have to go to Ebbw Vale via the 'muck hole' and Llanilleth. Down the 'muck hole' there were four running roads. '72xxs' went to Ebbw Vale with coal (from Aberbeeg) or to Hafodrynys (empties off and pick up coal), or scrap. To travel to Llanilleth from Crumlin Junction, the engine pulled the train around the corner and had the wagon brakes pinned down. At the bottom of the

Penar Halt, looking east on the same day. Eastbound freight trains would stop at the signal and the Crumlin banker would buffer up and be coupled to the rear of the train to begin banking to Cefn Crib.
M. Hale, Great Western Trust

Penar Halt was closed in 1917, and is seen here with an SLS Special on 12 July 1957 hauled by 0-6-0PT No 6434, which has stopped for water.
M. Hale, Great Western Trust

incline the brakes were picked up. On the way to Aberbeeg from Llanilleth there were sidings on both sides of the main line, including one for shunting off trains from Ebbw Vale for Pontypool. Steel from Ebbw Vale would travel to Pontypool Road to go north; if going south it would be taken down the valley to Newport.

Coal was moved from sidings at Hafodrynys, to where it had been brought via the Vale of Neath line. It was taken down the 'muck hole' to Llanilleth, and coal from Llanilleth was brought back up to Hafodrynys. Type 3 (later Class 37)

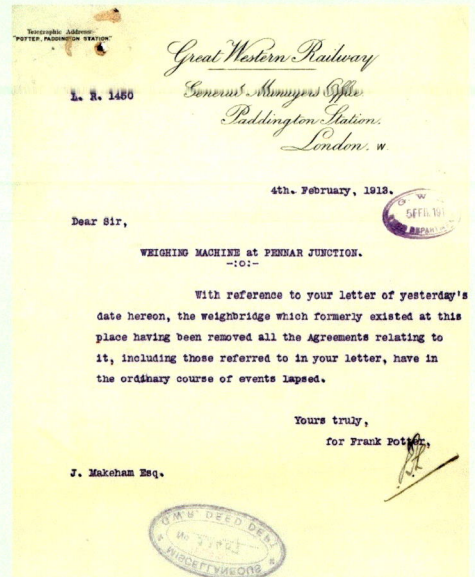

Above: The removal of a weighing machine at Penar Junction was discussed on 4 February 1913, as per this memorandum issued by the GWR at Paddington.
Phil Williams collection

Left: Ebbw Vale, showing the vast steelworks.
Phil Williams collection

Pontypool Road's '72xx' 2-8-2T No 7227 is seen at Ebbw Vale steelworks reception sidings in April 1962. *D. K. Jones collection*

diesels ran over this route, but it was closed when Crumlin Viaduct closed.

For banking duties a tender engine would be filled up with water and would last most of night, but a tank engine would take water twice in the night. The banker did three, four or five trips each night; it all depended on demand. It would take water at Penar Junction and at the Hafodrynys end of the viaduct (by a signal). Only freight trains were banked – steel sheets from Ebbw Vale and coal from Oakdale Colliery at Penar Junction are recalled.

I worked with Rollei Jones on the Crumlin banker. No 2385 was a 'Dean Goods' tender loco, and was regarded as being run-down. I worked this job with Rollei for the first time on a Monday night, and the engine wouldn't steam, it was rough to ride on, and didn't like heavy work. You had a job to keep steam going with it. It was a dirty night, and there was a tarpaulin sheet between the cab and tender, attached by springs like a pair of flippers. I was in the corner. Passing over Crumlin Viaduct on the way to Penar Junction the wind was catching the sheet and it was banging against the cab. When you got behind a train at Penar Junction, all you saw was a cloud of steam at the front of the engine.

When we got behind the train, Rollei showed me how to fire the loco before the train started away. When the loco started to move, the pressure steam pressure gauge dropped. 'Don't worry about it, Charlie – no one can get this to work.' We were behind the brake van and you couldn't see it for steam.

When we returned to Pontypool Road shed, Rollei filled in repair cards and gave them to the foreman. 'If it's there tomorrow, we shall come straight home to shed as it is not in a fit state of repair.'

The loco was booked for repairs but was later sent back to Swindon for scrapping. The rest of the week a pannier or a '56xx' or '66xx' was used on the job.

Ted Preece was another driver I worked with on this job, and he was enthusiastic. I recall banking a train from Penar Junction to Crumlin High Level, and when we arrived the smokebox door was glowing red hot for half its depth – the fire had been drawn through the tubes into the smokebox. With a pannier tank – a '36xx' or '46xx' – Ted would push the train and the train engine over the viaduct and continue pushing with great enthusiasm up to Cefn Crib signal box. The driver on the front engine would complain to me that he had to shut off steam coming through Glyn Tunnel when being banked. The smoke and steam blowing back onto the banking engine was awful, as it was the exhaust of two engines. At Cefn Crib I found that the smokebox door was still red hot as I went to change the red lamp from the back to the front of the engine, so we could cross over onto the opposite line and run back to Crumlin Junction.

I sat in the cabin by the signal box at Crumlin Junction in between banking turns. When the signalman dropped the signal arm he started shouting at me, 'Where's the driver?' I blew the whistle when the engine needed to assist another freight from Penar

Junction. Preece was courting at that time and when things were quiet he would nip off…

I couldn't get on with Ted Preece. He would thrash the loco and you'd be working hard doing nothing. You'd use three times the amount of coal – you would always struggle for coal when working with him. When working on the banker from Penar Junction you had to help yourself to loco coal from a wagon on a train of coal from Oakdale (going to Old Oak Common), stored in a siding, as your own supply of coal would be running low. He was a hard-hitter, and a strict driver.

I had an argument with him once after a 10-hour shift on nights on the Crumlin banker. I got home and found that my call-up papers for the Army were waiting for me. The next day, a Thursday, I went to work and saw Acker Gorman, the roster clerk. He

Driver Ted Preece and second man John Pike are seen at Hafodrynys New Mine sidings with a train of coal for Llanwern steelworks or Uskmouth Power Station, circa 1973. From around the end of March 1970 output from the drift at Hafodrynys New Mine was coal mined at Blaenserchan Colliery, and transported via an underground connection at Tirpentwys Colliery. *J. S. Williams*

was OK, you couldn't bend him – he had no favourites. The foreman was in the office by the viaduct, and said, 'You can't have Saturday off – I got too many men off sick.'

I said, 'I wasn't asking for Saturday off,' and showed him the call-up letter. I was due two weeks annual leave, which I took, as I was due to start in the Army in two weeks time. 'Good luck to you when you go in the forces – you won't be in work tonight.'

Harold Good was another hard hitter. I was in the banking link with him when I came out of the Army.

Tender engine working

Banking with tender engines was a menace – if it was snowing or raining you were running into it all the time. From Crumlin to Penar was only 4 miles, but you would get hellish wet going down there tender-first. When you got to Penar, you were put into a siding to wait for the next train to pull up to the starter for you to come up behind it.

Quite often you were sent light engine over the Vale to pick up a train of coal for Ponty at Nelson or Hengoed or somewhere. Tender engines were used on this quite a lot – '63xxs', '73xxs', '28xxs' or '38xxs'. You might be going into a storm without any protection at all, more or less. You couldn't get warm.

When booked to work with Driver Bert Hale, I went to across one morning with an engine and van to

Ocean Colliery at Treharris to pick up a train of coal with a '38xx'. It was the early hours of the morning and it was snowing. I went to the stores and got two tender storm sheets. I put one down from the cab to the tender and one from the tender to the cab.

We arrived at Penar Junction with the loaded train only to be told by the signalman that the banker had gone back to shed. It was about 5 in the morning. We backed the train up the Oakdale branch to wait for the banker to come, at about 8.00am. Then we would have to wait a few hours for another banker to bank our train to Cefn Crib at Hafodrynys.

I unhooked the two storm sheets from the tender and let them drop vertically from the cab roof, and Bert and I blocked up the cab cut-outs with our macs. Bert put the reversing lever in full forward gear, I rested my shovel against the cab front and we both got comfortable – Bert against the reversing lever, me against the shovel. I had

Ex-GWR '56xx' Class 0-6-2T No 5659 is seen at Treharris in August 1963 with an eastbound passenger service; the branch line to Taff Merthyr Colliery is to the right of this photograph. *ProRail*

the firedoors open with a good fire under the doors. We both nodded off for a sleep and were there for three hours.

When the signal come off I told Bert that I would make him some tea, but I needed some water for his tea can. I went to the box and asked the signalman for hot water. 'You were up in the van, were you?' he asked.

'No,' I said. 'I've been up on the engine.'

The signalman accused me of telling lies and having been in the brake van instead.

When I got back to the engine with Bert, we had a cup of tea and the train was banked to Cefn Crib at Hafodrynys.

The next night the same thing happened again, but the weather was better, and I didn't bother with the two storm sheets. At Penar Junction on the way back we had to stop again and wait for the banker. At the box the signalman apologised – he had spoken to the guard, who confirmed that we had been asleep on the engine.

Last trains over Crumlin Viaduct

Myself and Bert Hale were rostered to work the last week. We had tank engines and tender engines that week, the latter three times, being a '63xx' and a '68xx'. On the Friday night there was no engine allocated, but the foreman wanted Bert and me to work an engine to Newport. However, I wanted to go home and have a few pints – I had booked on at 1.00pm and it was now 9.00pm. Bert was of the same opinion; he worked a lot of overtime and was good to work with. As there was no engine booked, while Bert was talking to the foreman I chalked up '68xx' on the engine board by the shed doors – I wanted an easy day and a reliable engine.

A '63xx' or 'Grange', filled with water and coal, would go all the way to Neath, and the coal was easier to get at. You went to the shed or triangle at Neath to turn and come back, while a tank engine would have to go

Driver Bert Hale and fireman Charlie Reynolds pose with ex-GWR '41xx' Class 2-6-2T No 4157 at Quaker's Yard, looking east, during the last week of passenger services, 11 June 1964. *Rail-Online*

to Neath shed to turn. With a 4,000-gallon tender you could go all the way without taking water, otherwise water was taken three times with a tank loco.

No 6836 *Estevarney Grange* was the last tender loco to use Crumlin Viaduct on Saturday 13 June 1964. It left Pontypool Road at 2.25pm for Neath. John Williams, a lecturer at Pontypool College, was on the train and travelled as far as Aberdare with his wife and young son Nigel. At Aberdare he was looking at the engine and Bert Hale, the driver, asked him if he was interested in engines. He said he was, and Bert said he could have a ride back on the engine on the return trip, and would pull up at a disused halt outside Neath. John said he didn't have a ticket to get to Neath, but Bert told him to stay in the compartment next to the engine – they wouldn't be checking for tickets today as it was the last day. At Neath, another engine took the train on to Swansea.

On that last day at Neath, Bert had about eight people on the engine before coming back. The platform supervisor went berserk. 'You can't leave here with all those people on the engine!'

As they got off the engine, Bert said, 'There's a little halt up the road – get ready.'

About a mile from Neath was a disused halt, and there he stopped for his visitors to climb onto the engine for the ride to Pontypool Clarence Street. John Williams got on there, as did Wayne Perham from Pontypool, who recalls Bert showing him a photo of himself on a 'Castle'.

Pannier No 4639 from Pontypool Road, which would be working the last passenger train, was passed at Quaker's Yard on the way back. No 6836 slipped going through Glyn Tunnel, then going over Crumlin Viaduct John blew the whistle all the way back to Clarence Street station. All the footplate passengers got off there, as the footplate crew didn't want them to be seen getting off at Pontypool Road.

On the last day of the Vale of Neath as a passenger route, Saturday 13 June 1964, No 6836 *Estevarney Grange* leaves Pontypool (Clarence Street); it was the last tender engine to work to Neath from Pontypool. *R. H. Marrows*

The last eastbound passenger train from Pontypool to Neath enters Pontypool (Clarence Street) on the same day, again hauled by No 4639. *R. H. Marrows*

No 4639 then hauled the last train over the Vale of Neath line from Neath to Pontypool Road that Saturday night. At Aberdare the landlord of a local pub presented the footplate crew with a gift. When the engine went over Crumlin Viaduct, the viaduct was covered in detonators to signal a farewell to the route. The noise was heard in Ebbw Vale.

Arthur Llewellyn, a railway enthusiast born in the Sovereign at Crumlin, recalls watching the loco enter Hafodrynys Halt and Glyn Tunnel, and watching the steam disappear from the end of the tunnel.

At Clarence Street station there was difficulty in getting the brake off the

The same train waits to leave Clarence Street station. No 4639 would be the last engine to traverse Crumlin Viaduct in the eastbound direction later that evening. Dick Griffin is the fireman. *R. H. Marrows*

Ex-GWR 0-6-0PT No 4639 leaves Crumlin High Level station with the last westbound passenger train on Saturday 13 June 1964. *R. H. Marrows*

engine and the train was stopped a long time there. David Williams, a Pontypool railway enthusiast, recalls the train arriving at Pontypool Road station at the main platform, as the bay was occupied. His friend Clive Lamb's uncle, Dick Griffin, was the fireman on this last trip. After the engine was uncoupled and ran round its train, David and Clive had a footplate ride light engine, in reverse, back to the loco shed at Pontypool Road.

On the Tuesday before, a photographer had been taking photos and Bert gave him a ride to Pontypool. Bert gave him a photo to be copied, which he had a job to get back. Bill Prescott was the signalman at Hafodrynys, and knew the gentleman concerned, so got the photo back for Bert. Bert retired shortly after this last trip.

The end of an era: No 4639 arrives at Pontypool Road station with the last eastbound passenger train to cross Crumlin Viaduct on 13 June1964. *Paul Chancellor collection (Colour-Rail)*

86G

Index

86G